CROSS-CULTURAL PERSPECTIVES IN LANGUAGE ASSESSMENT AND INTERVENTION

Katharine G. Butler, PhD
Editor, *Topics in Language Disorders*
Syracuse University
Syracuse, New York

TOPICS IN LANGUAGE DISORDERS SERIES

AN ASPEN PUBLICATION®
Aspen Publishers, Inc.
Gaithersburg, Maryland
1994

Editorial Resources: Ruth Bloom

ISBN: 0-8342-0594-7
Series ISBN: 0-8342-0590-4

Printed in the United States

1 2 3 4 5

Table of Contents

Cross-Cultural Perspectives in Language Assessment and Intervention

Preface

Topics in Language Disorders is a transdisciplinary journal that is devoted to discussion of issues surrounding language acquisition and its disorders. *TLD* has as its major purposes (1) providing relevant information to practicing professionals who provide services to those who are at-risk or have language disabilities; (2) clarifying the application of theory and research to practice; (3) bringing together professionals across disciplines who are researchers and clinicians from the health and education arenas both as authors and as readers; (4) clarifying the application of theory to practice among professionals and students-in-training; and (5) contributing to the scientific literature while making each issue accessible and relevant to an interdisciplinary readership.

Typically, each *TLD* journal is devoted to a single topic, although the constellation of articles may vary. A few may be wholly clinical in nature, while most blend practice and research. In the *TLD* book series, each book provides a critical but highly sensitive evaluation of current research and translates that analysis into a framework for service delivery. Hence, in this *TLD* book, the reader will find a distillation of the best of the journal's current offerings as well as some seminal articles that may enhance the reader's conceptual knowledge. Offerings are provided from a variety of disciplines: speech-language pathology, educational psychology, reading, curriculum and instruction, including the teaching of English, applied psycholinguistics, special education, ethnography, and bilingual instruction.

This text focuses on the cross-cultural aspects of language acquisition and disorders among cultural minority children and those with limited English proficiency. Language specialists have been struggling for many years with the difficulty of assessing and treating language disorders among speakers of other languages and from other cultures. Many language specialists are monolingual and, even if bilingual, may not have facility with the language of the child or under-

stand the cultural barriers that often exist between those professionals immersed in America's mainstream classroom culture and the abilities and expectations of students whose backgrounds and language form, content, and use differ on many dimensions. This book is designed to begin to bridge the chasm that all too frequently exists.

PART I. PREREQUISITES TO THE DELIVERY OF SERVICES TO THOSE FROM OTHER CULTURES: DEBATING THE DIFFERENCES

Crago opens Part I with her discussion of "Ethnography and Language Socialization: A Cross-Cultural Perspective." In so doing, she notes that communicative options open to children who speak normally in their own language differ from those of individuals with language disorders. The vulnerability of learners with language impairments is reflected in the social-communicative aspects of their interactions. She points out the importance of addressing the linguistic as well as the social-communicative needs of such learners. She concludes that the ethnographic perspective is important in dealing with those aspects of communicative difficulty that were formerly referred to as "pragmatics."

In the article that follows, Iglesias asks the important question "Communication in the Home and Classroom: Match or Mismatch?" He notes that simplistic solutions, attempted in the past, have failed to solve complex problems. He follows with suggestions for working with teachers and parents. He dissects the language of the classroom, revealing how it fails to match the past experiences of children from other cultures in their homes and communities.

García continues the theme as she picks up the historical threads in "Ethnography and Classroom Communication: Taking an 'Emic' Perspective." She expands upon the role of sociolinguists and classroom ethnographers who have described home-school cultural discontinuities and have urged taking an emic perspective—the ability to empathize and understand others' actions and perspectives. The author's suggestion for bridging the differences through changing one's perspective is of critical importance to those professionals who deal with these discontinuities.

Rees and Gerber continue the focus on "Ethnography and Communication: Social-Role Relations." They highlight the importance of social errors in language use, since such errors can cause serious disruption in social relations. The authors propose that there are a number of speaking "options," which include (1) to speak or not to speak, (2) choosing an appropriate topic of conversation, (3) selecting the words and phrases, (4) varying speech patterns, i.e., dialect, variations in pronunciation, pausing, rate, and so forth, (5) selecting syntactic structures to specify direct or indirect comments or questions, and (6) discourse features, i.e., how power is conveyed, beginning and terminating conversations, and interruptions, as, for example, in "teacher talk." Rees and Gerber point out that language assessment must therefore address children's ability to manage speaker-speaker relationships, and intervention must address linguistic *and* social-communicative skills simultaneously.

"Taking a Cross-Cultural Look at Narratives" by Heath provides readers with an anthropological perspective. Noting that language learning is cultural learning and that language socialization is required for an individual's self-identification and self-esteem, Heath discusses the four universal types of narrative (recounts, eventcasts, accounts, and stories) and speaks to the need for caution until *community-level* language research is available. Educators and evaluators should not use tests in which only certain narrative genres are made available. She concludes with practical suggestions for classroom teaching and testing.

The theme continues in Kawakami and Au's suggestions for "Encouraging Reading and Language Development in Cultural Minority Children." They provide a seminal report on the Kamehameha Elementary Education Program (KEEP). This well-known program highlights the interactional language style of Hawaiian children, in which overlapping speech known as *talk story* is channeled by teachers to incorporate more standard English forms in a natural context. The authors provide a whole-class story reading lesson as an exemplar. The principles of using a culturally compatible interactive style are provided. Readers will find their suggestions for building on children's strengths in devising instructional procedures most helpful.

In the final article in Part I, Fishman looks at reading through the lens of two case histories in "Ethnography and Literacy: Learning in Context." She takes into account children's response to their environments, e.g., children's reading and writing may reflect what they have been taught to do, what they already know, what they care about, and who they know rather than what they are *able to do*, what they are *able to learn,* and who they *could know.* Using the portfolio approach, she presents pictures of Daniel and Mitch, the former is the oldest of five children in an Old Order Amish family and the latter an African-American child in a residential school for adjudicated juveniles. Both stories permit readers to gain insight well beyond that which can be obtained by standardized assessment techniques. Both address the core issues of the literacy debate and provide helpful suggestions.

PART II. ASSESSMENT PROCEDURES, PROBLEMS, AND PROTOCOLS

Bernstein provides a review of the changing patterns of assessment as language specialists are involved in "Assessing Children with Limited English Proficiency: Current Perspectives." There are many significant problems that constitute barriers for the monolingual speech-language pathologist in providing adequate assessment of those with limited English proficiency. While use of an interpreter may remove some of those barriers, a goodly number remain. Bernstein makes a plea for the more than three and a half million linguistic minority persons in the U.S. who have speech, language, and hearing disorders, noting that skilled language specialists who are competent foreign language users is very limited. She closes by suggesting alternative language assessment procedures that are culturally and pragmatically appropriate.

Taylor and Payne report on "Culturally Valid Testing: A Proactive Approach." Readers will find a clearly articulated review of the types of bias in speech and language assessment instruments and a model for identifying and minimizing potential sources of child evaluation bias. They move on to discuss text modifications within the constraints of professionally ethical techniques. A most helpful checklist for determination of potential discrimination inherent within certain assessment instruments is provided. The authors have provided numerous strategies for a constructive solution to a real clinical problem. They propose compensatory strategies as a way of approaching culturally valid testing.

Wolfram endorses Taylor and Payne's approach and contributes a complementary approach in "Test Interpretation and Sociolinguistic Differences." He reports on a well-known but oft ignored phenomenon, i.e., that the studies of nonstandard English varieties reveal that the majority of "differences" may be found at the more superficial levels of language organization and that dialectical differences fade at the deeper structural levels. However, as he so rightly points out, standardized tests tend to focus on the most superficial level and, therefore, may be inappropriate when used with other than the population on which they were normed. Suggestions for test interpretation follow, based on task characteristics. He closes with a warning: without a more complete understanding of what language assessment is really all about, serving

diverse populations holds the potential for disservice rather than service.

Leonard and Weiss speak to the central theme through their discussion of the "Application of Nonstandardized Assessment Procedures to Diverse Linguistic Populations." They provide an analysis of spontaneous speech samples and their usefulness in examining a variety of language functions and conversational behaviors. Readers will find their description of the use of probes in the language evaluation of nonstandard English speakers' productions to be instructive. Similarly, they address the use of probes and procedures in determining speakers' comprehension of Standard English.

The final article in this section looks at "Second Language Learners' Use of Requests and Responses in Elementary Classrooms." Wilkinson, Milosky, and Genishi begin by analyzing the unspoken assumptions that adult speakers make about the "language of the classroom." They provide the student characteristics that contribute to being an effective speaker in an academic setting. They then report on a study of 50 second language learners in third grade classrooms where the primary home language was Spanish. Readers will be interested in the twenty-minute language screening process used and the use of reading activities scored by a procedure generated by Loban. Again we see the use of "request" patterns of second language speakers as a window on the conversational role-taking of culturally diverse groups.

PART III. INTERVENTION WITHIN A MULTICULTURAL CONTEXT

Cheng brings her multilinguistic talents to bear on "Intervention Strategies: A Multicultural Approach." She presents two major aspects of intervention planning for Limited English Proficient (LEP) students: (1) a basic philosophy that calls for an experiential approach to intervention and (2) the necessity to develop appropriate intervention materials, i.e., those procedures and products that incorporate the student's culture into the intervention activities. She concludes her encyclopedic suggestions by addressing issues of LEP students' transition into the mainstream culture through the use of role playing and scripts.

Westby and Rouse return to the framing of cultural concerns through anthropological perspectives in "Culture in Education and the Instruction of Language Learning-Disabled Students." In this seminal work, they describe the organization of activities in an elementary classroom of language learning-disabled Hispanic children, and through the use of ethnographic research methods reveal how the culture of the child and the culture of the school may be at variance. To do this, they focus on high-context and low-context cultures. Hispanic and Native American children tend to come from relatively high-context cultures and therefore, may experience some difficulty as they enter the low-context culture of the American classroom. They suggest multiple teacher-child interaction strategies for readers' use.

Holland draws attention to an important, albeit frequently not attended to, dilemma. While much concern has been focused on children from diverse cultures, there is much less information on the "Nonbiased Assessment and Treatment of Adults Who Have Neurologic Speech and Language Problems." She presents four brief case histories to illustrate the principles she proposes as appropriate for dealing with LEP or speakers of other languages who suffer from neurologically-based speech-language disorders. To avoid stereotyping one's patients, her first principle is "In the absence of corroborating evidence, make the fewest possible assumptions." Her second principle is that cultural minorities exist even in white America and it is especially important to be sensitive to this fact in an aging population. Sorting out dialectal problems from dysarthria or from stroke is not as simple as it seems. The third principle is that it is more important to preserve the elderly patient's

perception of dignity than it is to practice speech intervention. Holland points out that the elderly are often coerced into an active therapy regime, willing or no, and that this may be inappropriate. Fourthly, she proposes that clinicians must be extremely aware of dialectal variations (regional, social class, race) and the effects that result from the imposition of speech-language disorders upon them. Knowledge of the patient's pretraumatic dialect is vital prior to an evaluation. These, and other caveats, are liberally sprinkled throughout Holland's provocative article.

PART IV. ADDRESSING THE NEEDS OF SOME SPECIFIC POPULATIONS

Cheng returns to present a model for "Service Delivery to Asian/Pacific LEP Children: A Cross-Cultural Framework." She provides both background information regarding Asian/Pacific populations, and stresses the knowledge that is required of professionals who wish to become cross-cultural communicators. Cheng advocates that professionals provide assessment and intervention using all available resources from both cultures.

Harris provides readers with further documentation of cross-cultural variability in "Considerations in Assessing English Language Performance of Native American Children." She notes that even though external markers, such as dress, language spoken, and location may change, the influence of Native American culture on child rearing practices remains. Thus, cultural identity is internalized and may not be apparent to the casual observer. For example, Navajo mothers may not verbally communicate with their infants; rather they attract their baby's attention by eye gaze. Citing ethnographic analysis of the assessment process, Harris agrees with many of the authors in this volume, providing guidance for establishing local norms (as in her studies involving Native American Indian children), and comparing children's performance to that of their cultural age mates.

Walker reflects on "Learning English: The Southeast Asian Refugee Experience." In so doing, she addresses a continuing problem for professionals who deal with children and adults from the Asian rim. She analyzes the linguistic and tonal differences between English and the various languages used by recent refugees. For example, since Southeast Asian languages have no final consonants, speakers of those languages experience considerable difficulty in becoming proficient in English. Readers will find her suggestions for gaining communicative competence and building fluency in basic communication patterns helpful.

Matsuda has had considerable experience in "Working with Asian Parents: Some Communication Strategies," which she shares with professionals who are intimately involved with parent conferences. For those whose task it is to involve parents in the Individualized Educational Plan (IEP), she suggests a number of strategies designed to enhance the IEP process. Matsuda describes the interpersonal style of Asians as well as the possible linguistic and cultural differences. She provides eight communication guidelines to assist monolingual professionals while reminding them that it is important to establish one's status as an authority figure, a suggestion that might seem to vary from the family-focused assessment and intervention procedures emanating from the early childhood literature.

The final article in Part IV addresses "A Socio-Cultural Framework for the Assessment of Chinese Children with Special Needs." Lee discusses educational evaluations from the perspective of the Chinese family. Using two case histories of three-year-old Chinese preschoolers with presumed language disorders, she provides a number of diagnostic questions that would need to be answered since there are no standardized language tests in Chinese. She concludes that assessing culturally and linguistically diverse children is a difficult but not impossible task.

This volume is dedicated to those who face a difficult but not impossible challenge: the clinicians and educators who address the needs of multiple minorities who are changing the face of America. In many of the country's largest school districts, the majority of students are members of a minority group. The authors herein have shared their theoretical, clinical, and educational expertise, derived from years of "hands-on" experiences with individuals whose lives have varied on many important dimensions from the American "mainstream" culture and from earlier waves of immigrants. Vast changes are in store for us all:

> When *we* are *they* and *they* are *we*
> However shall we know the world to be?
> A land of tongues that to our ears
>   do stand apart,
> A land of customs strange to both
>   eye and heart.
> A land of many a culture, color and hue,
> A changed America, a land truly new.
> However shall we know the world to be
> Now *we* are *they* and *they* are *we*?
> (Adapted from K.G. Butler, 1989, p. iv).

REFERENCE

Butler, K.G. (1989). (Ed.) From the Editor, Language assessment and intervention with LEP children: Implications from an Asian/Pacific perspective. *Topics in Language Disorders,* 9:3, pp. iv-v. (Issue Editor: Li-Rong Lilly Cheng).

—*Katharine G. Butler, PhD*
Editor, *Topics in Language Disorders*

Part I
Prerequisites to Delivery of Services to Those from Other Cultures: Debating the Differences

Ethnography and language socialization: A cross-cultural perspective

Martha B. Crago, PhD
Assistant Professor
School of Human Communication
Disorders
McGill University
Montreal, Quebec, Canada

CHILDREN LEARN and use language in interpersonal and societal contexts. They also learn it in a cultural context. The study of how children acquire the communicative competence necessary to be appropriate members of their society and culture was termed *language socialization* by Schieffelin and Ochs (1986a). Schieffelin (1990) has described language socialization in the following way:

The study of language socialization has as its goal understanding how persons become competent members of their social groups and the role language has in this process. Language socialization, therefore, concerns two major areas of socialization: socialization through the use of language and socialization to use language. (p. 14)

Language, then, is both sensitive to and constructive of culture. Language indexes social life and situational context (Ochs,

The author thanks Elisabeth Handsley for her expertise in preparing the manuscript and Judith Ball, Northern Outreach Coordinator of the University of Western Ontario, for her judicious reading.

Top Lang Disord, 1992,12(3),28–39

1990). In other words, when caregivers use language with and in the presence of children they are providing cues (indexes) to children about what the members of their culture are doing. In this way, children acquire the tacit knowledge of, and competence to deal with and understand, the social organization of activities and events within the framework of their culture. They also acquire the knowledge to use language in the creation and recreation of the events, social relations, and social organization that are central to their culture. Acquiring language and becoming a cultural member are intertwined processes that are deeply embedded within each member.

HISTORICAL BACKGROUND AND METHODS OF LANGUAGE SOCIALIZATION STUDIES

The roots of language socialization research can be traced to Hymes (1974), who described the importance of linking anthropological study to linguistic study. As noted by Rees and Gerber (in this issue) Hymes coined the term *ethnography of speaking* to describe this new cross-disciplinary area of study. Hymes also signaled the importance of studying the link between children's acquisition of language and their acquisition of cultural membership. From the mid-1970s onward, a number of researchers have pursued the study of language socialization in a variety of cultures (Boggs, 1985; Clancy, 1986; Crago, 1988; Demuth, 1986; Eisenberg, 1982; Heath, 1983, 1986, 1989, 1990; Ochs, 1988; Philips, 1983; Schieffelin, 1990; Scollon & Scollon, 1981; Smith-Hefner, 1988; Watson-Gegeo & Gegeo, 1986).

These language socialization studies combine the tradition of developmental psycholinguistic studies (Bloom, 1970; Brown, 1973; Halliday, 1975) with the ethnographic methodology that derives from the general tradition of anthropology (Geertz, 1973; Malinowski, 1935; Marcus & Fischer, 1986; Pelto, 1970; Spradley, 1979, 1980). In keeping with the psycholinguistic tradition, naturalistic recordings of children and their caregivers are made from which detailed verbal and nonverbal information is transcribed. Information from the detailed analysis of such transcripts is then linked with ethnographically derived information gathered from several sources by using a combination of participant observation and ethnographic interviews. It is this linking of the microlevel analysis of discourse with the macrolevel information on social practices, social organization, and cultural values that has become the hallmark of language socialization studies. It is what differentiates them from observational studies and other developmental research into pragmatics.

Before the use of ethnographic methodology in the cross-cultural study of the acquisition of communicative competence, a group of child-language researchers had described a set of tasks and experiments that they intended to carry out in various cultural settings with speakers of various languages (Slobin, 1967). The aim was to collect a set of data that would help uncover the universal properties of language acquisition. Instead, the researchers discovered themselves engaged in a number of untenable communicative situations (Schieffelin, 1979). Some of the specified tasks and procedures required people to carry out culturally inappropriate tasks. For instance, language samples were to be collected as a mother fed a baby. In some cultures, it is not the mother who feeds the baby. In other cultures, talking while eating is discouraged (Crago, 1988). The discontinuity between the prescribed tasks designed by white middle-class North American researchers and the cultural realities of communication between caregivers and children in the cultures they were studying signaled the need for a more sensitive and flexible approach to the cross-cultural study of children's acquisition of communicative competence. Ethnographic methodology, developed by the discipline of anthropology for the study of people in the naturalistic context of their everyday lives, provided an excellent tool for language socialization studies.

VARIATION: A CENTRAL ISSUE IN LANGUAGE SOCIALIZATION

The comparison of language socialization practices across cultures requires a few caveats. First, no culture is a monolith (Schieffelin & Ochs, 1986b). Variation exists in communities, families, and individuals. This variation is as true for language socialization as it is for other behaviors. Second, particular language socialization practices are not the unique holding of any one culture. Third, language socialization is not done in the same way, nor in the same context, nor by the same people within any given culture. What is unique to a culture is the particular dose of "who," "how," "when," and "where" that is associated with language socialization. In cultures in which children live with extended

families or are socialized by several community members, they have early communicative interaction with a number of partners of differing ages who play a number of social roles that are associated with varying status. Part of what they learn as they acquire language is who speaks to whom about what, in what manner of discourse, and in the context of what activity. In doing so, they come to understand the hierarchy and tapestry of the ways of talking and listening in their culture.

Another important form of variation related to language socialization is variation across sociohistorical time. Cultures are not static phenomena. Cultural patterns of communicative interaction evolve over time (Crago, Annahatak, & Ningiuruvik, in press; Heath, 1990). The evolution is sometimes sparked by the disruptive effects of schooling, second language acquisition, acculturation, and the impact of certain social policy changes.

Heath (1990) has documented how changes in housing policy that led to the isolation of young African American mothers and their children served to disrupt the tapestry of language and the web of language users, speakers and listeners, and performers and spectators. These disruptions had negative consequences for these young children's language acquisition and

---

Part of what [children] learn as they acquire language is who speaks to whom about what, in what manner of discourse, and in the context of what activity.

---

cultural socialization. Crago et al (in press) have described the difference between the language socialization practices of older Inuit mothers and those of young mothers and have shown how this difference is related to issues of acculturation, schooling, and cultural dominance. Results of both of these studies have demonstrated that

fewer and fewer individuals in some minority groups define themselves in terms of webs of significance that they, themselves, spin, and many may be caught without understanding, interpreting, or transmitting anything like the cultural patterns into which they themselves were socialized. (Heath, 1990, p. 517)

CONTRIBUTIONS OF LANGUAGE SOCIALIZATION STUDIES TO THEORY

How are the findings of ethnographic studies of child language different from those of other studies of child language? Language socialization study findings have not confirmed the universal nature of the particular modified caregiver register ("motherese") described in psycholinguistic studies (Snow, 1977, 1984). Indeed, the often unmentioned fact in North American psycholinguistic research is that this research has been largely restricted to one particular culture, the white middle class. Ochs and Schieffelin (1984) have referred to this phenomenon as "the invisible culture" of child-language studies. "There has been a tacit assumption that readers can provide the larger cultural framework for making sense out of the behaviors documented, and, consequently, the cultural nature of the behaviors and principles presented have not been explicit" (pp.

283–284). These two authors contrasted three developmental stories of language learning: a Kaluli story, a Samoan story, and an American white middle-class story. The latter story was constructed from a composite of pieces of psycholinguistic research to which Ochs and Schieffelin (1984) provided an explicit cultural perspective. In doing so, they illustrated that the modified caregiver register documented in studies of the North American white middle class is a culturally related phenomenon, reflecting the values and beliefs of that particular sociocultural group. Theories regarding the universal nature of this register, therefore, need to be reframed.

A continuum of communicative accommodation

Instead, Schieffelin and Ochs (1986a) have described a continuum of communicative accommodation along which cultures vary with regard to their caregiver–child discourse. Different types of accommodation lead to different modifications of the caregiver register addressed to young language learners. One extreme is child-centered accommodation in which "the caregiver takes the perspective of the child in talking to and understanding the child" (p. 174). Alternately, situation-centered communication is one in which "the child is expected to accommodate to activities and persons in the situation at hand" (p. 174). According to Schieffelin and Ochs (1986a), societies vary in their use of these forms of accommodation. Their variation is determined by the cultural values, structures of caregiving, and social organization of the culture in question (Schieffelin & Eisenberg, 1984). The white middle-class culture has been described as making largely child-centered accommodations (Lieven, 1984). Crago (1988), however, documented that child-centered and situation-centered accommodations cooccur in the Inuit culture. Furthermore, she pointed out that the Inuit culture both shares with and is different from the white middle-class culture in certain of its forms of child-centered and situation-centered accommodations. Watson-Gegeo and Gegeo (1986) have described how forms of accommodation can vary during a child's development.

Implicational universals of language socialization

Heath (1988) proposed that implicational universals of language socialization be determined and described. She expressed the hope that "we shall eventually be able to establish fundamental social communicative operating principles that enable children to come to their sense of identity and to function as communicating members of their particular primary group" (p. xi). Her notion was that the specifics of how a particular cultural group interacts with its young children are structured from the specifics of its social organization. Because certain cultures share in certain aspects of their social organization, it is also true that certain communicative practices will intersect across cultures. Implicational universals of language socialization would describe the links between a given set of societal and cultural features and the concomitant communicative patterns between caregivers and children. For instance, Heath (1989) pointed out that several hunting and gathering societies in the world have similarities in their social orga-

nization and structures of caregiving. They also exhibit certain similarities in language socialization practices. Understanding how such practices intersect across different cultural groups serves as a means both for understanding the extent of the variation and of demonstrating the degree of the commonality.

Commonality and variation

Language socialization studies have indeed revealed a number of commonalities related to children's acquisition of language. To begin with, children in various cultures appear to develop language at approximately the same age. They also show individual variation in their development of language. Furthermore, caregivers in all cultures interact with language and with affection in one way or another with their children. Caregivers in all cultures also guide their children's participation and provide support for their learning (Rogoff, 1990). Language socialization studies have also revealed a great deal about cultural variation. Rogoff (1990) has described the essence of this variation in the following way: "The most important differences across cultures, in guided participation, involve variation in the skills and values that are promoted according to the cultural goals of maturity" (p. 114). In different cultures, then, different communication skills are considered important, different approaches to their teaching are valued, and different situations and people are available for their teaching. The relation of language and culture is a nexus of interpenetrated features. The values, orientations, activities, and historical status of a culture interact to affect the communicative status and patterns of children and their caregivers. In turn, the communicative interactions of children and their caregivers construct cultural awareness and cultural membership.

CONTRIBUTIONS OF LANGUAGE SOCIALIZATION STUDIES TO EDUCATIONAL AND CLINICAL PRACTICE

How does educational and clinical practice fit into the linguistic and cultural interweave of language socialization? Are clinicians and educators caught in webs into which they, themselves, were socialized without understanding or interpreting what they transmit to the children and the families that they serve?

The culture of clinics and classrooms

Most North American clinical and educational practitioners assume a particular cultural stance with regard to the patterns of communication and language socialization that they propose to, and engage in with, their clients. This invisible culture of clinics and schools is, in fact, the mainstream North American middle-class culture. Without conscious recognition of it, most classroom discourse and clinical intervention and assessment practices have been based on the language socialization patterns of their mainstream practitioners and on the theoretical perspectives that have emerged from culturally decontextualized psycholinguistic research. In contrast, large numbers of the children caught in this particular cultural, clinical, and educational web are not from the mainstream (Cole, 1989).

Education literature (Duranti & Ochs,

1988; Erickson, 1987; Heath, 1983; Philips, 1983) has documented the problematic effects of school practices that are discontinuous with home socialization practices. For many Native American, African American, and immigrant children, most North American schools represent a secondary form of socialization. These children have to learn academic subject matter while unlearning many patterns of language use that they were brought up with and relearning culturally different ways of communicating. In many instances the result is systematic school failure (Trueba, 1988). On the other hand, efforts to adapt classroom discourse and patterns of learning and instruction to the socialization practices of the children's homes and families have had positive educational outcomes (Heath, 1983; Tharp et al., 1984; Vogt, Jordan, & Tharp, 1987). The net effect of these particular educational experiments has been that nonmainstream children's learning has been maximized and their cultural loss minimized.

Language socialization and clinical assessment

Issues related to language socialization directly impinge on clinical assessments in speech-language pathology. Taylor and Payne (1983) and Erickson and Iglesias (1986) have described different forms of bias that exist in the assessment of nonmainstream children. Among them is format bias. This means that the testing situation, for instance, has components in it that are culturally unfamiliar to certain children. In some cultures, adults do not ask children questions to which they, the adults, already know the answer (Crago, 1988). In others, children are not expected to be alone with adults (Westby, 1985). In cultures in which children are socialized to do much of their talking with peers, talking in the presence of an adult can be uncomfortable (Crago, 1988). Hence, these children may be quite taciturn in the testing situation, a behavior that makes them appear to be less capable than they actually are.

Despite the fact that nonstandardized approaches to assessment have been proposed as a solution to the assessment of nonmainstream children (Holland & Forbes, 1986; Leonard & Weiss, 1983), commonly used procedures for language sampling are very susceptible to differences in the ways clinicians and children have been socialized to use language. Mainstream clinicians attempting to elicit language samples from nonmainstream children frequently assume the role of communicative partner with these children. Yet, they may not be aware of what the nature of caregiver accommodations to these children has been. Schieffelin (1990), in describing how she collected her naturalistic data for her language socialization study of Kaluli children, wrote the following:

I collected speech between children and those individuals with whom they usually interacted in everyday family situations.... I did not want to act in a way that would elicit the data I was analyzing for many reasons. Not being a member of Kaluli society, I would not presume to know the culturally appropriate ways of speaking to and interacting with children, nor would children know how to talk to me. (p. 27)

This ethnographic awareness of the cultural dimensions of communication and of socialization has significance for clinical language samples. A clinician who is not knowledgeable about a child's culture is not likely to be an adequate communicative partner. Furthermore, without knowing the cultural situations, interactions, and interactants in a child's life, the clinician may not be able to structure the situation and the participants in the language-sampling process in an effective way. Unless the clinician knows, for example, that Native American children talk more with peers than with adults, he or she may not think to structure the elicitation of language samples in such a way that it involves the interaction of children and not parent–child or clinician–child dyads. Awareness of clients' language socialization histories, then, can help practitioners form clinical assessment practices.

Language socialization and clinical intervention

Clinical language intervention with nonmainstream children and their families also needs to be influenced by how these children's families have socialized their children to use language. Parent–infant intervention programs need to have special sensitivity to this. Most early intervention literature and practices in the field of communication disorders have been based on theory derived from culturally decontextualized accounts of caregiver–child interaction (Cole, 1991; Cole & St. Clair-Stokes, 1984; Cross, 1984; Fey, 1986;

A clinician who is not knowledgeable about a child's culture is not likely to be an adequate communicative partner.

Fitzgerald & Fischer, 1987; Manolsen, 1983; McDade & Varnedoe, 1987; Snow, Midkiff-Borunda, Small, & Proctor, 1984; Tiegerman & Siperstein, 1984). Disrupting the fiber of caregiver–child communicative interactions by recommending forms of linguistic accommodation and discourse that are culturally foreign to a family could have deleterious effects on the parent–child relation, the nature of communication in the home, and, more simply, the effectiveness and willingness of the parents to carry out the proposed intervention (Crago, in press). On the other hand, the ethnographic documentation of a given culture's language socialization practices can provide the basis that speech-language pathologists and educators can use to adapt their parent–infant intervention programs, so that they become culturally appropriate (Crago, 1990).

Preschool intervention projects designed to prepare nonmainstream children for the communicative interaction, discourse, and pragmatic structure of language uses in school are similarly vulnerable to the effects of language socialization. Westby (personal communication, May 1991) has described an intervention program for Hispanic preschoolers designed to increase their pragmatic uses of language, so that the uses will match those required of them in school. Preliminary results have shown that the children are talking more but that their pragmatic categories are limited and unexpected. For instance, directives became heavily used by these children. This may well reflect the communicative forms used by their caregivers at home.

Increasing nonmainstream school-aged children's awareness of different forms of discourse has also been suggested in the education literature (Delpit, 1988). Possibly, school-aged intervention programs to increase nonmainstream children's abilities to code switch between their home patterns of communication and those of the classroom or clinic would work more successfully when children's metalinguistic skills are better developed. In any case, innovative intervention programs need to be designed, so that mainstream teachers and clinicians shift their discourse patterns to accommodate those of nonmainstream children and their families.

If successful intervention for nonmainstream children follows the patterns outlined for successful education of such children, one has to presume that intervention that is maximally congruent and minimally discontinuous with the home culture's patterns of language socialization will be most effective. Clinicians, as a result, must become culturally literate and knowledgeable about other cultures' discourse patterns, so that children can be served effectively. This means becoming aware of their own assumptions about language socialization and learning about other people's ways with words.

The intersection of language socialization and bilingual education

Finally, in both the intervention and the education of preschool and school-aged children whose mother tongue is not the language of the school or the clinic, there is another important issue related to language socialization. Once children start to learn a second language in nonbilingual preschools and schools, a considerable shift in their use of their first language (L1) at home takes place (Wong-Fillmore, in press). Their parents also increase their use of a second language (L2). This is especially true where presumably well-meaning interventionists counsel parents to speak more of the second language at home (Cummins, 1989). One of the results of this counseling is that home patterns of communication are seriously interrupted. First, children are exposed to severely limited language input because their parents are as much learners of the second language as they are (Wong-Fillmore, 1991). Second, the usual language socialization practices are not easily carried out by caregivers who are trying to raise their children across the barrier of nonproficient language. Affectionate and culturally patterned language routines, for instance, can become uncomfortable and meaningless in a second language that is not well known.

Language socialization and practitioner change

Clinicians and educators are not faced with an easy task. They must learn to recognize their own invisible cultural curricula while learning the cultural dimensions of their clients' and students' communication patterns and language use. Furthermore, in educational and treatment facilities that provide service to numerous different cultural groups, this can represent a considerable amount of information to master.

Several approaches to the problem can help empower clinicians and educators in their dilemma. First, their practice can now be increasingly informed by the results of language socialization studies. Second, they and the institutions for which they work can initiate projects to work

hand in hand with ethnographic researchers designing and documenting experimental classroom and clinical programs as well as practitioner training programs that are similar to those whose effectiveness has already been documented (Heath, 1983; Tharp et al., 1984). Third, service providers can involve themselves in collaborative relations with nonmainstream parents and teachers to identify culturally appropriate educational and clinical goals and practices. This collaboration may span a continuum with individual information sharing at one end and actual parent and paraprofessional and professional training at the other end. Such training must be a mutually informing, two-way dialogue in which the mainstream professional is trained by the cultural members in question and in which this same professional shares his or her knowledge of speech and language disorders with nonmainstream families, other professionals, and paraprofessionals. Although the process is not likely to be a speedy one, there is ample evidence in the literature to indicate that, through a gradual shaping and developing of educational and clinical practice, more effective outcomes should be possible.

• • •

The socialization of children to their culture is an essential and vulnerable process in which language plays a crucial role. Ignoring nonmainstream children's cultural and socialization histories by not accepting this relation leads to inappropriate intervention and assessment procedures. The lack of recognition of the strength of the relation of language and culture by many educators and clinicians has led to changes in the patterns of communicative interaction that are almost exclusively unidirectional. Nonmainstream children and their caregivers have had the burden of change. Their communicative patterns are expected to be drawn in line with the mainstream despite the fact that educational studies have documented the gains that result from educating (and presumably remediating) children in a culturally congruent manner. Practitioners who are ignorant of, or refuse to alter their practices in ways that recognize the strength of, cultural patterns of communicative interaction can, in fact, be asserting the hegemony of the mainstream culture and can thereby contribute, often unknowingly, to a form of cultural genocide of nonmainstream communicative practices.

REFERENCES

Bloom, L. (1970). *Language development: Form and function in emerging grammars.* Cambridge: MIT Press.

Boggs, S.T. (1985). *Speaking, relating, and learning: A study of Hawaiian children at home and at school.* Norwood, NJ: Ablex.

Brown, R. (1973). *A first language.* Cambridge: Harvard University Press.

Clancy, P.M. (1986). The acquisition of communicative style in Japanese. In B.B. Schieffelin & E. Ochs (Eds.), *Language socialization across cultures* (pp. 213–250). New York: Cambridge University Press.

Cole, E.B. (1991). *Listening and talking: A guide to promoting spoken language in young hearing-impaired children.* Washington, DC.: A.G. Bell Association for the Deaf.

Cole, E.B., & St. Clair-Stokes, J. (1984). Caregiver-child interaction behaviors—A videotape analysis procedure. *The Volta Review, 86*(4), 200–216.

Cole, L. (1989). E pluribus pluribus: Multicultural imperatives for the 1990s and beyond. *Asha, 31*(8), 65–70.

Crago, M.B. (1988). *Cultural context in communicative interaction of young Inuit children.* Unpublished doctoral dissertation, McGill University, Montreal.

Crago, M.B. (1990). The development of communicative competence in Inuit children of Northern Quebec: Implications for speech-language pathology. *Journal of Childhood Communication Disorders, 13*(1), 54–71.

Crago, M.B. (in press). The sociocultural interface of communicative interaction and L2 acquisition in Quebec Inuit. *TESOL Quarterly.*

Crago, M.B., Annahatak, B., & Ningiuruvik, L. (in press). Changing patterns: The interface of education and Inuit parenting. Unpublished manuscript submitted.

Cross, T.G. (1984). Habilitating the language-impaired child: Ideas from studies of parent-child interaction. *Topics in Language Disorders, 4*(4), 1–14.

Cummins, J. (1989). *Empowering minority students.* Sacramento: California Association for Bilingual Education.

Delpit, L. (1988). The silenced dialogue: Power and pedagogy in educating other people's children. *Harvard Educational Review, 58*(2), 78–95.

Demuth, K. (1986). Prompting routines in the language socialization of Basotho children. In B.B. Schieffelin & E. Ochs (Eds.), *Language socialization across cultures* (pp. 51–79). New York: Cambridge University Press.

Duranti, A., & Ochs, E. (1988). Literacy instruction in a Samoan village. In E. Ochs (Ed.), *Culture and language development: Language acquisition and language socialization in a Samoan village* (pp. 189–209). New York: Cambridge University Press.

Eisenberg, A. (1982). *Language acquisition in cultural perspective: Talk in three Mexicano homes.* Unpublished doctoral dissertation, University of California, Berkeley.

Erickson, F. (1987). Transformation and school success: The politics and culture of educational achievement. *Anthropology and Educational Quarterly, 18,* 335–357.

Erickson, J.G., & Iglesias, A. (1986). Assessment of communication disorders in non-English proficient children. In O.L. Taylor (Ed.), *Nature of communication disorders in culturally and linguistically diverse populations.* San Diego: College-Hill Press.

Fey, M. (1986). *Language intervention with young children.* San Diego: College-Hill Press.

Fitzgerald, M.T., & Fischer, R. (1987). A family involvement model for hearing-impaired infants. *Topics in Language Disorders, 7*(3), 1–18.

Geertz, C. (1973). *The interpretation of cultures.* New York: Basic Books.

Halliday, M. (1975). *Learning how to mean: Explorations in the development of language.* London: Edward Arnold.

Heath, S.B. (1983). *Ways with words: Language, life and work in communities and classrooms.* New York: Cambridge University Press.

Heath, S.B. (1986). Sociocultural contexts of language development. In *Beyond language: Social and cultural factors in schooling language minority children* (pp.

143–186). (Developed by the Bilingual Education Office, California State Department, Sacramento.) Los Angeles: Evaluation, Dissemination and Assessment Centre.

Heath, S.B. (1988). Foreword to E. Ochs, *Culture and language development: Language acquisition and language socialization in a Samoan village* (pp. vii–xiii). New York: Cambridge University Press.

Heath, S.B. (1989). The learner as cultural member. In M.L. Rice & R.L. Schiefelbusch (Eds.), *The teachability of language* (pp. 333–350). Baltimore: Paul H. Brookes.

Heath, S.B. (1990). The children of Trackton's children: Spoken and written language in social change. In J.W. Stigler, R.A. Shweder, & G. Herdt (Eds.), *Cultural psychology* (pp. 496–519). New York: Cambridge University Press.

Holland, A., & Forbes, M. (1986). Nonstandardized approaches to speech and language assessment. In O.L. Taylor (Ed.), *Treatment of communication disorders in culturally and linguistically diverse populations* (pp. 49–66). San Diego: College-Hill Press.

Hymes, D.H. (1974). The ethnography of speaking. In B.G. Blount (Ed.), *Language, culture, and society: A book of readings* (pp. 189–223). Cambridge: Winthrop.

Lieven, E.V.M. (1984). Interaction style and children's learning. *Topics in Language Disorders, 4*(4), 15–23.

Leonard, L., & Weiss, A.L. (1983). Application of nonstandardized assessment procedures to diverse linguistic populations. *Topics in Language Disorders, 3*(3), 35–45.

Malinowski, B. (1935). *Coral gardens and their magic: II. The language of magic and gardening.* Bloomington: University of Indiana Press.

Manolsen, A. (1983). *It takes two to talk: A Hanen early language parent guide book.* Toronto: Hanen Early Language Resource Centre.

Marcus, G.E., & Fischer, M.M.J. (1986). *Anthropology as cultural critique.* Chicago: The University of Chicago Press.

McDade, H.L., & Varnedoe, D.R. (1987). Training parents to be language facilitators. *Topics in Language Disorders, 7*(3), 19–30.

Ochs, E. (1988). *Culture and language development: Language acquisition and language socialization in a Samoan village.* New York: Cambridge University Press.

Ochs, E. (1990). Indexicality and socialization. In J.W. Stigler, R.A. Shweder, & G. Herdt (Eds.), *Cultural psychology* (pp. 287–308). New York: Cambridge University Press.

Ochs, E., & Schieffelin, B.B. (1984). Language acquisition and socialization: Three developmental stories and their implications. In R.A. Shweder & R.A. LeVine (Eds.), *Culture theory: Essays on mind, self, and emotion* (pp. 276–322). New York: Cambridge University Press.

Pelto, P.J. (1970). *Anthropological research: The structure of inquiry.* New York: Harper & Row.

Philips, S.U. (1983). *The invisible culture.* New York: Longman.

Rogoff, B. (1990). *Apprenticeship in thinking: Cognitive development in social context.* Oxford: Oxford University Press.

Schieffelin, B.B. (1979). Getting it together: An ethnographic approach to the study of the development of communicative competence. In E. Ochs & B.B. Schieffelin (Eds.), *Developmental pragmatics* (pp. 93–108). New York: Academic Press.

Schieffelin, B.B. (1990). *The give and take of everyday life.* New York: Cambridge University Press.

Schieffelin, B.B., & Eisenberg, A. (1984). Cultural variation in children's conversations. In R.L. Schiefelbusch & J. Pickar (Eds.), *Communicative competence: Acquisition and intervention* (pp. 377–422). Baltimore: University Park Press.

Schieffelin, B.B., & Ochs, E. (1986a). Language socialization. *Annual Review of Anthropology, 15,* 163–246.

Schieffelin, B.B., & Ochs, E. (Eds.). (1986b). *Language socialization across cultures.* New York: Cambridge University Press.

Scollon, R., & Scollon, S. (1981). *Narrative, literacy and face in interethnic communication.* Norwood, NJ: Ablex.

Smith-Hefner, N.J. (1988). The linguistic socialization of Javanese children in two communities. *Anthropological Linguistics, 30*(2), 166–198.

Snow, C.E. (1977). Mother's speech research: From input to interaction. In C.E. Snow & C.A. Ferguson (Eds.), *Talking to children* (pp. 31–50). New York: Cambridge University Press.

Snow, C.E. (1984). Parent-child interaction and the development of communicative ability. In R.L. Schiefelbusch & J. Pickar (Eds.), *Communicative competence: Acquisition and intervention* (pp. 69–108). Baltimore: University Park Press.

Snow, C., Midkiff-Borunda, S., Small, A., & Proctor, A. (1984). Therapy as social interaction: Analyzing the contexts for language remediation. *Topics in Language Disorders, 4*(4), 72–85.

Spradley, J.P. (1979). *The ethnographic interview.* Orlando, FL: Holt, Rinehart & Winston.

Spradley, J.P. (1980). *Participant observation.* Orlando, FL: Holt, Rinehart & Winston.

Taylor, O.L., & Payne, K. (1983). Culturally valid testing: A proactive approach. *Topics in Language Disorders, 3*(3), 8–20.

Tharp, R.G., Jordan, C., Speidel, G.E., Hu-Pei Au, K., Klein, T.W., Calkins, R.P., Sloat, K.C.M., & Gallimore, R. (1984). Product and process in applied developmental research: Education and the children of a minority. In M.E. Lamb, A.L. Brown, & B. Rogoff (Eds.), *Advances in developmental psychology* (Vol. 3, pp. 91–144). Hillsdale, NJ: Erlbaum.

Tiegerman, E., & Siperstein, M. (1984). Individual patterns of interaction in the mother-child dyad: Implications for parent intervention. *Topics in Language Disorders, 4*(4), 50–61.

Trueba, H.T. (1988). *Raising silent voices: Educating the linguistic minorities for the 21st century.* New York: Harper & Row.

Vogt, L., Jordan, C., & Tharp, R.G. (1987). Explaining school failure, producing school success: Two cases. *Anthropology and Education Quarterly, 18,* 276–286.

Watson-Gegeo, K.A., & Gegeo, D.W. (1986). Calling-out and repeating routines in Kwara'ae children's language socialization. In B.B. Schieffelin & E. Ochs (Eds.), *Language socialization across cultures* (pp. 17–50). New York: Cambridge University Press.

Westby, C. (1985, November). *Cultural differences in caregiver-child interaction: Implications for assessment and intervention.* Paper presented at the American Speech-Language-Hearing Association Conference, San Francisco, CA.

Wong-Fillmore, L. (1991, April). *Language loss: The price to children, families, and society.* Invited talk presented at the Sixteenth Annual Conference of the Canadian Association of Speech-Language Pathologists and Audiologists, Montreal.

Wong-Fillmore, L. (in press). Learning a language from learners. In C. Kramsch & S. McConnell-Ginet (Eds.), *Text and context: Cross-disciplinary perspectives on language studies.* Lexington, MA: Heath.

Communication in the home and classroom: match or mismatch?

Aquiles Iglesias, PhD
Assistant Professor
Department of Speech
Temple University
Philadelphia, Pennsylvania

I felt like an alien. The children just sat there and stared. They did exactly what they were told. Of course, there were a few who came in with a lot of communication, maybe 6 out of 28.

(Bilingual-bicultural kindergarten teacher, personal communication, 1984)

ALL SOCIETIES have formal or informal procedures through which children acquire the values, behaviors, and knowledge necessary for socialization. In the majority of Western societies, the socialization process is carried out partially through formal classroom instruction. The educational institutions in these societies often reflect familial, economic, political, and religious aspects of the dominant society. As such, the expectations and demands placed on children enrolled in these institutions are congruent with the values, traditions, and behaviors of the mainstream society. The U.S. educational system is one that "serves primarily to prepare middle class children to partici-

Top Lang Disord, 1985, 5(4), 29-41
© 1985 Aspen Publishers, Inc.

pate in their own culture" (Saville-Troike, 1979, p. 141).

At least for the first few years, the curriculum in these educational institutions is organized so that the academic skills that middle-class children have learned at home are reinforced and practiced. In addition, during the preschool years, the instructional approaches used by the middle-class parents to train these skills are almost identical to the ones that the children will later experience in the classroom. For example, the question-answer routines the parents use to train colors, shapes, names of objects, and so on, are the same type of routines used by mainstream teachers to train that particular content. Thus, before entering school, middle-class children have considerable experience in academic content as well as the rules for interacting in the classroom. As a result of this early training, success is virtually guaranteed for normal, middle-class, majority children.

But what happens when children enter an educational system that differs markedly from their own cultural and linguistic background? Middle-class children would not be as successful in a program in which instruction is in a language other than their own, in which the content of the curriculum was different from that trained by the parents, or in which the rules of classroom interaction violated the rules of home discourse. Middle-class children, as a group, would do as poorly in this type of educational system as cultural-linguistic minority children, as a group, have done in mainstream, middle-class American classes.

Although it is not the sole source of academic success or failure, the ability to communicate in the classroom is essential to success in school. Children must possess the linguistic skills (phonology, morphology, and syntax) necessary to understand the teacher and to transmit newly acquired knowledge when required. In addition, children must possess the discourse rules of their particular classroom.

The child's communication skills may match or mismatch the communication skills demanded by the teacher. Mismatches, and in some cases matches, affect cultural-linguistic minority children's ability to succeed in the U.S. educational system. In addition, communication difficulties encountered by these children are further aggravated by educational policies that are insensitive to their needs. The term *cultural and linguistic minority* refers here to the group of individuals who are culturally and linguistically different from their English-speaking, middle-class peers. This minority is heterogeneous with respect to socialization practices at home, linguistic skills, and communication styles. Differences exist between and among the various subgroups. As such, generalizations cannot, and should not, be made.

COMMUNICATION IN THE HOME

Communicative interactions in the home setting reflect child-rearing attitudes and practices that vary across cultural groups around the world (Blount, 1982; Heath, 1983; Super & Harkness, 1982; see also Harris, this issue). Through these interactions, children acquire not only their significant others' linguistic system but also the rules for participating in linguistic dialogues within their culture. Children's acquisition of these communication skills is gradual, and their communication system will undergo transformations as a function of the communicative demands placed on them by their significant others in various social situations. For example, some children might be involved in "reading routines" with their parents in which the children are expected first to be passive listeners (e.g., the children are required only to look at pictures); then to be active, nonverbal participants (the parents ask the children to point to objects in the pictures); and finally to be active verbal participants (children are asked to label pictures or answer questions about the story).

The nature of the interactions in which the children are engaged at home has a considerable effect on the communication skills they acquire before entering school. The type, quantity, and quality of these interactions will be the result of numerous variables, such as the sex of the parent and the child, the parents' educational level, the home language, ethnicity, economic status, and so on. The field of child language development has not yet established a method for ascertaining the exact effect of any of these variables on a particular aspect of a child's communication skills. The only claim that can be made at this point is that these factors do affect, to some extent, either directly or indirectly, the type of communicative interactions in which the children are engaged.

Through their daily interactions with their parents and others, children learn the discourse rules of their particular speech community: how and by whom topics are introduced and terminated, how topics are developed, what type of utterance can follow other utterances, what role different members of the community may play in an interaction, and so forth. The following miniscripts illustrate how two mothers, who happen to be members of the same nonmainstream cultural group, interact with their children during a free-play situation.

Family 1

C: Mom. Mom. Mom. Mom.

M: (Looks at the child)

C: I saw one of those at Joe's house. *(Points to a puppet named Grover)* His mother gave it to him for his birthday. *(Child moves to other end of room and climbs chair in order to get car from the shelf).*

M: Don't stand on it, you're going to fall.

C: (Grabs car from shelf and brings it to mother, taps mom's hand three times) Can I take it home?

M: No, I'll buy you one when we get home.

C: When are we going home?

M: In a little while.

C: I want to go home now. I'm hungry. What are we having for dinner?

M: Well, we can have spaghetti or tuna casserole.

C: Let's have spaghetti.

Family 2

M: Look here. I think this is Grover. What's his name?

C: I like to play with Ernie better.

M: What's his name? *(Holds Grover up)*

C: Grover.

M: (Pretends that Grover is walking up the steps) What is Grover doing now?

C: He is walking.

M: Yes, but where is he going?

C: He is going upstairs. I think the . . .

M: Oh, he just went down to the kitchen. What is he going to eat?

C: I don't know.

M: Well, what food do we have here? What is this?

C: Corn.

M: And this?

C: Oranges.

Assuming that the miniscripts are typical of the interactions between the two dyads, what interaction rules are being trained? In Family 1, the child is being trained to use attentionals, either verbal or nonverbal, before initiating a topic; to initiate any topic using a variety of speech acts; and to terminate a topic by walking away. In Family 2, the child is being trained to expect topics to be initiated and terminated by others; that a questioner knows the answer to the questions he or she asks; and that the questions must be answered in the way the questioner expects. Although Family 2's interaction may seem stifling to the child's creativity, the child is learning the interaction and academic skills that will be necessary to function successfully in the first years of the U.S. educational system.

One factor that has considerable influence on the degree to which parents

Parents, as a result of their experiences with particular educational systems, make assumptions about the communication and academic skills that will be demanded of their children in the school situation.

engage in teaching routines similar to those found in Family 2 is parental assumptions about school expectations. Parents, as a result of their experiences with particular educational systems, make assumptions about the communication and academic skills that will be demanded of their children in the school situation. The parents will then teach these skills,

consciously or unconsciously, in their daily interactions with their children. For example, if the parent assumes that the child will be expected to label items and events, the parents will engage in question-and-answer routines in which the questioner knows the answer; on the other hand, if the parents assume that prereading skills will not be required of children entering school, they may not practice this routine with their children.

Sometimes parental assumptions about school demands, and the skills they teach accordingly, are compatible with the communication norms of their own community. In these cases, the parents train skills that are consistent with the community's way of using language. In other cases, parental assumptions of school demands force parents to modify the nature of their interaction in a way that is inconsistent with the norms of their particular speech community. This process of modifying communicative interactions to meet assumptions of school demands is best illustrated by the following comment made by the parent of a cultural-linguistic minority child:

I raised my first child the same way I was raised. I taught him those things that children in my hometown are supposed to learn before they go to school. What I taught him was not what the teacher wanted. He has done very poorly in school. I don't want my second child to have the same problems. I now talk to him differently than to my first child (Parent, personal communication, May, 1984).

In addition to acquiring interactional and academic skills, children will acquire the linguistic skills necessary to interact with members of their community. Parents of cultural-linguistic minority children and other individuals with whom the child interacts are a linguistically heterogeneous group; some are monolingual speakers of the majority language; some are monolingual speakers of the minority language; and the large majority are bilingual, falling between the ends of the continuum.

Only in rare cases are cultural-linguistic minority children exposed solely to individuals at one end of the continuum. The most probable scenario is that of a child who is exposed to some monolingual speakers of the minority language and a large number of bilingual speakers. Some of the bilingual speakers with whom the child interacts might speak to the child using one language at a time; others might code-switch (e.g., "Come here y ponlo aqui"); and others might speak in the minority language with words borrowed from the majority language interspersed throughout their utterances (e.g., "El tro cruzo el traque/The truck crossed the railroad track").

In order to become effective communicators within their community, the children must acquire the forms appropriate to the speaker and the situation. In some cases, children might be expected to speak only one language; in other cases they might be permitted to code-switch; and in other cases they might be allowed to use borrowed words. The particular forms the children are exposed to and expected to use will vary across children as a function of the linguistic skills of the participants with whom they interact.

In summary, there is a wide variation in the communication skills of cultural-linguistic minority children entering school. The variation is the result of the wide range of interactions children may have with a linguistically heterogeneous group of individuals.

COMMUNICATION IN SCHOOL

Each classroom is in itself a minicommunity controlled by the teacher. The teacher's goal is to train particular skills in a short period of time to a large group of children. In order to accomplish this goal, the teacher determines the physical layout of the classroom, the activities or tasks to be accomplished, and the rules for participating in these activities. These teacher-controlled situations will place different communication demands on the children. The following is an example of such a situation.

Situation 1. Children sit in a semicircle; teacher shows pictures; children are asked to say how many objects there are in the picture.

T: How many dogs in this picture? (*Monica, Peter, Brian, and Michael raise their hands. Teacher looks at Monica.*)

P: Five.

T: (*Looks at Peter*) Did I say you could answer? (*Teacher looks at Monica.*) Monica, how many?

M: Five.

T: No. Let's count them.

M: Oh, I didn't see the little one. Why did you cover the puppy with your finger?

T: I'm sorry, Monica, I didn't mean to.

M: There are six.

T: That's right. Does everyone see the six dogs?

(*Chorus*) Yes!

In this situation, the teacher is following the question-answer routine similar to that found in many classrooms (Mehan, 1979). Any child may answer the teacher's questions provided that he or she raises a hand. Once the children are allocated a turn, they may continue the interaction for several turns. It should be noted that in this situation the demands are placed only on the children who are both willing to participate and are selected. Thus, unless the teacher changes the rule of participation, children who do not want to or do not know how to participate will have no demands placed on them.

Sometimes teachers set up activities in which all children are required to participate. Situation 2 is an example of such activity.

Situation 2. All children line up in the rug area. They each take a turn at rolling a ball and knocking down bowling pins. They then count the number of pins knocked down and go to the end of the line when finished.

T: John, roll the ball. (*John rolls the ball*) How many pins did you knock down?
J: One, two, three. Three. (*J. goes to the end of the line*)
T: OK, next. (*Maria rolls the ball*) How many?
M: (*No response*)
T: Let's count. One, two, three, four, five. You knocked down five. Cuantos tumbastes? [*How many did you knock down?*] Five.
M: Five.
(*Activity continues until each child has had one turn*)

Although all children are expected to communicate in this situation, the communicative demands placed on individual children vary. The first child is expected to understand and comply with the

request for action and the request for information. The second child is also expected to understand and comply with a request for action, but in this case the teacher does not specify what the child is to do, just that it is the child's turn. Maria's nonresponsiveness to the teacher's question is first interpreted by the teacher as Maria's inability to perform the academic task. After providing the answer, the teacher asks a more specific question using a different language, answers her own question without providing Maria the opportunity to answer and Maria provides an answer that may be considered an imitation.

Not all activities require the children to be verbal participants. For example, in Situation 3, the children are required only to comply with the teacher's request for action. Although the teacher asks a series of questions, the children never have an opportunity to answer them.

Situation 3. All children are sitting at their desk coloring a drawing of a rabbit. They are to make an exact copy of the teacher's sample rabbit.

C1: (*Uses another child's crayons*)
T–C1: Take your own. Don't you know your name?
T–C2: Sit down, dearie. Sit down!
T–C3: I'll be around with the paste.
T–C4: Pick up the crayon from the floor.
T–C5: You know why she is covering hers? Because she didn't do the face right.
T–C2: Sit down and be quiet! (*Inaudible*)
T–C3: Well, use it.
T–C6: Pay attention.
T–All: Whose crayons are these?
T–C3: Yours? Hers?
T–C4: These are hers. You find your own box.

As can be seen from the three situations, the communicative demands placed on the children depend on the task and the rules of participation. In some cases, teachers make minor adjustments in order to accommodate children with different communication and academic skills.

The specific language used by teachers when interacting with cultural-linguistic-minority children depends on both school

---

Some districts require all children who are not "English dominant" to enroll in classes in which the instruction is provided by a bilingual staff member; that is, the teacher or the aide is bilingual.

---

policy and personal preference. Some districts require all children who are not "English dominant" to enroll in classes in which the instruction is provided by a bilingual staff member; that is, the teacher or the aide is bilingual. Other districts do not provide such services, and the children are enrolled in classes in which the staff does not speak the minority language.

Except in school districts in which the bilingual staff is closely monitored, the language used by teachers for instructional purposes is one of personal preference. Some teachers and aides use English as the primary language of instruction and the minority language only for clarification; others use only the minority language; and others use different languages depending on the task and the participants.

In summary, teachers organize their classrooms in the way in which they feel

curricular objectives are best achieved. The procedures teachers use to accomplish these objectives determine the communicative demands placed on each individual child.

COMMUNICATIVE MATCH AND MISMATCH

Erickson and Iglesias (1984) propose the communicative match/mismatch model illustrated in Figure 1. According to this model, a set of factors (H) influences the communication skills the child brings from home in ways that are yet to be determined. Teachers in turn place certain communicative demands on these children as a function of the procedures they select to accomplish curricular objectives. The factors (S) influencing teachers' selection of particular procedures include grade level, educational background, ethnic background, and so forth. As in the case with the child's communicative skills, the only claim that can be made at this point is that these factors do affect, to some extent, directly or indirectly, the type of procedures used by teachers to carry out their curricular objectives. The model shows that in later years the child's communication skills will be the combined result of home factors and previous classroom experiences (C).

Communicative mismatch occurs when a child's communication skills are not equivalent to those demanded and expected by the teacher. The most obvious mismatch occurs when a teacher addresses the child in a language that the child does not understand. However, communicative mismatch extends beyond the use of different "languages" by the child and the teacher. For example, if a teacher asks a

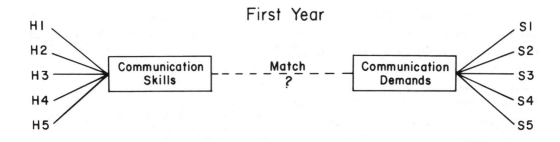

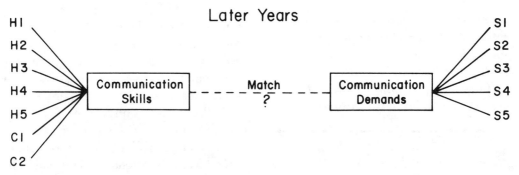

Figure 1. Communication match/mismatch model proposed by Erickson and Iglesias (1984). H = home factors; C = previous classroom experiences; S = factors influencing teacher's selection of procedures.

child to tell a story (expecting the child to tell a story with a beginning, middle, and end) and the child provides only a very elaborate description of the characters in a story, then a communicative mismatch has occurred.

Different combinations of children and teachers produce different outcomes. In some cases the child's skills closely resemble those demanded by the teacher. For example, there should be little chance of a breakdown in teacher–child communication if the child comes from a home in which directives are used most of the time and the teacher requires the child only to comply with requests, as in Situation 3. On the other hand, a greater chance of a

communication breakdown exists if the same child is in a classroom in which the teacher individually nominates him to answer questions, such as, "Juan, how much is two plus two?" Here the distance between the child's communication skills and those demanded by the teacher is greater than in the previous case.

On the surface, it appears that the greater the match between the child's skills and the teacher's demands, the greater the chance for the child to succeed in school. This assumption is correct only if the demands made by the teacher are consistent with the demands made by teachers the child will encounter in higher grades. In order to be successful, the child must learn to use language differently in different situations and with different tasks and different teachers.

When cultural-linguistic minority children are in the first years of school, teachers often blame the mismatch between teacher and children on the children's background. When a child's behavior is considered to be inappropriate, the teacher may attempt to minimize the mismatch by teaching a particular skill the teacher considers the child to be "missing." Teachers often comment that although they understand what the children are trying to communicate, they refuse to accept that particular way of communicating because "it is not the way they will need to communicate in higher grades." It should be stressed that a communication match between a particular teacher and a child does not imply that the child will not have a mismatch with other teachers.

After the first few years, mismatch between the child's communication skills and the teacher's demands tend not to be attributed by the teachers to the child's cultural and linguistic background. This is especially true for English-speaking minority children. The problems children in higher grades encounter are more often attributed to low intellectual capacity and/or to a communication disorder. What teachers at this level often fail to realize is that the communicative demands of their classrooms are different from those of earlier grades, and that many of these children have not been taught, either at home or in their previous classes, the particular skills required for success in the higher grades. Like the Roadville children (Heath, 1983), these

children are not prepared for the type of tasks necessary for higher-level school work.

Communicative matches and mismatches have considerable implications for educational policy. First, cultural-linguistic minority children should be placed in classes in which little or no mismatch exists between the child's communication skills and the teacher's demands. In other words, the teacher should speak the child's native language and the teacher's communication demands should be similar to those to which the child has been exposed at home. Second, since the teacher's goal is to ensure that children function adequately in mainstream classes, the teacher must gradually train them in the communicative skills required in those classes. Providing children only with some basic linguistic skills in English is not sufficient. Although the U.S. government has not necessarily used the same rationale, the transitional bilingual approach is the educational policy that was advocated by the government from the mid-1970s until the early 1980s.

EDUCATIONAL POLICIES

Until the late 19th century, school laws either made no mention of the language of instruction or permitted instruction in a language other than English (Castellanos, 1983). In the early 1900s, individual states began requiring English as the medium of instruction. Prohibition of non-English languages in the school continued until the late 1960s, when the Bilingual Education Act of 1968 (PL 90–247) was enacted. The goal of this act and its 1974 amendments

(Equal Opportunity Act of 1974) was to provide appropriation for transitional programs that used the child's native language in conjunction with English instruction before children entered English-only classes.

Also in 1974 the U.S. Supreme Court, in the landmark *Lau v. Nichols* case, held that school districts must devise programs to ensure equality of educational opportunities for students of non-English-speaking background. In 1975 the Office of Civil Rights proposed a set of guidelines, referred to as the Lau Remedies, intended to help school districts comply with the Supreme Court decision. The Lau Remedies specified that when school districts had 20 or more Limited English Proficient (LEP) students from one language group, the children's native language was to be used for instruction until each child had sufficient English skills to function in an English-only classroom. Enrollment of a child in English as a Second Language (ESL) classes without the benefit of instruction in the child's native language

was not considered to be sufficient. Use of the Lau Remedies has varied considerably across the country. O'Malley (1982) estimated that 58 percent of LEP students are enrolled in English-only classes and 11 percent were enrolled in ESL-only classes. Thus less than one-third of non-English-speaking children are enrolled in educa-

---

Children are grouped on the basis of their linguistic skills, usually their English skills, even though their communication and academic skills may vary.

---

tional programs in which the teacher speaks the children's native language.

Generally, school districts that offer instruction in children's native languages and/or ESL follow the identification and placement procedure illustrated in Figure 2. Children are grouped on the basis of their linguistic skills, usually their English skills, even though their communication

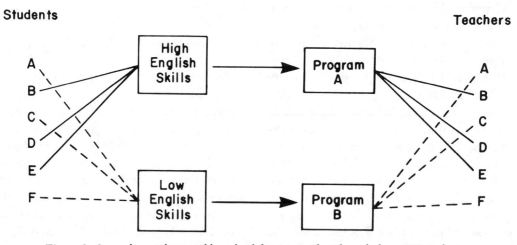

Figure 2. General procedure used by school districts to identify and place LEP students.

and academic skills may vary. Children who fall in the same category are then placed in the "same" program. For example, the procedure used by the New York City School District involves administering the Language Assessment Battery (LAB) to all language-minority students. Spanish-speaking children are entitled to bilingual education if they score below the 20th percentile on the English version of the LAB and their scores on the Spanish version of the LAB are higher than their scores on the English version of the test. Since only the English and Spanish versions of the test are available, language-minority students whose language is other than Spanish are given only the English version. Thus their placement is based solely on their linguistic skills in English.

School districts that follow the procedure illustrated in Figure 2 make two assumptions. First, they assume that children who demonstrate the same linguistic skills on a particular test have the same communication skills. Second, they assume that all teachers in classrooms in which a particular educational philosophy is advocated (bilingual, English-only, etc.) will place the same communicative demands on their students. Neither of these two assumptions is valid. Children with the same linguistic skills in English do not demonstrate the same communication skills (Politzer, Shohamy, & McGroarty, 1983), and teachers in the same programs do not place the same communicative demands on their students (Iglesias, in press).

Because of the transitional nature of the bilingual programs, students are expected to transfer to a regular English-only class after the third year, if not sooner.

Although most schools advocate the use of multiple exit criteria, the greatest weight is usually given to children's linguistic skills in English (i.e., their scores on an English dominance/performance test). Little or no emphasis is given to the children's ability to use their newly gained linguistic skills for academic purposes. Once exited from a bilingual program, the children are viewed as "proficient communicators."

Educational policy has been guided by the premise that cultural-linguistic minority children's limited proficiency in English is the sole cause of their academic difficulties. Some school districts operate as if the time spent teaching the child in his or her native language is wasted time that can be best spent teaching English skills to the child. Other districts have opted for an approach in which English is gradually introduced as the child learns subject matter in his or her native language, thus guaranteeing that the child does not fall behind in the content areas. What policy makers and practitioners using these two approaches have failed to realize is that the premise on which their policies and practices are based is incorrect.

There is no question that a lack of linguistic skills contributes to the difficulties encountered by these children. However, numerous other factors are involved, including invalid assessment tools used to place the children, educational programs that do not teach the children how to communicate in different settings, exit criteria that do not mirror the communicative demands that will be placed on the children when they enter mainstream classes, and so forth. Unless educational policies and practices begin to reflect current knowledge about communication, cultural-linguistic minority children will continue to encounter difficulties in the U.S. educational system.

IMPLICATIONS FOR PROGRAM DEVELOPMENT

Despite pleas for educational reform to accommodate linguistic and ethnic minorities (e.g., Labov, 1969), substantial changes have not occurred. Success within the educational system still means learning and following "their" rules and speaking "their" language.

The moment a child encounters academic difficulties in the U.S. educational system, individuals begin to blame the home environment or the school. Parents are accused of providing an environment that is not linguistically and cognitively stimulating, or schools are accused of being "insensitive to the culturally different linguistic and cognitive style that he [child] brings to the classroom" (Baratz & Baratz, 1970). Those who blame the home have advocated remedial programs that would "counteract the deleterious effect of the home situation" (p. 39) by using the same teaching strategies but training the child in "missing" skills. Those who blame the school setting advocate using procedures and materials that are culturally relevant. Thus they advocate modifying the teaching and ignoring the home situation. Neither of these two approaches has achieved the success anticipated by their advocates. In both cases, the problem lies in attempting to use simplistic solutions to solve a complex problem.

No one program can be advocated for a diverse population. However, for any program to succeed in meeting the needs of cultural-linguistic minority children, it must incorporate systematic and intensive training of the children's parents and teachers.

Parents are often unaware of the communication demands that are placed on their children in the school situation. They often do not incorporate the content the children learn at school into their home routines. Thus parents must be made aware of this content and, if necessary, taught how to reinforce what the child is learning in the classroom. Parents must also be informed about how this content is assessed by the teacher. Merely enumerating the particular skills that the child must learn is not sufficient. Since the communicative demands change throughout the school year, the parent and the teacher must remain in constant and frequent contact.

Teachers often fail to realize that the communicative demands they place on individual students vary with the procedures they select for implementing their curricular goals. Teachers must become aware of the communicative demands they are placing on their students, and if necessary, they must be trained in ways to modify their instructional approach to ensure that each child has the opportunity to participate in classroom interactions. In addition, teachers must ensure that they train children in the communication skills that will be required in higher grades.

• • •

The educational programs presently available for cultural-linguistic minority children are primarily based on "authority (laws and experts), personal experience of educators, and common sense reasoning of program designers and planners ... rather than on research based theoretical

frameworks" (Office of Bilingual Education, CA, 1981, p. ix). It is hoped that this article has contributed to such frameworks, which are desperately needed.

REFERENCES

Baratz, S.S., & Baratz, J.C. (1970). Early childhood intervention: The social science base of institutional racism. *Harvard Educational Review, 40*, 29–49.

Blount, B.G. (1982). Culture and language of socialization: Parental speech. In D. Wagner & H.W. Stevenson (Eds.), *Cultural perspectives on child language* (pp. 54–76). San Francisco: W.H. Freeman.

Castellanos, D. (1983). *The best of two worlds. Bilingual-bicultural education in the U.S.* Trenton, NJ: New Jersey Department of Education.

Erickson, J., & Iglesias, A. (1984). *Communication match/mismatch.* Unpublished manuscript.

Heath, S. (1983). *Ways with words.* Cambridge, UK: Cambridge University Press.

Iglesias, A. (in press). School discourse problems. In D. Ripich & F. Spinelli (Eds.), *Educational discourse and the communicatively impaired children.* San Diego, CA: College Hill Press.

Labov, W. (1969). The logic of nonstandard English. *Georgetown Monographs on Language and Linguistics, 22*, 1-31.

Mehan, H. (1979). *Learning lessons.* Cambridge, MA: Harvard University Press.

Office of Bilingual Education, CA (1981). *Schooling and language minority students: A theoretical framework.* Los Angeles: Evaluation, Dissemination and Assessment Center, California State University.

O'Malley, M. (1982). *Children's English and services study. Educational needs assessment of language minority children with limited English proficiency.* Rosslyn, VA: National Clearinghouse for Bilingual Education.

Politzer, R.L., Shohamy, E., & McGroarty, M. (1983). Validation of linguistic and communicative oral language tests for Spanish-English bilingual programs. *Bilingual Review, 10*, 3–20.

Saville-Troike, M. (1979). Culture, language and education. In H.T. Trueba & C. Barnett-Mizrahi (Eds.), *Bilingual multicultural education and the professional: From theory to practice* (pp. 139–148). Rowley, MA: Newberry House.

Super, C.M., & Harkness, S. (1982). The development of affect in infancy and early childhood. In D. Wagner and H.W. Stevenson (Eds.), *Cultural perspectives on child language* (pp. 1–19). San Francisco: W.H. Freeman.

Ethnography and classroom communication: Taking an "emic" perspective

Georgia Earnest García, PhD
Assistant Professor
Department of Curriculum and
*   Instruction*
Center for the Study of Reading
University of Illinois at
*   Urbana-Champaign*
Champaign, Illinois

Have you ever hurt
    about baskets?
I have, seeing my grandmother weaving
    for a long time.
Have you ever hurt about work?
I have, because my father works too hard
    and tells how he works.
Have you ever hurt about cattle?
I have, because my grandfather has been
    working on the cattle for a long time.
Have you ever hurt about school?
I have, because I learned a lot of words
    from my school,
And they are not my words (Anonymous; cited
in Cazden & Dickinson, 1981, p. 458)*

THIS POEM, written by an Apache
child in Arizona, captures the focus
of this article. A teacher in a kindergarten
classroom in the Midwest also helped to

---

*Reprinted with permission from Cazden, C.B. & Dickinson, D.K. (1981). Language in education: Standardization versus cultural pluralism. In C.A. Ferguson & S.B. Heath (Eds). Language in the U.S.A. New York: Cambridge University Press. Copyright 1981, Cambridge University Press.

Top Lang Disord, 1992,12(3),54–66
© 1992 Aspen Publishers, Inc.

set the tone for this article when she told me how she refers African American children to the school's speech-language pathologist (SLP), not because she suspects that the children are language delayed, but because she cannot understand them.

In this article, findings from ethnographic and microethnographic research are reviewed to further the understanding about how classroom interaction patterns can affect student achievement. This line of research should be of particular interest to SLPs and other special educators, not just because many of their referrals come from the classroom teacher, but because they are increasingly being called on to work within the classroom setting as part of the collaborative model of service delivery.

This article draws on findings from two research groups: (a) sociolinguists and classroom ethnographers who focus on understanding the role of language in classroom instruction and (b) educational anthropologists who study the cultural role of language in home, community, and school settings. After the concept of communicative competence, in general and in the classroom setting in particular, is discussed the findings from studies of home–school cultural discontinuities are reviewed to illustrate the importance of understanding the different norms that may govern language interactions in the home, community, and classroom. The article concludes by discussing how an *emic* perspective—the ability to empathize and understand other participants' perspectives and actions—can help teachers and clinicians bridge these differences between home and school.

COMMUNICATIVE COMPETENCE

Individuals are considered communicatively competent within a particular speech community when they know how to participate in socially appropriate ways (Florio-Ruane, 1987; Saville-Troike, 1989). *Communicative competence* is the knowledge that allows the individual to understand and act in concert with the expectations of the other participants. Young children learn how to communicate appropriately within the speech community in which they are raised. By the time they are five years old, most have acquired the linguistic and grammatical rudiments necessary to become competent speakers of the dialect and/or language heard around them (Lindfors, 1987). In addition to acquiring linquistic and grammatical rules, children become sensitive to the context, function, and meaning of interaction patterns. Depending on the speech community and one's role within that community, different ways of interacting and talking with parents, siblings, grandparents, other adults, and peers are learned (Saville-Troike, 1989).

Because communicative competence reflects what is appropriate in one speech community, there will be some variation in what is appropriate in a different speech community, even within the same country. These variations in communicative competence are called *sociolinguistic styles.* García, Pearson, and Jiménez (1990) point out that the "persistence of different sociolinguistic styles, even when children are exposed to the mass media and to universal schooling, suggests that these styles are acquired at an early age through socialization" (p. 54). It is likely that children's willingness to acquire new styles is affected by their motivation to participate not only in other speech communities but also in the larger society (see Ogbu & Matute-Bianchi, 1986).

Speech-language pathologists need to understand that children who speak a distinct dialect of English or who are learning English as a second language face problems that are different from those of a child who has not learned the appropriate sociolinguistic styles for his or her own speech community. In working with a dialect mismatch between the teacher and the child, the SLP needs to be sensitive to the fact that all English-speaking Americans speak a dialect of English, although some dialects are closer to standard English than others. Speech-language pathologists and classroom teachers need to understand that dialects, especially African American dialects, are not deviant forms of language (Labov, 1982). In fact, there is evidence that teachers' negative reactions to children's use of dialect, and not the children's use of dialect itself, is what appears to adversely affect their academic performance (García et al., 1990). Many children who speak a distinct dialect of English cease to participate when SLPs or teachers continually interrupt their speech to correct a dialect feature or insist that they only use standard English (García et al., 1990; Smitherman, 1986). Acquiring the type of standard English characteristic of written text is a relatively new task for all children. The task is eased, however, when the teacher shares the same dialect as the child or when the teacher is bidialectal and can help the child acquire two dialects (Delpit, 1988; Smitherman, 1986).

Children acquiring English as a second language are knowledgeable about appropriate ways of communicating in their native language but may need help in understanding and acquiring pragmatic skills in English. As an example, sixteen-year-old María, a Spanish-English bilingual student enrolled in a general equivalency degree (GED) program, appeared to be extremely fluent in both languages. Yet, she startled her adult education teacher when she authoritatively commanded that a worker at a McDonald's fast-food restaurant "give her" the food that she desired. Although the worker understood what

---

Children acquiring English as a second language are knowledgeable about appropriate ways of communicating in their native language but may need help in understanding and acquiring pragmatic skills in English.

María had said, he was taken aback by her tone of voice and the imperative nature of her command. María had not acquired the appropriate courtesy protocol for this particular American social setting. Here is a situation in which the SLP and María's classroom teacher could work collaboratively to develop such activities as role playing or the use of videotapes to teach her the appropriate courtesy protocols in English.

Communicative competence encompasses knowledge about the linguistic features of language, the interaction patterns necessary to participate successfully in a variety of roles, and the cultural knowledge necessary to understand how communication (both verbal and nonverbal) is shaped and interpreted within a particular culture or speech community (Saville-Troike, 1989). Most adults have acquired communicative competence as young children immersed in the language and culture that surround them. Encountering new contexts of language use, children add to their communicative competence repertoire, increasing the sociolinguistic styles with which they are familiar.

CLASSROOM INTERACTION

The role that sociolinguistic styles play in determining school success may depend on the extent to which learning in the classroom is a function of the ability of the teacher and the child to sustain meaningful interaction in the classroom (see Gumperz, 1982; Leacock, 1972). A basic assumption underlying many of the current studies of classroom interaction is that teaching and learning are "interactive processes that require the active participation of teachers and students to ensure that information is conveyed as a precondition for learning" (Gumperz, 1982, p. 57).

Successful participation in the classroom requires a different type of communicative competence than that brought to school by most children (Cazden, 1988; Saville-Troike, 1989). The teacher's role and status differ from those of other adults with whom the child has interacted or continues to interact. For example, teachers tend to be more absolute in their authority, controlling not only how children verbally and nonverbally interact with them, but also how they interact with

other children. This is true both in traditional classrooms and in more open-ended whole language classrooms. Saville-Troike (1982) points out that communication in the American classroom traditionally has been characterized by "rigid turn-taking, with a raised hand to request a turn; [a definite] spacial arrangement, with children seated in rows of desks or around tables; and peer interaction which is initiated and controlled by adults" (p. 240). Although whole language classrooms provide students with more freedom (Goodman, 1989), the teacher still is the primary authority figure in the classroom. Children have to learn how to get the teacher's attention, when it is appropriate to speak to the teacher in private or in front of the group, how to respond appropriately, with whom they can interact and when, and what the different spacial arrangements are for the different activities.

Classroom discourse in traditional and whole language classrooms is characterized by identifiable patterns that students must learn if they are to acquire classroom communicative competence. For example, one of the most common patterns of classroom interaction in the United States occurs when the teacher initiates an interaction, the student responds, and the teacher evaluates the student's response (Cazden, 1988; Mehan, 1979). This pattern of interaction may occur in whole-class settings, in small group settings, or in teacher-student conferences. Teachers may use it to request an answer:

Teacher: John, what is the answer to #4?
John: Six.
Teacher: Good.

Other times, they may use it for clarification or to request unknown information:

Teacher: Diane, were you absent yesterday?
Diane: Uh-huh.
Teacher: Okay.

To avoid answering the question would be a breach of communicative conduct on the student's part. This pattern of interaction tends to characterize most teacher-led lessons, whether the lesson is reading, arithmetic, or social studies (Cazden, 1988). Teachers tend to use questions and answers within this pattern of interaction to elicit known information from children, so that they can monitor the children's comprehension of material and evaluate their performance (Cazden, 1988; Heath, 1982).

Throughout their interactions with children, teachers also use certain types of speech acts to control behavior and solicit cooperation. Because the functions of these acts may vary from one context to the other, children have to learn how to interpret their teacher's use of these acts (Sinclair & Coulthard, 1975). For example, it is not unusual for middle-class Anglo teachers (especially female teachers) to pose a command as a question (e.g., "John, will you please close the window?") (Delpit, 1988; Heath, 1982). Delpit (1988) points out that not all children are socialized in their speech communities to respond to this type of command. She contends that some African American children get into trouble in school because they respond to it literally, interpreting it as a request that can be denied and not a command.

Classroom activity also is characterized by routinized speech events, such as show and tell, taking roll, storybook time, round robin reading, and independent silent reading (Cazden, 1988; Saville-Troike, 1982).

Children learn to recognize these speech events by paying attention to the contextualization cues—verbal, paralinguistic, and kinesic behavior—that teachers routinely use to introduce them (Cazden, 1988; Gumperz, 1982). When children recognize the cues and are aware of the shifting activities or emphases that the cues represent, they are then free to focus on the content of the lesson (Cazden, 1988; Harker & Green, 1985).

Because many whole language teachers eschew telling students what to do, students in this type of classroom setting may need to rely more on their implicit understanding of classroom communicative competence and contextualization cues to understand the type of communicative behavior that is appropriate. For example, these students will need to know when the classroom activity has shifted and when it is appropriate to discuss information with a peer, call out information, wait for a turn, whisper, or be silent.

Children's entry into the classroom speech community is eased when children and their teachers participate in the same speech community outside the school (see Byers & Byers, 1972; Delpit, 1988; Heath, 1982; Michaels, 1981). In this situation, the teachers are familiar with the communicative competence that these children bring to school. As a result, they are able to shape these children's interactions, so that they become socialized into the school environment. When teachers are unfamiliar with the sociolinguistic styles of children, numerous opportunities for miscommunication and misassessment exist (Delpit, 1988; García, 1991; García et al., 1990; García & Pearson, 1991).

Classroom communicative competence

involves knowing and understanding the classroom rules that govern classroom interaction. Sometimes the rules are explicitly stated (e.g., "Raise your hand and wait to be called on before you talk."). Other times, they are implicit, and children must learn them through observation and trial and error, just as they acquire communicative competence in their speech community. Speech-language pathologists who collaborate with classroom teachers and work with children who are having difficulty interacting in the classroom need to understand the type of classroom communicative competence that the teacher expects. It also helps if the SLP is familiar with the type of communicative competence that the children are likely to bring with them to school. In this way, the SLP can help the teacher understand potential areas of miscommunication and help the child acquire the type of classroom communicative competence necessary to participate successfully in the classroom activities that the teacher deems necessary for instruction and evaluation.

HOME–SCHOOL DISCONTINUITIES

Differences in sociolinguistic styles in the American classroom have been noted in terms of participant structures (verbal and nonverbal patterns of interaction), discourse organizational patterns, and contextualization cues. Florio-Ruane (1987) points out that ethnographers who have contributed to this knowledge typically have studied home, school, and community settings through extensive participant observations and detailed analysis of recorded speech events. Their conclusions are the result of data triangulation—comparison and integration of data from a variety of sources—across home, community, and school settings.

Participant structures

Differences in the social conventions of verbal and nonverbal interaction can affect classroom teaching and learning. Who gets to speak when, how an individual holds the floor, and the way in which questions and answers are formulated and sequenced are aspects of communicative competence. As Hymes (1972) explains,

it is not that a child cannot answer questions but that questions and answers are defined in terms of one set of community norms rather than another, as to what counts as questions and answers, and as to what it means to be asked or to answer. (p. xxxi)

Findings from several ethnographic studies suggest that some children hold different expectations for their participation, which, if not accommodated by the teacher, may adversely affect their involvement in speech events that are an integral part of classroom instruction. For example, Philips (1972, 1983) found that Native American students from the Warm Springs Indian Reservation in Oregon did not willingly respond when the teachers solicited individual volunteers or when they called on students to respond as a group or

---

Who gets to speak when, how an individual holds the floor, and the way in which questions and answers are formulated and sequenced are aspects of communicative competence.

---

individually in front of the group. Students' participation level increased, however, when they interacted on a one-to-one basis with the teacher or when they participated in small groups directed by themselves. Interestingly, the latter participant structure paralleled the type of interaction that was most common for the students on the reservation.

Similar types of home–school discontinuities were reported by Boggs (1972, 1978) for Hawaiian dialect-speaking children, by Heath (1982) for African American children, and by Delgado-Gaitan (1987) for Mexican immigrant children. Boggs noted that the Hawaiian children in his study tended to respond as little as possible when a question was directed to them, but would not hesitate to blurt out the answer when the question was directed to another student or when the teacher directed the question to a group of students. This type of participant structure was similar to a discourse pattern, termed *talk story,* that was common in the children's speech community (see also Kawakami & Au, 1986).

Heath (1982) found that working-class African American students in the Carolina Piedmonts were not supposed to interact with their parents as conversational partners until they were considered "competent speakers." As a result, the children listened to adult conversation but did not actually participate in it. If an adult asked a child a question, it was one that required a "real" answer. Children learned to gain and hold the floor in their interactions with each other by using a story-starter style and analogies. Questions were not used to elicit known information for display purposes, the very type of question that most teachers use in the classroom to monitor and evaluate classroom learning.

Delgado-Gaitan (1987) discovered that Mexican immigrant children were more accustomed to a cooperative working environment than a competitive environment. At home, the children were allowed to negotiate how they would complete assigned tasks; whereas, at school, they were not. When the children tried to work cooperatively at school, the teacher misinterpreted their actions, viewing their efforts as cheating or disruptive.

Because classroom communication involves "the language of curriculum, the language of control, and the language of personal identity" (Cazden, 1988, p. 3), cultural discontinuities between home and school can result in lost teaching and learning opportunities, as well as incorrect assessment of children's capabilities (see García & Pearson, 1991). Speech-language pathologists, psychologists, special educators, and classroom teachers need to be aware of the social context of the testing situation, regardless of whether it is a formal or informal setting. Leap (1982), for example, found that a Native American student hardly responded when she was asked to retell a story read in class. She produced an extensive narrative, however, when she was asked to make up a story about a classmate's picture. Edwards and García (1989) also discovered that an African American child, who was labeled language delayed by the classroom teacher, was very verbal but reticent to participate in adult–child storybook interactions because these interactions did not characterize her home life.

Discourse organization patterns

Cultural differences in how students structure their speech and writing also have been documented. Several study findings suggest that teachers do not always understand why some groups of students may structure their oral speech in ways that vary from the classroom norm (Cooley & Lujan, 1982; Michaels, 1981). For example, Cooley and Lujan explored why college instructors said that their Native American students, who also happened to be monolingual English speakers, tended to ramble when they gave formal presentations in class. Through a comparative analysis, these researchers found that the structure and the content of the Native American students' oral speeches tended to parallel those of their tribal elders. Both groups structured their speeches so that several topics were introduced in sequence without much transition, although coreferencing helped to provide cohesion within the topics. The students also tended to emphasize their sources of information more than the information itself, a characteristic of Native American culture.

Michaels (1981) found differences in discourse patterns among Anglo and African American first graders during sharing time. The Anglo children tended to use a topic-centered style, whereas the African American children used a topic-associating style that consisted of a series of "implicitly associated personal anecdotes" (p. 429). There were no explicit statements of overall themes or points, but the anecdotes all related to a particular topic or theme that had to be inferred. Topic shifts were signaled prosodically and appeared to be difficult for the teacher to follow. The end result was that the Anglo teacher was able to use questions to shape the Anglo children's narratives, helping them to approximate the type of decontextualized, orderly sequenced prose that she thought they would later encounter in their reading. The teacher's attempts to help the African American children, however, were mistimed and inappropriate. She eventually stopped calling on these children because she could not understand the focus of their presentations.

Contextualization cues

The importance of contextualization cues in forming the content and surface style of interaction in the classroom should not be overlooked. Contextualization cues can include formulaic expressions; code, dialect, and style switching; prosodic signs, such as gaze direction, proxemic distance, and kinesic rhythm or timing; choices among lexical and syntactic options; phonetic and rhythmic signs; and conversational openings, closings, and sequencings (Erickson & Shultz, 1977; Gumperz, 1982). As Gumperz explains, these cues allow the activity to be interpreted, "the semantic content to be understood, and the relationship of each sentence to the next to be foreseen" (p. 31). When a listener does not perceive a cue or does not know its function, misunderstandings and different interpretations may occur. In the classroom this may result in misinterpretation of behavior and loss of feedback.

Gumperz (1982) suggests that misinterpretation of contextualization cues in the classroom especially may occur because children use stress, rhythm, and intonation to communicate what adults customarily might put into words. For example, African American children he studied in Berkeley tended to respond to the teachers' requests for action or information by saying, "I don't know," "I can't read," "I don't want to do this," or "I can't do this." The teachers' usual response was to ignore the children or to halt any further interaction. An analysis of the contextualized cues used by the students, however, revealed "similar intonational structures, characterized by a high pitch register, sustained tone, and vowel elongation on the last syllable" (p. 19). When a panel of African American adults reviewed the speech samples, they said that the children actually were saying that they did not like to work alone and needed help.

Differences in the timing of nonverbal gestures also have been noted. For example, Byers and Byers (1972) discovered that an Anglo teacher did not maintain the same type of eye contact with her Anglo children as she did with her African American children. Although the African American children and Anglo teacher actually gazed at each other more often than did the teacher and Anglo children, their pauses were mistimed. As a result, less eye contact was realized. Byers and Byers suggest that differences in contextualization cues may mean that students will miss "subtle interconnections" in the presentation of information. As a result, students will not feel secure "in what [they have] learned and in what the significance of learning is" (p. 27).

There are several reasons why children and teachers from different speech communities may miscommunicate. Home–school discontinuities may be reflected in dif-

ferent participant structures, discourse organization patterns, and contextualization cues. Clinicians need to be aware of these differences and take the time to find out whether a child's communication problem represents such a discontinuity. To do this, they will need to observe both the teacher and the child in the classroom, documenting the points of miscommunication and the type of classroom communicative competence that the teacher expects. In addition, they will have to find out more about the child's background and the type of communicative competence that prevails in the child's speech community. They especially need to be open to input from the child's parents and other members of the community. Heath (1982) began her longitudinal study of literacy and communicative behavior in the Carolina Piedmonts when the African American children's parents told her that they did not understand why the teachers said that their children could not answer questions. Juxtaposing conflicting points of information is one way to discover home–school discontinuities that have the potential for successful resolutions.

BRIDGING DIFFERENCES

Several researchers and educators have suggested that school professionals (classroom teachers, SLPs, special educators, administrators, and psychologists) need to be aware of the emic perspective. That is, they need to understand the importance of viewing school events from the cultural perspectives of the participants. To do this, these professionals not only have to be open to understanding how communicative events are interpreted by others, but also have to acknowledge that their own patterns of interaction are influenced by their own socialization. A key component of the emic perspective is the ability to observe others from their perspective and to understand how one is conditioned by one's own perspective.

Educators who have been willing to bridge differences in communicative competence have met with some success. For example, the Kamehameha Early Education Program (KEEP) in Hawaii (Au, 1980) has had considerable success in increasing Hawaiian children's reading comprehension by allowing the students to engage in the type of talk story that Boggs (1972,

---

A key component of the emic perspective is the ability to observe others from their perspective and to understand how one is conditioned by one's own perspective.

1978) described. Although teachers in the KEEP program generally initiate reading comprehension questions, the students respond by calling out their answers and building on each other's responses until the group as a whole has reacted to the teachers' questions. The interaction pattern that dominates during this part of the instruction is quite different from the teacher initiates–student responds–teacher evaluates type of pattern that generally characterizes most reading group instruction.

Two other examples are provided by Heath (1982) and Erickson and Mohatt (1982). In Heath's study (1982), the teach-

ers were able to bridge differences in interaction patterns by incorporating more of the African American students' questioning patterns in their own classroom instruction and by attempting to introduce the African American students, in a risk-free manner, to the types of questions that they preferred. Erickson and Mohatt (1982) found that an Anglo teacher was able to interact successfully with his Native American students when he accommodated to cultural differences in sociolinguistic styles throughout the year by increasing his one-on-one interactions with the students and reducing the "spotlighting" of student interactions in front of an audience.

Many times observant teachers will naturally adjust to what they perceive to be a lack of communication. Other times, they will need to rely on outside help to explain a classroom occurrence they do not understand. Carrasco (1981) found that even a well-intentioned bilingual teacher misread the potential capability of one of her bilingual students. In response to a bilingual aide's comment that the Latino children talked more often in groups, Carrasco began to videotape one of the bilingual children whom the teacher was considering retaining. He found that this child was the one who was helping the other students complete work that the teacher did not think she could do on her own.

Genishi (1985) points out that teachers frequently may not be able to do systematic observations because of the nature of their jobs. Clinicians should be able to help teachers in this area. The clinician may be able to discover why communication has gone awry by observing or videotaping (or both) the classroom; interviewing the teacher, the child, and the child's parents; and visiting the child's home and community. The clinician can share this information with the classroom teacher and use what she or he knows about language acquisition, classroom communicative competence, and potential home–school discontinuities (see Harker & Green, 1985) to help the teacher develop a plan to bridge communication differences.

Sometimes, bridging communication differences may involve a radical change in how the teacher presents material or facilitates interaction, such as found in the KEEP program (Au, 1980). Other times, it may involve a simple change, such as not interrupting the oral reading of a dialect-speaking student when the student uses a dialect feature that preserves meaning, or becoming aware of how students from a particular speech community use language, as described by Gumperz (1982). Still other times, it may involve an instructional modification, in which the teacher modifies the ways in which she or he elicits students' active participation in a communicative event deemed necessary for learning and instruction, at the same time that he or she makes explicit, or introduces students to, those aspects of classroom communicative competence that tend to prevail in the American classroom, as in Heath (1982).

• • •

If school professionals are to take an emic perspective, in which the focus is on understanding the situation from the different cultural perspectives of the participants, they need to step out of their roles as participants in the school's speech community. They need to recognize that there are other patterns of communication that are just as viable as those they are accustomed to in school. School professionals also have to be willing to search for alternative explanations when children are not performing well in school. They have to be willing to accept the interpretations and the observations of not just the teacher, but also of the child, the child's parents, and the community members.

The clinician can help in this effort. By using ethnographic techniques, such as home–school observation, interviews, and data triangulation, the clinician can determine whether a communication problem is due to a mismatch between the child's communicative competence and the classroom communicative competence expected at school. An ethnographic approach not only can help clinicians understand the source of communication problems, but also can help them work with the classroom teacher, the student, and the student's parents to design a plan, so that differences in communicative competence can be bridged.

REFERENCES

Au, K.H.-P. (1980). Participation structures in a reading lesson with Hawaiian children: Analysis of culturally appropriate instructional events. *Anthropology and Education Quarterly, 11,* 91–115.

Boggs, S.T. (1972). The meaning of questions and narratives to Hawaiian children. In C.B. Cazden, V.P. John, & D. Hymes (Eds.), *Functions of language in the*

classroom (pp. 299–327). New York: Teachers College Press.

Boggs, S.T. (1978). The development of verbal disputing in part-Hawaiian children. *Language in Society, 7,* 325–344.

Byers, P. & Byers, B. (1972). In C.B. Cazden, V.P. John, & D. Hymes (Eds.), *Functions of language in the classroom* (pp. 3–31). New York: Teachers College Press.

Carrasco, R.L. (1981). Expanded awareness of student performance: A case study in applied ethnographic monitoring in a bilingual classroom. In H.T. Trueba, G.P. Guthrie, & K.H. Au (Eds.), *Culture and the bilingual classroom: Studies in classroom ethnography* (pp. 153–177). Rowley, MA: Newbury House.

Cazden, C.B. (1988). *Classroom discourse: The language of teaching and learning.* Portsmouth, NH: Heinemann.

Cazden, C.B. & Dickinson, D.K. (1981). Language in education: Standardization versus cultural pluralism. In C.A. Ferguson & S.B. Heath (Eds.), *Language in the USA* (pp. 446–468). New York: Cambridge University Press.

Cooley, D., & Lujan, P. (1982). A structural analysis of speeches by Native American students. In F. Barkin, E.A. Brandt, & J. Ornstein-Galicia (Eds.), *Bilingualism and language contact: Spanish, English, and Native American languages* (pp. 80–92). New York: Teachers College Press.

Delgado-Gaitan, C. (1987). Traditions and transitions in the learning process of Mexican children: An ethnographic view. In G. Spindler & L. Spindler (Eds.) *Interpretive ethnography of education: At home and abroad* (pp. 333–359). Hillsdale, NJ: Erlbaum.

Delpit, L. (1988). The silenced dialogue: Power and pedagogy in educating other people's children. *Harvard Educational Review, 58*(3), 280–298.

Edwards, P.A., & García, G.E. (1989, November). *A case study of one low-income mother learning to share books with her four-year-old daughter.* Paper presented at the National Reading Conference, Austin, TX.

Erickson, F., & Mohatt, G. (1982). Cultural organization of participation structures in two classrooms of Indian students. In G. Spindler (Ed.), *Doing the ethnography of schooling: Educational anthropology in action* (pp. 132–174). Orlando, FL: Holt, Rinehart & Winston.

Erickson, F., & Shultz, J. (1977). When is a context? Some issues and methods in the analysis of social competence. *The Quarterly Newsletter of the Institute for Comparative Human Development, 1,* 5–9.

Florio-Ruane, S. (1987). Sociolinguistics for educational researchers. *American Educational Research Journal, 24*(2), 185–197.

García, G.E. (1991). Factors influencing the English reading test performance of Spanish-speaking Hispanic children. *Reading Research Quarterly, 23*(4), 371–392.

García, G.E., & Pearson, P.D. (1991). The role of assessment in a diverse society. In E. Hiebert (Ed.), *Literacy in a diverse society: Perspectives, practices, and policies* (pp. 253–278). New York: Teachers College Press.

García, G.E., Pearson, P.D., & Jiménez, R.T. (1990). *The at-risk dilemma: A synthesis of reading research* (study 2.2.3.3b). Urbana-Champaign, IL: University of Illinois, Reading Research & Education Center.

Genishi, C. (1985). Observing communicative performance in young children. In A. Jagger & M.T. Smith-Burke (Eds.), *Observing the language learner* (pp. 131–142). Newark, DE: International Reading Association; and Urbana, IL: National Council of Teachers of English.

Goodman, K.S. (1989). Whole language research: Foundations and development. *The Elementary School Journal, 90*(2), 207–221.

Gumperz, J. (1982). *Discourse strategies: Studies in interactional sociolinguistics I.* New York: Cambridge University Press.

Harker, J.O., & Green, J.L. (1985). When you get the right answer to the wrong question: Observing and understanding communication in classrooms. In A. Jagger & M.T. Smith-Burke (Eds.), *Observing the language learner* (pp. 221–231). Newark, DE: International Reading Association; and Urbana, IL: National Council of Teachers of English.

Heath, S.B. (1982). Questioning at school and at home: A comparative study. In G. Spindler (Ed.), *Doing the ethnography of schooling: Educational anthropology in action* (pp. 102–131). Orlando, FL: Holt, Rinehart & Winston.

Hymes, D. (1972). Introduction. In C.B. Cazden, V.P. John, & D. Hymes (Eds.), *Functions of language in the classroom.* New York: Teachers College Press.

Kawakami, A.J., & Au, K.H.-P. (1986). Encouraging reading and language development in cultural minority children. *Topics in Language Disorders, 6*(2), 71–80.

Labov, W. (1982). Objectivity and commitment in linguistic science. The case of the Black English trial in Ann Arbor. *Language in Society, 11,* 165–201.

Leacock, E.B. (1972). Abstract versus concrete speech: A false dichotomy. In C.B. Cazden, V.P. John, & D. Hymes (Eds.), *Functions of language in the classroom* (pp. 111–134). New York: Teachers College Press.

Leap, W.L. (1982). The study of Indian English in the U.S. Southwest: Retrospect and prospect. In F. Barkin, E.A. Brandt, & J. Ornstein-Galicia (Eds.), *Bilingualism and language contact: Spanish, English and Native American languages* (pp. 101–119). New York: Teachers College Press.

Lindfors, J.W. (1987). *Children's language and learning* (2nd ed.). Englewood Cliffs, NJ: Prentice-Hall.

Mehan, H. (1979). *Learning lessons.* Cambridge: Harvard University Press.

Michaels, S. (1981). Sharing time: Children's narrative styles and differential access to literacy. *Language in Society, 10,* 423–442.

Ogbu, J.U., & Matute-Bianchi, M.E. (1986). Understanding sociocultural factors: Knowledge, identity, and school adjustment. In *Beyond language: Social and cultural factors in schooling language minority students* (pp.

73–142). (Compiled by California State Department of Education.) Los Angeles: Evaluation, Dissemination & Assessment Center.

Philips, S. (1972). Participant structures and communicative competence: Warm Springs children in community and classroom. In C.B. Cazden, V.P. John, & D. Hymes (Eds.), *Functions of language in the classroom* (pp. 370–394. New York: Teachers College Press.

Philips, S. (1983). *The invisible culture: Communication in classroom and community on the Warm Springs Indian Reservation.* White Plains, NY: Longman.

Saville-Troike, M. (1982). *The ethnography of communication: An introduction* (1st ed.). Baltimore: University Park Press.

Saville-Troike, M. (1989). *The ethnography of communication: An introduction* (2nd ed.). New York: Basil Blackwell.

Sinclair, J. McH., & Coulthard, R.M. (1975). *Toward an analysis of discourse: The English used by teachers and pupils.* London: Oxford University Press.

Smitherman, G. (1986). *Talkin and testifyin: The language of Black America.* Detroit: Wayne State University.

Ethnography and communication: Social-role relations

Norma S. Rees, PhD
President
Office of the President
California State University, Hayward
Hayward, California

Sima Gerber, PhD
Assistant Professor
Communication Arts and Sciences
Queens College
Flushing, New York

FOR PRACTITIONERS whose fascina- tion with language has led them to language disorders as a field of study and a professional commitment, language in use has turned out to be of bottomless complex- ity and, yet, of central importance. As they have struggled to understand what it is that language users do (and what language- disordered persons do not do well enough), helpful insights from ethnographic ap- proaches to the study of communication have become apparent. From this work, it has been learned in a systematic way from the observations of language users that communicative competence requires not only linguistic skills but also skills for the use of language in interactive communica- tion. Furthermore, these skills include knowledge of how things are done, linguis- tically and communicatively, in the cul- ture in question (Bauman & Sherzer, 1989; Saville-Troike, 1989). In their work on language in the classroom, Shuy and Griffin (1981) state that

Top Lang Disord, 1992,12(3),15–27
© 1992 Aspen Publishers, Inc.

one of the answers to the "What did you do at school today?" asked at dinner tables across the nation could be "I exhibited my competence at using language but nobody noticed because it's so common and, besides, I didn't do it to be noticed but because I have to use language to make it through the day with my friends and my teachers and ideas." p. 285

It was not long ago that practitioners, who considered themselves knowledgeable about language and language acquisition, simply assumed that when a child had a lexicon and syntactic structures sufficient to produce sentences as complex as those ordinarily produced by similar-age children, the rest would simply follow. It was learned, however, that language structure and language content are not sufficient to make a language user. Practitioners have learned to ask serious questions about what is going on in circumstances in which people use language to get things done. More than an understanding of phonology and grammar is essential to understand the social rules for language use in a culture. Hymes (1962) was the first researcher to propose a theoretical and methodological approach to the study of communication focusing on socially based modes of linguistic organization rather than on grammar. Combining constructs from the disciplines of anthropology, linguistics, sociology, and folklore, Hymes proposed the discipline of ethnography of speaking. This ethnographic approach to the study of communication provides an understanding of community norms, operating principles, strategies, and values that guide the production and interpretation of speech and language (Bauman & Sherzer, 1989).

Probably the most studied aspect of what it means to be a language user is the use of language in conversation. Scholars have provided extensive information about such topics as speech acts, coherence, turn taking, and conversational repair. This article, however, addresses language and social role in an attempt to outline how the options of spoken language use in conversation create, affect, and reveal social-role relations among speakers. One of the most subtle yet powerful uses of language is to establish, maintain, and vary the social bonds between persons. By their choices of what to say and how to say it, speakers convey information about their own and their conversational partners' identity, role, status, social relations, and context of speaking. Although language is by no means the only mechanism for communicating social information—aspects of dress, gaze, posture, and other facets of nonverbal communication have important effects as well—there has been much productive study of the social rules for language use, both in this culture and in other cultures.

When language users engaged in conversation formulate utterances, they express what they know about the participants in conversation and the social structures relevant to the speaking situation. Because speakers are also listeners, listeners as well as speakers have to know how all this works, so that they can derive social information from what speakers say. Language users, therefore, must not only be familiar with status systems and social role variables, but also know how these variables are expressed in language in their sociocultural communities. Many of the articles in this issue consider social-role relations. Crago discusses parent–child relations, DeFrancisco considers gender role communication, García reviews the literature on student–teacher roles, Fishman considers role relations in the use of literacy, and Kovarsky and Maxwell examine communication in clinician–client relations.

Speech acts theory teaches that speakers have options about how to do things with language. To illustrate, it is recognized that when one person would like another to perform an action such as moving some books, various specific forms of the message are possible, and each carries information beyond the core content. If one hears someone say,

Get those books off the dinner table.

one knows that the speaker wants the listener to move some books from a particular piece of furniture. Even more is known, however, because the speaker could have said, with approximately the same goal,

Would you mind clearing the books off the dinner table?
                    or
Please move those books. I'm about to set the table for dinner.
                    or
You know how mother hates clutter.

When one hears,

Get those books off the dinner table.

one knows something about the speaker and listener and the relation between them. One knows that the speaker might be a father talking to his son, but not the other way around. One also knows that the place is probably the home and that persons outside the family are probably not present. The speaker could have chosen to express his meaning in any one of a number of different ways. The example conveys a considerable amount of information about the self-perception of the speaker in relation to the person being addressed, as well as about where they were at the time and who else was present.

It might seem that the rules for this behavior are learned painlessly at the same time that the language user learns the grammar and the vocabulary of his or her language. To some extent, of course, that is so. The rules vary so much from one kind of community to another and from one setting to another, however, that people who come in contact with a variety of communities are always making mistakes— and, presumably, learning from them. Social errors in language use occur all the time and sometimes cause serious disruption in social relations. More often, however, they are probably ignored or repaired quickly. Children, of course, are relatively limited in experience of the variety of settings and circumstances in which adults may find themselves and, thus, are more likely to make social errors. A child may ask a visitor to the family home how old he or she is or how much his or her camera cost and might learn from the resulting discomfort or laughter that something was wrong with the question. Children and adults with language and learning disorders are at risk with respect to their ability to find their way among the options and variations needed for managing social-role relations.

This article addresses the concept of communication and social role. First the dimensions of speaker–listener relations are discussed. Next, speaking options in these relations are presented, and, finally, implications of language-learning disabled individuals' failure to appreciate these dimensions and options are considered.

DIMENSIONS OF SPEAKER–LISTENER RELATIONS

The *Get those books off the dinner table* example suggests how language in use provides quick and subtle ways to express relations between speakers and listeners. Two dimensions of speaker–listener relations that pervade conversational interchanges might be described as "Who's on top" and "Who's inside" or, put more formally, the *status dimension* and the *solidarity dimension.* (See Brown & Gilman, 1960, for the seminal work on this subject.) Each dimension, in turn, has two poles: the poles of status are dominance and deference, whereas the poles of solidarity are insider and outsider.

Where participants in conversational discourse find themselves on the dimensions of status and solidarity determines who may speak, what can be talked about, who is allowed to speak first, who is allowed to establish the topic of conversation, and what words and structures may be used. This view, of course, presumes that individuals have a repertoire of "ways of speaking" and can make conscious choices among the options available to suit the role relations of the particular circumstances of a conversational context. The greater the language user's combination of skill and experience, the more likely that he or she will have a large repertoire of ways of speaking and, hence, the ability to adapt quickly to varying circumstances.

The status dimension is expressed in language through various devices for indicating dominance or deference relative to

> *The greater the language user's combination of skill and experience, the more likely that he or she will have a large repertoire of ways of speaking and, hence, the ability to adapt quickly to varying circumstances.*

the other person. It is not absolute but, rather, relative status that applies, because a given speaker is likely to be in an authority or a dominant position in some contexts but in a deferent status in other instances. Furthermore, expressing deference may have more than one function: the speaker may be signaling that his or her status is lower than that of the listener or may be merely using a strategy for appearing polite. One way of expressing deference is to appear hesitant or indecisive when asked to make a choice. For example, when visiting a friend and being offered something to drink one might say, "Don't bother" or "Whatever you've got."

In the United States, differences in status associated with social class are not drawn as sharply as they may be in other countries. There are, however, still asymmetries, such as parent–child, adult–child, employer–employee, physician–patient, physician–nurse, judge–lawyer, teacher–student, and man–woman dyads. Many of the articles in this issue consider some aspects of status differences in role relations. To signal inequalities of this kind, a particularly effective mechanism is forms of address. Physicians, for example, are addressed as "Doctor" plus last name, whereas patients are called by their first name. Teachers and professors are usually title plus last name, whereas students are first name, though this practice varies from setting to setting. As for the adult–child asymmetry, some families teach their children always to address adults by their last name, preceded by Mr. or Mrs. (or, in more intimate family or even non-family relations, Uncle or Aunt), whereas other families expect children to call by first name anyone the parents feel comfortable addressing by first name. So there are rules and variations, and children must learn both. In fact, they usually do learn these rules, apparently quite easily if they have the requisite experience.

The other dimension, solidarity, refers to the uses of language for signaling the insider–outsider status of the speaker relative to that of the listener. It is also necessary to signal this solidarity status to others who may be present. The linguistic options for expressing solidarity are complex and sophisticated. They are also essential to any understanding of how language is used in conversational interaction.

One device for expressing solidarity, or "who's inside," is the speakers' use of what would ordinarily be insults in a context in which everyone is expected to be polite. Two persons with equal power may make jokingly demeaning remarks to each other and effectively create the perception to listeners that they are close friends. If persons are not of equal power, the same remarks would be interpreted as insulting. The effect of these jokingly demeaning remarks is one of solidarity between the speakers. It signals who is inside (the speakers) and who is outside (the audience) the group. Less oblique ways of expressing solidarity are the reciprocal use of first names or nicknames, the use of

slang or off-color expressions, the introduction of certain sensitive topics, the use of direct rather than indirect directives, and so forth. It becomes apparent that these various dimensions of the speaker–listener relation can be conveyed in several ways.

SPEAKING OPTIONS

Ways of speaking may also be thought of as options or possible variants in how messages may be formulated. The kinds of options speakers have, and the rules that affect choices among these options, are described below.

Option #1: To speak or not to speak

Language in use reflects social role in terms of the rules for whether speaking is permitted at all and, if so, who may and who may not speak. Rules about who may speak, of course, vary with culture and within culture over time. In Victorian times children were expected to be seen and not heard in the presence of adults. Among the Quakers, the meeting for worship was ideally conducted in silence, so that the members could "wait in the light" for understanding until a member had reached a spiritual message he or she believed was intended to be shared with others (Bauman, 1974). In some cultures women may not speak in public or in the presence of men (Hymes, 1971). Among the Western Apache, it is customary to refrain from speaking, for a time at least, when meeting strangers, during the initial stages of courting, and on returning home after a prolonged absence (Basso, 1971).

In other words, the language user must learn not only when to speak but when not to speak. Thus one must know what is culturally acceptable behavior, as well as the consequences of violating rules in this sphere. In terms of the dimensions of status and solidarity, ordinarily the dominant or powerful individual has the right to speak (or to speak first), whereas the deferent or powerless individual may be barred from speaking or required to wait until asked to participate. Members of the group (insiders), by definition, have the right to speak, but outsiders may not. The concepts of *distance* and *access* apply here as well: the speaker who may speak (or who may speak first) is the one who has access to the other, whereas the one who must keep silent lacks access. Furthermore, choosing to be silent can also be used as a means of distancing oneself from the other.

At times the topic of conversation determines its participants, as in the following exchange between two men in the presence of a woman:

A: What do you know about the Metropolitan Health Club?
B: I hear you can get everything there except women.

The contents of this sequence made it clear to the woman that, although present, she was not a participant in the conversation.

Option #2: Choosing a topic of conversation

Not all topics are equally available to all speakers in all situations. In a somewhat earlier time, the subjects of politics, business, and religion were considered improper for conversation in social situations

in which both sexes were present. In the course of sociological change that restriction has loosened, but other rules persist. For example, it is still unlikely that persons who know one another socially but casually will discuss the details of one another's income, health, or sex life. People who do not know one another well may stick to safe topics, of which the weather is surely among the safest.

Both the choice of topic and who may choose the topic are at stake here. In a given conversation, whether one participant initiates new topics or permits the other to do so, or a speaker cooperatively maintains the previous speaker's topic or changes it, and if, when changing the topic, the speaker utters, "By the way," or just proceeds without the introductory phrase of apology, something about the speaker's perception of his or her own status in the conversational configuration is stated. To put it simply, the higher the speaker's perceived status relative to the listener, the more likely that the speaker will select the topic of conversation and be successful in getting the topic established and maintained.

In Erickson's analyses (1982) of dinner table conversations among Italian-Americans, he described the effect of the presence of the father in one instance (in contrast to another dinner table conversation in which the father was absent):

The father had a significant role in leadership in the conversation; many of the new topics that came up were either introduced by the father, or were ratified by him through giving attention to the speaker who introduced the topic. (p. 50)

Goffman (1967) presented an example of deference and access in the workplace.

In American business organizations the boss may thoughtfully ask the elevator man how his children are, but this entrance into another's life may be blocked to the elevator man, who can appreciate the concern but not return it. (p. 64)

A motive for choosing safe topics, then, is to avoid the pitfalls of presuming access when distance might be more appropriate. The speaker's place on the dimensions of status and solidarity is a significant determinant of choice of conversational topic.

Option #3: Selecting words and phrases

The English language is rich in alternatives, and time and place affect the suitability of choices. In the courtroom, for example, the victim of an assault may be described as comatose rather than unconscious and the witness may be more likely to say, "The patient was not ambulatory," than "Mrs. Davis was not able to walk" (O'Barr, 1982). Certain bodily functions may not be spoken about at all in some situations but, in others, may be variably addressed by using colloquialisms or technical terms, depending on the degree of informality the speaker considers to be appropriate to the situation. In the following example, the words used cause three sentences of similar construction and meaning to convey distinctly different social implications:

They are holding a meeting to discuss the issue.
They are getting together to talk it over.
They're sittin' down to rap about it. (Gumperz & Herasimchuk, 1975, p. 81)

Choices among terms of address, men-tioned earlier, are especially powerful for signaling status as well as dominance and deference. In *The Chronicle of Higher Education* the following tip was recently offered for conference participants, with women and minorities in mind:

It is inappropriate to use first names for women and not men. It conveys a great deal about your view of women's status in the organization if you say, *I had Suzie type this speech, then I checked it with Mr. Harper.* (*The Chronicle of Higher Education*, July 17, 1985, p. 23)

When speakers in the office refer to one person by title plus last name and another person by first name only, they are signaling that these persons have different status relative to themselves. The consistent use of colloquial terms in the "rappin'" example signals not only informality but *insiderness*, to coin a new word.

Lexical choice used to convey information about group membership occurs also in the use of *registers*, that is, inventories of terms associated with distinctive groups and especially with certain occupations or hobbies. A particularly specialized and delightful example is cited by Berger and Bradac (1982):

Some toadster on a disco chip orned me on that last set and put gnarly snackle in my rhino chaser. (p. 55)

According to the authors, the speaker of this utterance would be recognized (in Southern California, anyway) as a surfer.

Option #4: Varying speech patterns

Variation in dialect is a major social marker. A woman who grew up in West Texas, for example, can and does speak as the natives of that area do when she visits her family and friends, but she adopts the more neutral pattern found in the state capital when she returns to her job in that city—usually without thinking about it much. Dialectal variations are important markers of speakers' identification with ethnic groups and social strata and, therefore, are effective tools for establishing solidarity.

An anecdote from a teacher (who is also a linguist) illustrates the effect of dialectal variation.

When I originally moved North, I talked in a marked Southern drawl, and when I took my first teaching job at the University of Toronto, I talked about anthropology in that drawl. I soon discovered that my students weren't paying a bit of attention to the content of my lectures. The truth of the matter seems to be that you cannot talk science to a Northern audience with a Southern accent. A lecturer knows that you had better talk in Standard Professor if the content of your words is going to be attended to. (Birdwhistell, 1974, p. 204)

In addition to variation in pronunciation, there may be variations in speech parameters, such as tone of voice, rate of speaking, loudness, hesitations, and so on. For example, increased loudness, rapid rate, and wide intonational contours are associated with conversation between persons who know one another well. In contrast, these parameters tend to be more

Dialectal variations are important markers of speakers' identification with ethnic groups and social strata and, therefore, are effective tools for establishing solidarity.

moderate in the talk of persons whose relation is distant or formal. Furthermore, solidarity between speakers in conversation is demonstrated by pausing less frequently, whereas conversation between strangers is characterized by more frequent pausing (Markel, 1990). Authority and control may be expressed by raising pitch and increasing loudness, as when the teacher uses her "come to order" voice when saying

Everyone return to your seats and take out your math sheets.

Listeners tend to associate frequent or unusually long pauses with lack of control and uncertainty, whereas rapid rate suggests anxiety or enthusiasm. Regional differences may be apparent. New Yorkers, for example, are characterized as "fast talkers," whose pauses between speaker turns are shorter than those of speakers of English from other regions or countries.

The whining tone of a child leads a listener to guess that the child is talking to a parent rather than to another child or to a strange adult, in which case the voice is more normal (Gleason, 1973). When adults talk to very young children, they use higher pitch and wider pitch ranges than when they talk to older children or adults (Garnica, 1977). Interestingly, these latter features do not appear in all languages and cultures (Ratner & Pye, 1984).

Use of a rising question intonation in declarative responses to questions, such as

Q: When will dinner be ready?
A: Around six o'clock? (O'Barr & Atkins, 1980, p. 96)

seems to give the listener a choice and to convey powerlessness or, perhaps, lack of interest.

Option #5: Selecting syntactic structures

Among the well-known options for expressing relative status and power is the choice of direct and indirect forms for indicating what the speaker wants the listener to do, as in the *Get those books off the dinner table* example. Generally speaking, the speaker who has greater status, or more power, or more control, can be more direct in telling the listener what to do.

Questions are also formulated so as to avoid making the listener look bad. Aronsson and Rundstrom (1989) offer a useful analysis of how a pediatrician in an allergy consultation can find out what the child wears at home by asking the child "You wear shorts at home?" and the mother answers "Yeah." If addressing the mother directly, the pediatrician might have been more likely to ask "What does he wear at home?" thus avoiding the implication that mother allows the child to dress improperly for his or her allergic condition. The example shows how the speaker can "exploit" the presence of a third party or "side participant" to use formulations that are more direct and, in this case, more efficient.

Children learn these conventions surprisingly early. In a role-playing situation, seven-year-olds had the "doctor" say "Nurse, go get the operating machine," but had the "nurse" say "Doctor, would you like to look at it?" (Andersen, 1978).

Option #6: Discourse features

Discourse features cover such matters as how power and solidarity are conveyed by who speaks first; who has the right to terminate the conversation; who can be interrupted, and by whom; and if interrupting, whether to barge right ahead or apologize first, like saying "By the way" or "Excuse me for intruding, but."

In the unequal power situation of physician–patient dialogue, physicians ask most of the questions and patients provide most of the responses. That arrangement is predictable, no doubt, from the purpose of the interaction. Nevertheless, the fact that the physician is entitled to ask most of the questions and can expect the patient to answer the questions as well as possible confers additional power on the physician. West (1984) noted that, in her data from routine patient visits, questions asked by physicians were almost always answered by the patients. Interestingly, many of the questions asked by patients "were stuttered, reformulated midway, and generally impeded by marked speech disturbances" (p. 109). Furthermore, not all the patients' questions were answered by the physicians. It seems a clear case of a situation where only one party has the right to ask questions and only one party has the obligation to answer questions; other possibilities exist, but are optional.

In contrast, an intensive analysis of the changes in speaking patterns of a patient and psychotherapist during a complete course of psychotherapy revealed that "the patient's style of speech changed in the direction of becoming less patientlike and more like that of an equal. Shares of the speech became more even in terms of both number of utterances per session and average speech length" (Winefield, Chandler, & Bassett, 1989, p. 81).

Some of the influential early work on language in the classroom was done by Mishler (1975, 1978), who called attention to the use of discourse features to establish and maintain the authority relation between teacher and pupil in the first-grade classroom. Teachers more often initiate dialogue by asking questions and keep the dialogue going by continuing to ask questions, which is unsurprising. Furthermore, the analyses show that, even when the child asks a question, the teacher is more likely than not to respond with a question, thus regaining control over the interaction. Children's responses to teachers' questions are more likely to be single words or phrases, whereas their responses to other children's questions are more likely to be complete sentences or more elaborate constructions.

The previous sections have outlined six categories of variables or options of speaking over which the participants in conversational interaction can exercise some choices, but about which there are social rules and therefore expectations about which choices are appropriate and which are not. Patterns that combine choices from several of the categories are also known as style, and able speakers make effective use of variations in style.

A lawyer, for example, is likely to address prospective jurors during *voir dire* in a casual colloquial style, as though seeking solidarity with jurors. He may joke frequently during this aspect of the trial and adopt a speech style "like ordinary folks." When questioning witnesses, he is likely to distance himself from hostile witnesses—by attempting to make colloquial or subcultural varieties appear "stupid" and unlike him, or attempting to suggest that expert witnesses for the opposition are using "big words to obscure relatively simple matters." (O'Barr, 1981, p. 396)

To carry the point still further, some choices will work and others will fail,

depending on the social expectations for the use of language in the environment in which the language user finds himself or herself as well as the language user's skill and the willingness of listeners to accommodate the speakers' choices.

IMPLICATIONS FOR UNDERSTANDING LANGUAGE-DISORDERED POPULATIONS

The array of communicative options for establishing and varying social-role relations is not necessarily fully available to language-disordered individuals. Regardless of the primary area of deficit of the communicatively disabled individual, his or her ability to use language in interpersonal communication is likely to be compromised in some way. As practitioners learn to understand the complexities of using language to signal and affect social-role relations, the potential areas of vulnerability for the language-disordered population become readily apparent.

Gallagher (1991) states, "The central role that language plays in social cognition, social competence, and social access to peer acquaintances places children with impaired language skills at social-communicative risk" (p. 34). For example, the child with a phonological disorder may be less effective in conversation because the listener has difficulty understanding the child. This situation would create a more frequent need to respond to requests for clarification. As a result, this child may be perceived as a less competent individual (Burroughs & Tomblin, 1990) and obliged to play a deferent role in relation to others in conversation. Children whose grammatical skills are limited may lack access to the variations in speaking style needed for accommodating to their listeners (Fey, Leonard, & Wilcox, 1981; Prinz & Ferrier, 1983). As Johnston (1988) puts it, "Language disordered children can use social and communicative schemes to adjust their speech in an age-appropriate manner, but only when this variation requires minimal grammatical knowledge" (p. 692).

In other instances, disruptions in interpersonal relations are at the very heart of communication. Pearl, Donahue, and Bryan (1985) found that learning-disabled children, telling classmates that they had been rejected for a role in the school play or had not been invited to go to the movies, gave less tactful messages than their non-learning-disabled classmates (compare "You can't go" with "You can go with me next time"). Inasmuch as the study of Pearl et al. controlled for linguistic sophistication, other factors had to be contributing to the form of the children's messages. Other study findings support the hypothesis that such difficulties stem more from learning-disabled children's understanding of social relations than from their structural linguistic skills (Donahue, 1981).

• • •

Practitioners have entered the decade with more than ten years of knowledge about language use, a great deal of research data about the performance of language-disordered children, and a growing armamentarium of clinical tools, protocols, and programs for assessing and teaching language use (Bedrosian, 1985; Prutting & Kirchner, 1987; Tattershall, 1988). Currently, methods of assessing social compe-

tence have been recommended to speech-language pathologists concerned with the impact of language disorders on social interaction (Gallagher, 1991). Because a key to competent negotiation in social-role relations is a repertoire of ways of speaking, the language-disordered individual is at risk socially as well as linguistically.

Clinical diagnosis should therefore address the child's ability to manage speaker-speaker relations. The social role dimensions of status and solidarity offer a useful framework for this purpose. In addition, techniques for ethnographic assessment will assist in understanding communicatively impaired individuals relative to their cultures and the social situations that make up their daily lives (Crago & Cole, 1991; Westby, 1990). Clinical intervention, similarly, must begin with the recognition that knowledge of language structure and knowledge of language use are inseparable at some points during the language-learning process. Accordingly, intervention should address linguistic skills together with social-communicative skills. Learning words and phrases will not result in effective language use unless form and function are learned together. The five-year-old needs to know not only how to form questions, but also how the use of interrogative forms ("Can I get some ice cream?" or "Would you play with me?") may be more effective in obtaining positive responses than the use of direct directives ("Gimme a cookie.").

Clinicians are familiar with children whose ability to create, reveal, and affect social-role relations is limited. Whatever the origins of the speech and language deficits, the use of language in social-role relations is a central concern for all clinical intervention. The ethnographic framework helps practitioners to understand what happens in a clinical session (Kovarsky, 1990) and how the interaction serves the goal of improving the language user's social-communicative experiences in a variety of settings. The ethnographic perspective has taught practitioners that "pragmatics can no longer stay off the streets" (Crago & Cole, 1991, p. 124).

REFERENCES

Andersen, E.S. (1978). Will you don't snore please? Directives in young children's role-play speech. *Papers and reports on child language development* (p. 15). Stanford, CA: Stanford University Press.

Aronsson, K., & Rundstrom, B. (1989). Cats, dog, and sweets in the clinical negotiation of reality: On politeness and coherence in pediatric discourse. *Language in Society, 18*, 483–504.

Basso, K.H. (1971). To give up on words: Silence in Western Apache culture. In K.H. Basso & M.E. Opler (Eds.), *Apachean culture history and ethnology*. Tucson, AZ: The University of Arizona Press.

Bauman, R. (1974). Speaking in the light: The role of the Quaker minister. In R. Bauman & J. Sherzer (Eds.), *Explorations in the ethnography of speaking*. New York, NY: Cambridge University Press.

Bauman, R., & Sherzer, J. (1989). *Explorations in the ethnography of speaking* (2nd ed.). New York, NY: Cambridge University Press.

Bedrosian, J. (1985). An approach to developing communicative competence. In D.N. Ripich & F.M. Spinelli (Eds.), *School discourse problems*. San Diego, CA: College-Hill Press.

Berger, C.R., & Bradac, J.J. (1982). *Language and social knowledge: Uncertainty in interpersonal relations*. London, England: Edward Arnold.

Birdwhistell, R.L. (1974). The language of the body: The natural environment of words. In A. Silverstein (Ed.), *Human communication: Theoretical explanation*. Hillsdale, NJ: Erlbaum.

Brown, R., & Gilman, A. (1960). The pronouns of power and solidarity. In T.A. Sebeok (Ed.), *Style in language*. Cambridge, MA: MIT Press.

Burroughs, E., & Tomblin, J.B. (1990). Speech and language correlates of adults' judgments of children. *Journal of Speech and Hearing Disorders, 55*, 485–495.

Crago, M., & Cole, E. (1991). Using ethnography to bring children's communicative and cultural worlds into focus. In T. Gallagher (Ed.), *Pragmatics of language: Clinical practice issues*. San Diego, CA: Singular Publishing Group.

Donahue, M. (1981). Requesting strategies in learning disabled children. *Applied Psycholinguistics, 2*, 213–234.

Erickson, F. (1982). Money tree, lasagna bush, salt and pepper: Social constructions of topical cohesion in a conversation among Italian-Americans. In D. Tannen (Ed.), *Analyzing discourse: Text and talk*. Washington, DC: Georgetown University Press.

Fey, M., Leonard, L., & Wilcox, K. (1981). Speech style modifications of language-impaired children. *Journal of Speech and Hearing Disorders, 46*, 91–96.

Gallagher, T. (1991). Language and social skills: Implications for clinical assessment and intervention with school-age children. In T. Gallagher (Ed.), *Pragmatics of language: Clinical practice issues*. San Diego, CA: Singular Publishing Group.

Garnica, O.K. (1977). Some prosodic and paralinguistic features of speech to young children. In C.E. Snow & C.A. Ferguson (Eds.), *Talking to children: Language input and acquisition*. New York, NY: Cambridge University Press.

Gleason, J.B. (1973). Code-switching in children's language. In T.E. Moore (Ed.), *Cognitive development and the acquisition of language*. New York, NY: Academic Press.

Goffman, E. (1967). *Interaction ritual*. Hawthorne, NY: Aldine.

Gumperz, J.J., & Herasimchuk, E. (1975). The conversational analysis of social meaning: A study of classroom interaction. In M. Sanches & B.G. Blount (Eds.), *Sociocultural dimensions of language use*. New York, NY: Academic Press.

Hymes, D. (1962). The ethnography of speaking. In T. Gladwin & W.C. Sturtevant (Eds.), *Anthropology and human behavior* (pp. 13–59). Washington, DC: Anthropological Society of Washington.

Hymes, D. (1971). Competence and performance in linguistic theory. In R. Huxley & E. Ingram (Eds.), *Language acquisition: Models and methods*. New York, NY: Academic Press.

Johnston, J. (1988). Specific language disorders in the child. In N. Lass, L. McReynolds, J. Northern, & D.

Yoder (Eds.), *Handbook of speech pathology and audiology*. Philadelphia, PA: B.C. Decker.

Kovarsky, D. (1990). Discourse markers in adult-controlled therapy: Implications for child-centered intervention. *Journal of Childhood Communication Disorders, 13,* 29–43.

Markel, N. (1990). Speaking style as an expression of solidarity: Words per pause. *Language in Society, 19,* 81–88.

Mishler, E.G. (1975). Studies in dialogue and discourse: II. Types of discourse initiated by and sustained through questioning. *Journal of Psycholinguistic Research, 4,* 99–121.

Mishler, E.G. (1978). Studies in dialogue and discourse: III. Utterance structure and utterance function in interrogative sequences. *Journal of Psycholinguistic Research, 7,* 279–305.

O'Barr, W.M. (1981). The language of the law. In C.A. Ferguson & S.B. Heath (Eds.), *Language in the USA*. New York, NY: Cambridge University Press.

O'Barr, W.M. (1982). *Linguistic evidence: Language, power and strategy in the courtroom*. New York, NY: Academic Press.

O'Barr, W.M., & Atkins, B.K. (1980). "Women's language" or "powerless language"? In S. McConnell-Ginet, R. Borker, & N. Furman (Eds.), *Women and language in literature and society*. New York, NY: Praeger.

Pearl, R., Donahue, M., & Bryan, T. (1985). The development of tact: Children's strategies for delivering bad news. *Journal of Applied Developmental Psychology, 6,* 141–149.

Prinz, P., & Ferrier, L. (1983). Can you give me that one? The comprehension, production, and judgment of directives in language impaired children. *Journal of Speech and Hearing Disorders, 48,* 44–54.

Prutting, C., & Kirchner, D. (1987). A clinical appraisal of the pragmatic aspect of language. *Journal of Speech and Hearing Disorders, 52,* 105–119.

Ratner, N.B., & Pye, C. (1984). Higher pitch in BT is not universal: Acoustic evidence from Quiche Mayan. *Journal of Child Language, 34*(11), 515–522.

Saville-Troike, M. (1989). *The ethnography of communication: An introduction*. Oxford, England: Basil Blackwell.

Shuy, R.W., & Griffin, P. (1981). What they do at school any day. In W.P. Dickson (Ed.), *Children's oral communication skills*. New York, NY: Academic Press.

Tattershall, S. (1988). Checklist of pragmatic language. *The Clinical Connection, 2,* 14–16.

West, C. (1984). Medical misfires: Mishearings, misgivings, and misunderstandings in physician, patient dialogues. *Discourse Processes, 7,* 107–134.

Westby, C. (1990). Ethnographic interviewing: Asking the right questions to the right people in the right ways. *Journal of Childhood Communication Disorders, 13,* 101–113.

Winefield, H.R., Chandler, M.A., & Bassett, D.L. (1989). Tag questions and powerfulness: Quantitative and qualitative analyses of a course of psychotherapy. *Language in Society, 18,* 77–86.

Taking a cross-cultural look at narratives

Shirley Brice Heath, PhD
Associate Professor
School of Education
Stanford University
Stanford, California

IN ANY testing session that takes place with young children in school, adults spend a great portion of time asking students to talk about two-dimensional drawings, or objects that they set in front of young learners. Tests of language proficiency, measures of reading comprehension, and assessments of oral language facilities increasingly depend on students' ability to talk about objects, sequences of events, or relations among actors and actions. In formal schooling, aside from multiple-choice testing, most judgments of students' performance depend on their oral production of certain kinds of narratives. Yet neither testers nor teachers give much thought to the fact that definitions of narratives and their roles in children's early language socialization vary greatly across sociocultural groups.

At the broadest level, *narratives* are verbalized memories of past or ongoing experiences. In all societies, one or several speakers can create narratives, and members of each sociocultural group recognize

Top Lang Disord, 1986, 7(1), 84–94
© 1986 Aspen Publishers, Inc.

and produce narratives in predictable, coherent, organized patterns of structure and content. In some societies, narratives occur only in oral form; in others, written narratives appear in a wide array of genres, ranging from literary forms to accident reports. For mainstream middle-class members of most Western societies, the term *narrative* is often synonymous with *story*, but in some sociocultural groups, such fictional narratives may be relatively rare, while other narrative forms abound. Anthropologists have described the types of stories valued by Hawaiian youngsters (Au, 1980), Native American children (Philips, 1983), and black and white working-class communities (Heath, 1983b), but they have rarely given attention to other types of extended discourse. Reports of past experiences, accounts of new or reformed ideas, and descriptions of current or projected activities occur in all societies. They appear in multiparty conversations as well as in monologic talk (such as lectures or formal addresses) that may be relatively independent of direct audience interaction.

Children learn how to recognize, anticipate, tell, read, and respond to narratives as part of their initial language socialization at home and in their primary communities. To understand the embedded nature of such language learning, anthropologists have linked early language learning with other sociocultural features that heavily influence the uses of language through which children display what they know outside school. Reviewed here are brief guidelines anthropologists follow in studying language socialization, some of their findings on narratives and the roles narratives play across sociocultural

groups, and suggestions of ways these findings might help those who must assess students' language use within school settings.

STUDYING NARRATIVES IN LANGUAGE SOCIALIZATION

Anthropologists who study young children learning their first language (or children growing up in situations in which two languages are needed) spend many months living with these groups and participating to the extent possible in the customary roles adults play with youngsters in any given society (Ochs & Schieffelin, 1983, 1985; Schieffelin, 1979; Schieffelin & Ochs, 1986). Such research must link the learning of language to: (a) roles adults play in their children's daily lives, (b) goals they have for their children's futures, and (c) connections these groups have to secondary groups or institutions, such as the school, voluntary associations, or organized recreational groups (Heath, 1986a).

Language learning is cultural learning. Language socialization is, in the broadest sense, the means by which individuals become members of their primary speech community and, later, the secondary speech communities beyond the family. Language socialization includes all the learning that enables a member of a family and community to behave appropriately within the group that is initially critical to self-identification and whose approval is necessary for self-esteem. For some children, the primary group provides the major learning environment for the preschool years; for other children, contexts for learning language extend to secondary social groups, such as churches, day-care programs, and peer groups. Children find their primary social group's uses of language (oral and written) differentially contradicted, confirmed, denied, or ignored by those of the secondary groups. For some children, these secondary settings provide occasions for using a language other than their home language and for using language to exchange information drawn from written sources or authorities who are not intimately known to the children or their primary caregivers.

Anthropologists who study child language socialization acquire, through a long-term relationship, an intimate knowledge of a particular sociocultural group and its language. Their data must be grounded in historically informed and currently sensitive descriptions of social organization and units of space and time within the primary group and between the primary and secondary groups. Moreover, such child language research should report ways in which group members assign roles that are critical to group functions, such as parenting. Descriptions must also take into account class relations between the child's primary network and the secondary institutions from which the child may also learn language and that may ultimately evaluate the child for socioeconomic participation. Finally, studies of language socialization must attend to the acquisition of both oral *and* written language. The artifacts and events of literacy and literate behavior impinge on the child's occasions for speaking, judging sources of authority, and categorizing and comparing actors and events of the world.

STARTING ON THE NARRATIVE ROAD

One of the most troublesome problems for researchers focusing on either perception or production in child language is determining the fundamental units that the child initially perceives. Very young infants can discern their mother's voice and detect and produce shifts in prosody—intonation and meter (Crystal, 1979). But as children get older they encounter complex streams of discourse, directed to them with increasing frequency. Aside from conversational exchanges that are marked primarily by single-turn exchanges, how do children discern the units of *extended discourse*—occasions when one speaker holds the floor for more than a single-unit response in a conversation? Current research from a variety of sources suggests that children learn very early to discern and produce larger units of discourse (Heath, 1986b; Peters, 1983).

Narratives contribute to the fundamental genres in any society, but every society includes genres other than narratives (e.g., jokes, sermons, magical rites, poetry). *Genres* are maps or plans for stretches of discourse, marked orally by prosody and by formulaic phrases (especially as openings), as well as by gestures. During the babbling stage, children can shift their intonational contours, and alert caregivers can interpret such contours as those of communicating need, providing commentary on the current scene, or remembering past events (Carter, 1979; Halliday, 1975, 1979). At this initial level, the infant is already capable of communicating beyond the usual focus of early child language research—conversations in which each party customarily contributes only a single unit within each turn of the speech exchange system (see Snow & Ferguson, 1977).

All communication is contractual, and part of the interactive contract of the speech exchange system is the expectation that speakers will express their experience in predictable ways that will allow the listener to anticipate the fundamental map or plan of the stretch of speech that is coming. Throughout the first years of their language learning, children come to recognize that certain conventions—repeated patterns of structures—mark different types or genres of discourse. Children learn to associate one form with similar forms they have heard in the past; for example, the particular intonational contour and the opening lines of the first jokes they hear soon set up expectant associations, and children learn to predict that a joke is coming by hearing only a brief fragment of its opening. Once children begin to hear, speak, or write different forms of these longer stretches of language, they "know" at some level the patterned organization of what is to come; without such anticipation, little or no comprehension or recall is possible.

Genre is an old term—its etymological root is the Latin word *genus* (kind). Prosody is the primary determinant of oral genres. The fundamental genres in every sociocultural group are narratives that capture verbally remembered or projected experiences. Listeners distinguish one genre from another not by a single characteristic, but by several in interaction (Dubrow, 1982). Each sociocultural group has fundamental genres that occur in recurrent situations of that group's daily life, and each group recognizes and uses only a few of the total range of genres that humans are capable of producing. Each speech community acknowledges and conventionalizes only some forms of narrative: some of these are purposely taught; others are not labeled, but are nevertheless used and recognized by members of the community. The range of genres that are overtly recognized, normed, and taught probably correlates in patterned ways with certain features of a group's social organization, as well as with its use of space and time and its modes of physical survival and socioeconomic classification.

Genres occur in *situations* (Cook-Gumperz, 1977; Goffman, 1964; Herrmann, 1983). Young children learn to expect certain features of situations in particular environments or settings, and they learn to monitor their own and others' behaviors and speech by associating these familiar situations with new experiences (Steffensen & Guthrie, 1984). Different sociocultural groups provide different situations for their children, and thus various types of narratives emerge as possible for children to learn in these situations. For example, some speech communities encourage children to give accounts of their experiences among adults; other groups either discourage or entirely reject such narratives. In some speech communities,

---

Different sociocultural groups provide different situations for their children, and thus various types of narratives emerge as possible for children to learn in these situations.

---

speakers sometimes verbalize the sequence and nature of their actions or those of others (e.g., a mother may provide an oral script of her actions as she helps an 8-year-old bake a cake). Other groups offer only praise or denunciation during activities (e.g., an adult says *Right, keep going*, or *Oops, try again*, as a youngster tries to walk a log). Adults of some societies openly verbalize problems and offer solutions through hypothetical situations; others reserve verbal problem-solving for adults only, omitting children for such deliberations.

FOUR UNIVERSAL TYPES OF NARRATIVE

Research in children's language socialization in widely varying sociocultural groups suggests that every society allows its young to hear and produce at least four basic narrative genres. The distribution and frequency of these genres vary greatly, as does the degree of elaboration of each genre. Three basic narrative genres that report factual scenes across stretches in time are: *recounts, eventcasts,* and *accounts*. The fourth narrative genre includes *stories*—fictionalized accounts of animate beings attempting to carry out a goal (Stein, 1982). All these narrative forms bring to consciousness past or imagined experience and require gestalt-level processes of linking similarities and dissimilarities across space and time.

The *recount*—a narrative that brings into present attention experiences of the past in which the speaker had one of several possible roles—is perhaps the most common genre of school performance, but it may be the most uncommon form in

early language socialization outside mainstream, school-oriented families. Parents or others in authority *ask* children to verbalize shared past experiences (e.g., *Tell your dad what happened to us at the grocery store today*); recounts are rarely volunteered. To give a recount, the child must have either observed a particular event, participated in it directly, or read or heard about it. Recounts tend to report an event or series of events with consecutive chronology and a consistent point of view. The base form of the recount across societies and languages is *paratactic*—clauses are strung together as roughly coordinate, with relatively little indication of their logical relation or relative importance. In some communities, such as those of mainstream, school-oriented groups, adults shape children's recounts to be *hypotactic* so that connections that seem causally or temporally related to that group are so expressed through grammatical relations—conditionals, temporal conjunctions, and so on. In a majority of societies, adults who request recounts from children place high value on verbal reiterations of events, not conclusive judgments children might make about how and why events occurred.

A second fundamental narrative genre in child language socialization across cultures is the *eventcast*, which is a verbal replay or explanation of activity scenes that are either in the current attention of those participating in the eventcast or are being planned for the future. Subgenres of this genre are often marked by an instrumental purpose—the goal is to obtain some result or some object either in the present or for the future. A child who notes that something is stored in a certain place, names the object, and indicates a desire for the object engages in a type of eventcast. Children who engage in dramatic play use this genre to negotiate a jointly achieved future scene, script, or redesignation of real objects and people (e.g., through verbal announcement, baskets become baby beds, or cats become tigers). Within such eventcasts, children must include subordination as well as some indication of hypothetical connectedness—from actions to results—as well as coordination (see Galda & Pellegrini, 1985).

Eventcasts are particularly susceptible to metalinguistic or metacognitive commentaries—which across societies seem to occur primarily when an implicit decision process is interrupted or encounters a snag. At such points of disruption of the normal communication flow, members of certain speech communities may stop talking about the topic at hand and instead talk briefly about language or thinking *per se*. Formal schooling encourages such stop-action framing—the segmentation of learning into discrete units so that each task is calibrated in its relation to the next. Much of what is currently taken to be literate behavior depends on the ability to segment language and to speak of it apart from its communicative stream (Olson, 1983).

The third genre, *accounts*, seems to be the preferred early narrative form that children produce spontaneously once their basic needs are met. Through accounts, individuals share what they have experienced. Initially, children set accounts apart from requests or directives only by an intonational contour, and later by opening formulas (*You know what?*),

intermittent requests for evaluation (*You don't believe me, do you?*), and so on. Children must initiate this narrative form, for accounts derive from children's experiences, from what they have been thinking, and not from what adults wish them to report. Sometimes children initiate accounts in response to objects in the current scene that remind them of past events, and sometimes they do so with no apparent objective reminder (Tizard & Hughes, 1984). In general, adults do not explicitly verbalize the conventions for successful accounts, and children must therefore internalize the norms for these narratives, recognizing that each account must cary within it a predictable progression that allows the listener to anticipate what is coming.

Accounts are highly susceptible to individual differences across speakers. In accounts, speakers may highlight their own views of segments of scenes or outcomes of actors' events. The listener or reader must, however, perceive the model underlying the segment in order to reconstruct the teller's or writer's mental sequence and thus respond to the consciously attended experiences that are narrated. Because initiation is from within the speaker or writer, not by invitation from external sources, the individual must obtain and hold the floor. To initiate, the speaker must signal that an account is forthcoming using prosodic cues and a formulaic opening; to hold the floor, the speaker must enable the listener to anticipate and thus comprehend what is coming (see Halliday, 1979).

Societies around the world know *stories* and acknowledge this fourth narrative genre in their midst. Stories differ from accounts by the extent of intentional focus they give to a known and anticipated pattern or structure. Moreover, listeners expect stories to contain some fictionalized elements and conscious reshaping of language beyond ordinary use, and they recognize that listeners play a necessary interpretive role for the story (and other literary forms as well, if these exist in the society). Fictional narratives embrace events, actors, and results that do not have to be "real"; that is, they do not have to exist outside the creator's imagination. It is highly likely that all societies have some verbalized conventions for this genre and recognize some members as being specialists in storytelling.

More research is needed on ways in which different speech communities enable children to distinguish real information from fictionalized knowledge. No doubt teasing—and the exchange of roles and manipulation of real events it allows—has a considerable effect on this kind of language learning (see Chapters 3 and 6, Heath, 1983b). In each society, such learning is interdependent with the situations in which children are allowed merely to observe and listen to, rather than to participate in or to create, recounts, accounts, or stories.

FACING THE RANGE OF VARIATION

The extent of variation of uses of these genres in the child's language socialization depends primarily, as indicated earlier, on three factors: (a) the extent to which adults see it as their responsibility to direct their child's language learning; (b) connections between the primary community and secondary institutions; and (c) the orientation of family and community to language as an instrument for future use and a resource for self-projection. Many combinations of these factors can exist among communities of the same socioeconomic class and geographic region, but with different cultural histories. Ethnographies of the communicative habits of different speech communities are needed to describe this diversity.

One such account (Heath, 1983b) describes the language socialization of Roadville, a white working-class community of families steeped for four generations in the life of Southern textile mills; and Trackton, a black working-class community whose older generations grew up farming the land but whose current members work in the mills. The townspeople, black and white mainstream middle-class families oriented to success in school for their children, provided their young with language socialization that reinforced narrative genres compatible with those of the school and work places of the region, but differing greatly from those of either Roadville or Trackton (Heath, 1983a, 1986c).

In mainstream families, the earliest genres modeled for children were event-

---

In mainstream families, the earliest genres modeled for children were eventcasts that occurred during nurturing activities, and later in connection with books, toys, and games.

casts that occurred during nurturing activities, and later in connection with books, toys, and games. These eventcasts began with preverbal children and continued throughout the preschool years between parent and child. Mainstream children heard many accounts and stories, and once they could talk, they were invited to give recounts as well as accounts and stories. By the time these children were 3, they were expected to recognize, appreciate, and produce accounts and stories as well as eventcasts; invitations to recount shared experiences decreased as children grew older. Before they were 2 years of age, mainstream children offered accounts to adults who asked for further explanation of the events the children reported, suggested alternative outcomes of the events, and assessed the attitudes and actions of the actors (see Ochs & Schieffelin, 1985).

For Roadville children, parents modeled eventcasts during play with young children and especially while planning family projects with older children. Frequent invitations—more than one or two a week—to give accounts did not begin until Roadville children were in school, and these did not come to predominate in communciation between young and old in Roadville until children were old enough to leave home. Stories were invited in a status-related hierarchy, and even young adults told few stories. Recounts, which were tightly scaffolded by those in power who had shared the event being retold, were the predominant genre throughout the preschool years.

For Trackton children, adults did not restrict participation in special genres or other language forms. Young children were active participants in rich, multi-party conversations, and they often imitated the ends of utterances going on about them. Their first accounts, however, came only when they could nonverbally attract the attention of adults and hold the floor with a genuine tale about an experience unique to them. Trackton children had minimal experience with recounts in their own communities; yet their earliest associations with secondary institutions were test situations in Head Start or kindergarten, in which they were asked to recount events demonstrated by the tester or to repeat instructions. The earliest genres Trackton children produced in their own communities were accounts or eventcasts—usually responses to real questions about their activities. The frequent teasing challenges by adults to toddlers soon resulted in stories, which were exaggerated accounts designed to hold the floor, often in cooperative production with others who joined in and created a fanciful tale.

The situations for hearing and producing genres of different types varied greatly across these three social groups. As long as these children remained within their primary socialization units, their linguistic and social performances enabled them to achieve and maintain positive self-identification. However, when they had to move into secondary institutions—such as the school or commercial establishments peopled by members of other social groups—they were expected to have already learned the genres of these secondary institutions. Trackton children who had had little or no experience with recounts, for example, found that in formal school, their facility with other narrative genres was dysfunctional. Children in the three groups had very different kinds and frequencies of experience with event-casts—narrative genres of the type teachers and test administrators expected when they asked children to describe a series of displayed objects or the events illustrated in a series of two-dimensional pictures. Similarly, there was great variation in the children's opportunities at home and in their communities to produce accounts or to participate in an interactive, reiterative process of building and testing hypotheses and challenging them—often drawing from written sources or from secondary authorities.

Vast differences marked the ways members of these three groups responded linguistically when something went wrong in thinking or speaking. Members of the mainstream froze ongoing talk—or written language—to do what they called "think out" what had happened. In doing so, they had to isolate units of language and consider them consciously, analyzing discrete points. The linguistic habit of stopping the normal flow of communication to frame language as a topic is highly variable across speech communities. Some groups have far more "meta" terms and mechanisms for applying them to ongoing language than others. Familiarity with some metalinguistic habits seems to cushion or smoothe the path of learning to read and write, especially in alphabetic languages. For language groups that do not stop their stream of speech to analyze discrete elements, the practice seems to be a first step before literacy habits, and the genres that schools and other secondary institutions will judge as acceptable and appropriate.

If such variation in language socializa-tion exists among English-speaking communities in the same geographic region, researchers can expect to find similar differences across communities that speak different languages (see Westby, Maggart, & Van Dongen, 1984; Heath, 1986a). Relatively recent anthropologically oriented child language research suggests, for example, that Chinese American families, both working-class and middle-class, strongly encourage their children to give accounts within, but not beyond, the family circle. Adults often add summative comments to children's accounts to focus on the appropriateness of the behavior for the child's role, age, or sex (Cheung, forthcoming).

Researchers working in speech communities that vary in migration history, social class membership, and degree of alignment with voluntary associations warn against overgeneralization of their findings. These scholars urge that educators and evaluators regard their findings as tentative until more community-level language research is available. However, even the current research that portrays an array of language socialization patterns across sociocultural groups should alert educators to the difficulty of basing test results on only certain narrative genres and motivate them to find ways to use a wide variety of narrative genres in classroom activities and develop and interpret tests accordingly (see Alvarez, 1986; Delgado-Gaitan, 1982; Desmond, forthcoming; Eisenberg, 1982).

The primary message from cross-cultural work on children's narratives is that the genres required in school performance should not be taken for granted as being "naturally" in place in any child's language repertoire. For the present, the research on differences in patterns of language socialization—especially reports of the extreme variation in children's access to different types of narrative genres—can provide background information that may make educators search for more varied ways of assessing children's language proficiency and development.

For example, teachers and resource center personnel can alert children to different types of narratives by asking them to bring in tape recordings or to simulate conversations they have had with representatives of secondary institutions (merchants, delivery personnel, etc.). With appropriate guidance, children can also be asked to provide recordings or simulations of cross-age play groups or other home and community situations that will not invade the privacy of the children's families. Resource centers should have available locally made videotapes of different types of narratives that take place in public situations (clerk–customer, lost tourist–local resident, etc.) for contrast with videotapes of types of narratives that usually take place only among family members and friends (accounts of events that took place at work, eventcasts of plans for visiting relatives, etc.). When teachers are aware of the need to do so, they can give much more specific explication and demonstration of what they expect in the narrative forms of recounts and eventcasts that underlie much of school performance in the early grades. Teachers of primary-level and remedial groups often ask for accounts only during the brief show-and-tell period of the day. Students vary greatly in their preparation for successful performance of such accounts, yet teachers rarely explicate the norms for them (see Heath, 1983b, Chapters 8 and 9; Michaels, 1981; Michaels & Collins, 1984).

Academic success depends not on the specific language or languages children know, but on the ways of using language that they know. This is a simple point, but one that teachers and testers find incompatible with customary ways of assessing children in school. As anthropologically oriented studies of child language socialization add to knowledge in the field (see Slobin, 1986), researchers and evaluators (test-makers as well as test administrators) must find ways of working together to use what children do with language in their homes and communities to extend and enrich the school's repertoire of narrative genres.

REFERENCES

Alvarez, C. (forthcoming). *Home and school contexts for language learning: A case study of two Mexican-American bilingual preschoolers*. Unpublished doctoral dissertation, Stanford University.

Au, K. (1980). Participation structures in a reading lesson with Hawaiian children. *Anthropology and Education Quarterly, 11*, 91–115.

Carter, A.L. (1979). Prespeech meaning relations: An outline of one infant's sensorimotor morpheme development. In P. Fletcher & M. Garman (Eds.), *Language acquisition*. Cambridge: Cambridge University Press.

Cheung, D. (forthcoming). *The Tao of learning: Socialization of Chinese American children*. Unpublished doctoral dissertation, Stanford University.

Cook-Gumperz, J. (1977). Situated instructions: Language socialization of school-age children. In S. Ervin-Tripp & C. Mitchell-Kernan (Eds.), *Child discourse*. New York: Academic Press.

Crystal, D. (1979). Prosodic development. In P. Fletcher & M. Garman (Eds.), *Language acquisition*. Cambridge: Cambridge University Press.

Delgado-Gaitan, C. (1982). *Learning how: Rules for knowing and doing for Mexican children at home, play, and school*. Unpublished doctoral dissertation, Stanford University.

Desmond, D. (forthcoming). *Language in a Mexican American community*. Unpublished doctoral dissertation, Stanford University.

Dubrow, H. (1982). *Genre*. London: Methuen.

Eisenberg, A. (1982). *Language acquisition in cultural perspective: Talk in three Mexicano homes*. Unpublished doctoral dissertation, University of California, Berkeley.

Galda, L., & Pellegrini, A. (Eds.). (1985). *Play, language and stories*. Norwood, NJ: Ablex.

Goffman, E. (1964). The neglected situation. In J.J. Gumperz & D. Hymes (Eds.), *The ethnography of communication. American Anthropologist*, 66 (6).

Halliday, M. (1975). *Learning how to mean: Explorations in the development of language*. New York: Elsevier North-Holland.

Halliday, M. (1979). Development of texture in child language. In T. Myers (Ed.), *The development of conversation and discourse*. Edinburgh: Edinburgh University Press.

Heath, S. (1983a). Research currents: A lot of talk about nothing. *Language Arts, 60*, 999–1007.

Heath, S. (1983b). *Ways with words: Language, life and work in communities and classrooms*. Cambridge: Cambridge University Press.

Heath, S. (1986a). Sociocultural contexts of language development. In *Beyond language: Social and cultural factors in schooling language minority students*. Sacramento, CA: Bilingual Education Office.

Heath, S. (1986b). Cross-cultural study of language acquisition. In *Papers and Reports in Child Language Development, 24*, 1–10.

Heath, S. (1986c). Separating "things of the imagination" from life: Learning to read and write. In W. Teale & E. Sulzby (Eds.), *Emergent literacy*. Norwood, NJ: Ablex.

Herrmann, T. (1983). *Speech and Situation: A psychological conception of situated speaking*. Berlin: Springer-Verlag.

Michaels, S. (1981). "Sharing time": Children's narrative styles and differential access to literacy. *Language in Society, 10*, 423–442.

Michaels, S., & Collins, J. (1984). Oral discourse styles: Classroom interaction and the acquisition of literacy. In D. Tannen (Ed.), *Coherence in spoken and written discourse*. Norwood, NJ: Ablex.

Ochs, E., & Schieffelin, B. (1983). *Acquiring conversational competence*. London: Routledge & Kegan.

Ochs, E., & Schieffelin, B. (1985). Language acquisition and socialization: Three developmental stories and their implications. In R. Shweder & R. LeVine (Eds.), *Culture and its acquisition*. New York: Academic Press.

Olson, D. (1983). The antecedents of literacy. In H. Goelman, A. Obert, & F. Smith (Eds.), *Awakening to literacy*. Exeter, NH: Heinemann Educational Books.

Peters, A. (1983). *The units of acquisition*. Cambridge: Cambridge University Press.

Phillips, S. (1983). *The invisible culture: Communications in classroom and community on the Warm Springs Indian Reservation*. New York: Longman.

Schieffelin, B. (1979). Getting it together: An ethnographic approach to the study of the development of communicative competence. In E. Ochs & B. Schieffelin (Eds.), *Developmental pragmatics*. New York: Academic Press.

Schieffelin, B., & Ochs, E. (1986). Language socialization. *Annual Review of Anthropology, 15*, 163–191.

Slobin, D. (1986). *The crosslinguistic study of language acquisition*. Hillsdale, NJ: Erlbaum.

Snow, C., & Ferguson, C. (1977). *Talking to children*. Cambridge: Cambridge University Press.

Stein, N. (1982). What's in a story: Interpreting the interpretations of story grammars. *Discourse Processes, 5*, 319–335.

Steffensen, M., & Guthrie, L. (1984). The effect of situation on verbalization: A study of black inner-city children. *Discourse Processes, 7* (1), 1–10.

Tizard, B., & Hughes, M. (1984). *Young children learning*. Cambridge: Harvard University Press.

Westby, C., Maggart, Z., & Van Dongen, R. (1984, July) *Oral narratives of students varying in reading ability*. Paper presented at the International Child Language Congress, Austin, TX.

Encouraging reading and language development in cultural minority children

Alice J. Kawakami, MEd
Educational Specialist

Kathryn Hu-pei Au, PhD
Educational Psychologist
CDEE–Curriculum Department
Kamehameha Schools
Honolulu, Hawaii

THE KAMEHAMEHA Elementary Education Program (KEEP) in Honolulu, Hawaii, was established as a research and development unit to create programs to increase the reading achievement of educationally at-risk students of Polynesian-Hawaiian ancestry. Efforts have centered on students in kindergarten through third grade who, in the past, had consistently scored at about the 30th percentile or lower on standardized tests of reading achievement. These students have scored near national norms when in the KEEP reading program (for further information on program evaluation, see Tharp, 1982). The evaluation data speak for the effectiveness of the program as a whole. The relative contributions of individual elements of the program, such as small-group comprehension instruction, have not been studied.

The present study was conducted in classrooms in the KEEP laboratory school. In developing the KEEP reading program, a model of least change was

Top Lang Disord, 1986, 6(2), 71-80

adopted. In taking this approach, the staff at KEEP sought to redesign familiar instructional events in critical ways to make them more effective for the target population. This strategy may be a more productive method of improving children's learning than strategies that require radically changing whole classrooms by introducing new materials, personnel, or management systems.

The first language of KEEP's Hawaiian students is the local English dialect or Hawaiian Creole English. The children have varying degrees of knowledge of standard English, but all are bidialectal to some extent. That is, they are all able to comprehend and use some features of standard English. In this regard, the children are similar to those in other cultural-minority, dialect-speaking populations in the U.S. mainland (Alexander, 1979).

The work to be described did not concentrate on remediating deficiencies in standard English, but instead followed a strategy of adjusting lessons to build on the children's strengths. Two areas of strength were targeted. The first was the children's familiarity with home and community speech events using a "talk story" interactional style. The second was the children's knowledge of real-world events. The redesigned lessons may thus be said to have two general properties: they are conducted in a culturally compatible interactional style, and they are oriented toward helping children draw relationships between text information and their own background experiences and knowledge.

INTERACTIONAL STYLE

In working to improve the reading and language learning of cultural-minority students, it is important to understand that their home preparation for literacy, and the interactional styles they bring to school, may differ substantially from those of mainstream students. Children from the dominant culture, and middle-class children in particular, often experience dyadic interactions with parents from their infancy (Taylor, 1982). Hawaiian children, and lower-income Hawaiian children in particular, do not frequently participate in one-to-one conversations with adults. Interaction in Hawaiian households tends to occur in group rather than dyadic form. It involves many adults and children and is based on norms that are consistent with the dynamics of groups (D'Amato, personal communication, April 1984).

Group interactions among Hawaiian children were studied by Watson (1975) and Watson-Gegeo and Boggs (1977). They examined a speech event called "talk story." Watson (1975) defines talk story as "a rambling personal experience narrative mixed with folk materials" (p. 54). In talk story, the children cooperate in producing narratives. That is, the first child begins a story, for example, about a camping trip. A second child will join in, adding another event or detail to the narrative. Other children may also join in the conversation. The children will then continue the narrative by speaking alternately with one another. Watson-Gegeo and Boggs (1977) discovered that Hawaiian children participating in talk story valued performance in collaboration with others over individual performance. This talk story pattern of speaking and interacting is seen in home events involving both children and adults, as well as in events involving only children.

As these studies of talk story show, the home experiences of cultural-minority children often differ from the experiences of their counterparts in the dominant culture. For example, children from the dominant culture, specifically middle-class children, experience bedtime story reading with a parent from a very young age. These experiences with books seem to play an important part in preparing children to learn reading and language skills (Clay, 1979; Teale, 1981). In the homes of educationally at-risk Hawaiian children,

> *In the homes of educationally at-risk Hawaiian children, such dyadic, book-centered interactions between parent and child often do not occur.*

such dyadic, book-centered interactions between parent and child often do not occur. However, group talk story sessions about television programs (with conarration, overlapping speech, and highly animated talk) are often observed (D'Amato, personal communication, April 1984).

This body of information suggests how school events may be structured to capitalize on students' knowledge about effective communication gained in the home culture. Previous KEEP research conducted by Au (1980), involving the close analysis of videotapes, shows that effective reading lessons can be carried out in the talk story style already familiar to young Hawaiian children. About half of the discussion time in these lessons occurs in *open turns*. In this type of turn, the teacher does not call on any one child to answer. Rather, any

student who knows all or part of the answer may speak in response to the teacher's question. Often, two, three, or even four children will appear to be speaking at the same time.

To those unfamiliar with the interactional style of Hawaiian children, so much overlapping speech may convey the impression of chaos. However, experienced teachers in the KEEP program have no trouble channeling all of this talk to further the group's understanding of the story being read. The teachers accomplish this by repeating or paraphrasing the best responses given by the children. After one question has been answered, the teacher goes on to ask another and again listens for and elicits the best responses. In another study, Au and Mason (1981) found that more academically engaged time occurred in lessons conducted in the talk story manner than in lessons in which dyadic or single-turn speaking was the rule.

Transcripts of sample lessons reveal that the children work cooperatively much of the time to answer the teacher's questions, with each child contributing one part of the answer. Several benefits for learning reading and speaking in standard English are made possible through the use of the talk-story style. First, the teacher always speaks in standard English, though permitting the children to speak in the dialect. Often the teacher repeats in standard English what the child has just said in the dialect. This procedure provides the children with models of standard English expression. Gradually, and in a completely natural way, they incorporate more and more standard English forms in their own speech.

Second, because the children are permitted to speak following already familiar rules for interaction, they feel comfortable participating in lessons and are almost always actively involved. Since the talk-story style allows more than one child to speak at a time, more responses can be given than would be possible in a conventional reading lesson. It can be argued, then, that in lessons conducted in the talk-story style, the children probably have more opportunity to discuss text ideas and to use standard English than would otherwise be the case.

BACKGROUND KNOWLEDGE

Background knowledge, or what the reader already knows, plays an extremely important role in reading for understanding, as many studies have demonstrated (for a review, see Langer, 1982). In fact, what the reader brings to the text seems to be as important in the process of constructing meaning as the wording of the text itself. For example, given the exact same text, black students may comprehend a passage as a description of "sounding," a ritual exchange of verbal insults, while white students assume it to be about a physical rather than verbal confrontation (Reynolds, Taylor, Steffenson, Shirey, & Anderson, 1982).

The instructional implications growing from these studies is that students need to be alerted to the importance of applying background knowledge when reading, because meaning resides as much in the mind of the reader as on the printed page. Thus, particularly when working with young children who have not had many home experiences with books, teachers

should help them learn to recall pieces of background knowledge that are pertinent to the understanding of a particular text.

At KEEP, the experience-text-relationship (ETR) method was developed to give teachers an instructional framework for helping students learn about the importance of background knowledge to reading with understanding (Au, 1979). ETR lessons consist of three phases. In the *experience phase*, the teacher asks the children questions about background experiences relevant to an understanding of the story.

Following this introductory discussion, the lesson moves into the *text phase*, during which the teacher sets a purpose for reading, generally based on the children's predictions about what might happen in the story. The story might be read aloud to the children, or they may read it silently to themselves. Generally, only a small part of the story is read at a time. After each interval of reading, the teacher helps the children validate or reject the predictions they made about story events, and generate new predictions. Other interesting or important story information is also discussed.

Text phases generally alternate with *relationship phases*, during which the teacher helps the children draw relationships between story ideas and experiences in their own lives. In this way, the teacher is able to communicate the idea that reading can be interesting and have a bearing on a child's life outside of school. Thus background knowledge and experiences come into play during both relationship and experience phases. Cultural-minority students, at risk educationally, will not necessarily learn to value reading unless teachers encourage them to explore these relationships, as they do during relationship phases.

WHOLE-CLASS STORY READING LESSONS

Thus, school experiences can profitably allow minority children to capitalize on their interactional skills and background knowledge and so learn to read and use standard English. Story-reading activities during the first years of school may be structured so that these students can participate confidently in discussions of text ideas.

A series of discourse analyses of videotaped story-reading lessons is currently in progress at KEEP. These analyses indicate that story-reading lessons provide young Hawaiian children with a solid foundation for literacy and language development (Kawakami, 1984). Redesigned story-reading lessons include the two important general principles: familiar interactional patterns and the knowledge that children bring with them from home.

The goal of these story-reading lessons in kindergarten classes is to encourage language and reading development. The primary objective of story reading is to make obvious the relationship between children's real-life knowledge and specific ideas in the text by allowing them to participate in culturally compatible interactions with a teacher and other children.

The following excerpt was taken from a transcript of a videotaped lesson of *Birthday Surprise* (Sabin, 1981). This sequence illustrates a typical experience phase during a story-reading lesson. In this KEEP kindergarten class, the children were seated on the floor in front of the teacher.

(Brackets indicate overlapping speech. The participants are the teacher, Kehau, Alan, and Moki; X = an unidentified student speaker, and _____ = undecipherable speech.)

T: And when it's your birthday, people usually do some kind of special thing for you, right?
K: Right
X: ⌈ Right
M: │ They buy some things.
T: │ What are some of the things
        ⌊ that people do for you?
X: ⌈ They give you something!
A: ⌊ They might give you a present.
X: ⌈ A fish
K: ⌊ They buy something.
A: Bring you presents
T: They might bring you presents.

In this sequence, the children were asked to share their ideas about birthdays before the story was read. In asking what the children knew about birthdays, the teacher began the lesson by tapping the children's prior knowledge of concepts that were an integral part of the text. The lesson was carried out in the talk-story style of interaction. Children spoke individually, with one or two other speakers, or in chorus with multiple speakers, as indicated by utterances in brackets. By using open turns rather than nominating individual children to answer, the teacher allowed discussion points to be constructed jointly as the story reading activity proceeded.

In the text phase of the lesson, the text rather than background knowledge became the focus of discussion. At this point in the lesson, the teacher had already read a few pages to the class, and the students were looking at a page showing the main character, Sammy the skunk. (Words printed in the book are capitalized. Brackets indicate overlapping speech. The participants are the teacher, Cheri, Liko, Bobbie, Violet, and Nona.)

T:	This is
C:	Summy
T:	**Sammy**
C:	**Sammy**
C,B,L:	**Is all alone.**
T:	Do you all see Sammy?
X:	
X:	Sammy
V:	Sammy, Sammy
Xs:	**Sammy**
	Is all alone.
T:	**Sammy is all alone.**
	I want you to look at his face.
N:	Sad!
X:	He's sad.
X:	
T:	He looks so sad.
	Why do you think he might be sad?
N:	He don't have no friends to play.
	with.
X:	
T:	There's no friends with him?

In this excerpt, the discussion was again carried out in the talk-story style, with ideas being presented both by single speakers and by the teacher and students speaking simultaneously. In this phase, the children commented on and speculated about text events. Interactions were not limited to talk about text ideas but also

included "reading along" with the teacher. This "reading along" allows children to become familiar with the language of books or patterns of written language that they do not normally encounter in their daily conversations.

In lessons such as these, children are guided by the teacher through the experience and text phases of the ETR approach. To increase students' knowledge of written texts, stories are selected from a wide variety of genres. These redesigned story-reading events promote language development as well as reading comprehension skills, because discussion about relevant background knowledge and text ideas allows students to practice organizing and talking about their thoughts.

Story-reading activities that build on the children's strengths offer cultural-minority children a bridge to literacy. Opportunities for interaction with texts allow them to move into more demanding instructional settings in which their skills in reading comprehension and language can be developed further.

SMALL-GROUP READING COMPREHENSION LESSONS

The principles of using a culturally compatible style of interaction and build-

---

The principles of using a culturally compatible style of interaction and building on students' background knowledge apply in small-group reading lessons as well as in large-group story-reading lessons.

ing on students' background knowledge apply in small-group reading lessons as well as in large-group story-reading lessons. Small-group reading lessons are at the heart of the KEEP reading program for students from the first grade on. Children in KEEP classes are homogeneously grouped for reading instruction on the basis of criterion-referenced tests that are part of the Kamehameha Reading Objective System (Crowell, 1981). Most classrooms have from 25 to 30 students and either four or five reading groups with approximately five students in each reading group. Each group meets daily with the teacher for a 20-minute to 25-minute reading lesson. In the meantime, the rest of the class works at learning centers on a variety of reading and writing activities.

The small-group reading lessons are also conducted following the ETR approach. Although trade books, magazine articles, and other materials may be used from time to time, most lessons center on selections from basal readers. In general, because the stories are read a few pages at a time, the reading of an entire story may take three to four days.

In a sample lesson, the teacher began by asking the children to read the title of the story, "A Surprise for Pat." She then pointed out that Pat was a nickname and asked if they knew anyone who might have that nickname. There happened to be a boy in the class named Patrick, and the children easily made the connection. Continuing on with the experience phase of the lesson, the teacher asked what kind of surprise Pat might have. The children guessed that it might be Pat's birthday and that he might receive a present.

After exploring the topic of surprises further, the teacher showed the children the illustration on the first two pages of the story. It showed, among other things, a leafless tree and snow on the ground. The teacher then drew upon the children's background knowledge by asking if they thought Pat lived in Hawaii. The discussion was conducted in the talk-story style, with much overlapping speech. Only on one occasion did the teacher call on a particular child to answer. (Brackets indicate overlapping speech. The participants are the teacher, Jeffery, Mickey, Cindy, and Brenda.)

T:	Do you think Pat
	⌈ lives in Hawaii?
J:	⌊ Maybe he might have
M:	Uh-uh.
T:	⌈ Why not?
M:	⌊ In the Mainland.
T:	⌈ How do you know he's
J:	⌊ Because he's in the winter.
T:	in the Mainland?
	⌈ It doesn't say.
J:	⌊ Because got snow.
T:	⌈ Cindy?
B:	⌊ Get snow.
C:	Because then it's snow.
T:	And what does it mean if it's snowing?
M:	Cause we don't have snow on our island.
T:	Yeah, we don't, do we, Mickey?
	⌈
C:	⌊ Only have sun.

This lesson exemplifies several of the ways in which teachers giving ETR lessons help children learn to read by building on existing background knowledge. The children are taught to read with the same texts as those used with children from majority-culture backgrounds. But to make the texts meaningful to the children, the teacher attempts to make explicit the connections between the text and what the children already know. In the case of the nickname Pat and the concept of surprises, the teacher simply helped the children tap existing background knowledge. But in the case of the setting of the story, in a locale cold enough to have snow, the teacher had to ask the children to contrast the place in which Pat lived with Hawaii.

SUMMARY AND IMPLICATIONS

The research described in this paper examined two types of events commonly found in elementary school classrooms: large-group story-reading lessons and small-group reading lessons. In both cases, by beginning the lessons with a prereading discussion of a topic that is already likely to be familiar to the children, teachers are able to involve them actively in lessons. This approach also allows the teacher to show the children the importance of background knowledge in constructing meaning from text. By conducting the lessons in a talk-story style of interaction, with open turns and overlapping speech, the teacher creates a comfortable environment for learning. Because the students are already proficient with this style of interaction, they are able to focus on learning to read rather than on figuring out how to participate appropriately in the discussion.

Teachers and language specialists should determine what their students already know and redesign reading and language lessons to capitalize on these strengths. Familiar patterns of interaction and prior knowledge are two aspects of students' culture-specific learning that were built on the redesigned lessons at KEEP, a strategy that can be adopted to other settings. Teachers of other cultural minorities might begin to gather similar information about children in their classes.

It has been argued here that teachers' use of the talk-story style of interaction helps educationally at-risk Hawaiian students to benefit from classroom reading lessons. For other minority groups, adopting styles of interaction that are consistent with the values of the students' homes might also have a positive effect on school learning. For example, Erickson and Mohatt (1982) found that Odawa Indian students were more responsive to teachers who made requests in an indirect manner, without putting the "teacher spotlight" on individual students. Another aspect of this interactional style was teachers' use of private conversations with students as opposed to a more public form of interaction, such as calling out to students from across the room. In studying a classroom of Mexican-American students, Cazden, Carrasco, Maldonado-Guzman, and Erickson (1980) discovered that much of teachers' effectiveness seemed to be related to their use of an interactional style that communicated a sense of caring. They asked questions reflecting their knowledge of the students' families and a concern for their well-being.

These studies bring out aspects of interactional style that may be important to students from particular cultural-minority backgrounds. Teachers should be aware of the importance of considering cultural differences in interactional style when attempting to redesign reading and language lessons (see Cazden, John, & Hymes, 1972; Chu-Chang, 1983; Trueba, Guthrie, & Au, 1981).

In addition to interactional style, the background knowledge that minority students bring to school should be considered. Generally, considerable information about students' background knowledge is available, but teachers and language specialists may not be making full use of this information for such purposes as planning prereading discussions. In the early grades, for example, "sharing" is a common and popular activity. During this time, children tell the rest of the class about things that are important in their lives outside of school. When students speak about visits from relatives, prized possessions, red-letter days, athletic achievements, and similar topics, the teacher can gain insights about their interests and abilities. Another source of information is students' writing. Dialogue jour-

nals (Staton, 1980) and writing following a process approach (Graves, 1983), with the children choosing their own topics, give teachers opportunities to become acquainted with students. Writing, for children as young as kindergarteners (Crowell, Kawakami, & Wong, 1984) can provide an outlet for concerns that a student may not want to share verbally with the whole class. If teachers are observant, daily interactions with students can also be a rich source of information.

To work effectively with cultural-minority children, the first question should be: "What strengths can I build upon?" By approaching instructional issues in this way, teachers are led to look at ways of changing school environments, as in the redesigning of reading lessons. Equally important, they are not led to look at the children's background as a problem. Many teachers and language specialists today work in classrooms or clinical settings in which the children are from a number of different cultural backgrounds. When they use students' strengths as a starting point for instruction, they can view cultural diversity as a resource rather than as a deficiency.

REFERENCES

Alexander, C.F. (1979). Black English dialect and the classroom teacher. *The Reading Teacher, 33*(5), 571–577.

Au, K.H. (1979). Using the experience-text-relationship method with minority children. *The Reading Teacher, 32*(6), 677–679.

Au, K.H. (1980). Participation structures in a reading lesson with Hawaiian children: Analysis of a culturally appropriate instructional event. *Anthropology and Education Quarterly, 11*(2), 91–115.

Au, K.H., & Mason, J.M. (1981). Social organizational factors in learning to read: The balance of rights hypothesis. *Reading Research Quarterly, 17*(1), 115–152.

Cazden, C.B., Carrasco, R., Maldonado-Guzman, A.A., & Erickson, F. (1980). The contribution of ethnographic research to bicultural bilingual education. In J. Alatis (Ed.), *Current issues in bilingual education* (pp. 64–80). Washington, DC: Georgetown University Press.

Cazden, C.B., John, V., & Hymes, D. (Eds.). (1972). *Functions of language in the classroom.* New York: Teachers College Press.

Chu-Chang, M. (Ed.) (1983). *Comparative research in bilingual education: Asian-Pacific-American perspectives.* New York: Teachers College Press.

Clay, M.M. (1979). *Reading: The patterning of complex behavior.* Auckland, New Zealand: Heinemann Educational Books.

Crowell, D. (1981). *Kamehameha reading objective system.* Honolulu, HI: Kamehameha Schools, Kamehameha Early Education Program.

Crowell, D., Kawakami, A.J., & Wong, J.L. (1984). *Emerging literacy: Observations in a kindergarten classroom.* Honolulu, HI: Kamehameha Schools, Kamehameha Elementary Education Program.

Erickson, F., & Mohatt, G. (1982). Cultural organization of participation structures in two classrooms of Indian students. In G.D. Spindler (Ed.), *Doing the ethnography of schooling: Educational anthropology in action* (pp. 132–174). New York: Holt-Rinehart and Winston.

Graves, D.H. (1983). *Writing: Teachers and children at work.* Exeter, NH: Heinemann Educational Books.

Kawakami, A.J. (1984, December). *Promoting active involvement with text through story reading.* Paper presented at the National Reading Conference, St. Petersburg, Florida.

Langer, J.A. (1982). The reading process. In A. Berger & H.A. Robinson (Eds.), *Secondary school reading: What research reveals for classroom practice* (pp. 39–57). Urbana, IL: National Conference on Research in English and ERIC Clearinghouse on Reading and Communication Skills.

Reynolds, R.E., Taylor, M.A., Steffenson, M.S., Shirey, L.L., & Anderson, R.C. (1982). Cultural schemata and reading comprehension. *Reading Research Quarterly, 17,* 353–366.

Sabin, L. (1981). *Birthday surprise.* Mahwah, NJ: Troll Associates.

Staton, J. (1980). Writing and counseling: Using a dialogue journal. *Language Arts, 57*(5), 514–518.

Taylor, D. (1982). *Family literacy: Young children learning to read and write.* Exeter, NH: Heinemann Educational Books.

Teale, W.H. (1981). Parents reading to their children: what we know and what we need to know. *Language Arts, 58,* 902–912.

Tharp, R.G. (1982). The effective instruction of comprehension: Results and description of the Kamehameha Early Education Program. *Reading Research Quarterly, 17*(4), 503–527.

Trueba, H.T., Guthrie, G.P., & Au, K.H. (1981). *Culture and the bilingual classroom: Studies in classroom ethnography.* Rowley, MA: Newbury House.

Watson, K.A. (1975). Transferable communicative routines: Strategies and group identity in two speech events. *Language in Society, 4,* 53–72.

Watson-Gegeo, K.A., & Boggs, S.T. (1977). From verbal play to talk story: The role routine in speech events among Hawaiian children. In S. Ervin-Tripp & C. Mitchell-Kernan (Eds.), *Child discourse* (pp. 67–70). New York: Academic Press.

Ethnography and literacy: Learning in context

Andrea R. Fishman, PhD
Assistant Professor
Department of English
Associate Director
Pennsylvania Writing Project
West Chester University
West Chester, Pennsylvania

MUCH HAS BEEN learned from ethnographic research about literacy in the past twenty years. Through ethnography, lessons have been taught on the basis of social realities (Heath, 1983; Taylor & Dorsey-Gaines, 1988) as well as cognitive realities (Cole, 1981; Wagner, 1983). In ethnography, lessons have been learned from individuals (Bissex, 1980; Calkins, 1983), from classrooms (Mehan, 1979; Michaels, 1983; Perl & Wilson, 1986), and from communities (Cazden & John, 1971; Fishman, 1988; Heath, 1983). Always, however, the lessons in ethnography have been learned and taught in terms of their cultural contexts, whether those cultures are the commonly recognized sort—the inner city (Taylor & Dorsey-Gaines, 1988) or the Amish settlement (Fishman, 1988)—or the less commonly recognized variety—the home (Bissex, 1980) or the first grade classroom

Top Lang Disord, 1992,12(3),67–75
© 1992 Aspen Publishers, Inc.

(Michaels, 1983). In fact, the contention in ethnography is that meaning only exists in context; there is no other kind (Mischler, 1979).

To understand what a particular school, curriculum, teacher, or clinician intends to convey by the term *literacy,* therefore, can be neither assumed nor generalized. There are no typical schools, classrooms, teachers, or students from an ethnographic perspective. An understanding of literacy can only be attained through participant observation in the particular setting in question. Ethnographers strive to understand how other people see and understand the world, assuming, as Smith states, that "people always act rationally to make sense of the world they are experiencing [and that] repeated patterns of behavior are doing something positive" (D. Smith, Personal Communication, September 1982) for those who use them. In terms of literacy this means that people read and write in ways that are useful and make sense to them, regardless of how their reading and writing may appear to outsiders.

Achieving this sort of contextual understanding is, obviously, labor intensive. It requires time, effort, involvement, and energy far beyond that of traditional literacy-assessment instruments. So the question becomes, What makes ethnographic understanding worthwhile? Why should context be accounted for in assessing, analyzing, or describing a child's literacy?

The answer is that context counts because children do not learn to read and write in a vacuum; they do not even learn to read and write in a laboratory or other sorts of testing contexts. Rather, children learn to read and write in school and classroom settings where they learn the setting along with the skills. When children read and write, the literacy, or the lack of literacy, displayed may reflect four dimensions of their learning that are crucial to understanding their work:

1. Children's reading and writing may reflect what they have been taught to do more than what they are able to do.
2. Children's reading and writing may reflect what they know about more than what they are able to learn.
3. Students' literacy may reflect what they care or do not care about doing more than what they are able to do.
4. Children's literacy may reflect who they know and know how to relate to rather than who they could know and learn how to relate to.

Thus, if educators and clinicians are to have some impact on children's future literacy development through their intervention, they must understand why children read and write as they do and how those factors can be addressed and perhaps adjusted to facilitate further growth. In other words, children may have all the ability they need; the key to further literacy development may rest in the needs the context establishes for such children.

To illustrate the power of ethnography to contextualize and thereby expand the understanding of literacy, this article presents two case studies. Both of these eighth-grade students attend school in southeastern Pennsylvania. A portfolio of each student's work will display their literacy, followed by ethnographic contextualization, which will interpret that work in light of the particular setting in which it was produced.

CASE STUDY #1: DANIEL

Case study #1 is Daniel, and sample #1 examines his reading comprehension. Daniel read a story called, "The Joker." It is about a boy named Dennis Conron who, along with his friends, played practical jokes on a schoolmate until one "joke" backfired and they all learned a predictable lesson. The questions (Q) are from the test; the answers (A) are written by Daniel.

Q: What was the joke that the boys played on Eddie Davis?

A: moved the furniture into Charlies room

Q: Why did they choose Eddie to play it on? What does the word GULLIBLE mean?

A: they could make him believe things that aren't so, easily tricked

Q: What type of person was Dennis Conron? Use parts of the story as evidence for what you say.

A: short and cheerful,

Q: Do you feel Dennis could be blamed for Eddie's accident? Write a paragraph explaining your feelings on this.

A: yes,

Q: Did Eddie ever understand the joke? Explain.

A: yes, because the joker did it

What questions does this test raise about Daniel's literacy and his ability to understand what he reads, to write in complete sentences, to explain himself fully, and to follow directions? Perhaps more important than the questions this test raises, what are the answers it suggests to those questions? On the basis of this test, where would Daniel be placed? What language-arts objectives would be written for him? What kinds of reading and writing exercises would he be assigned? Results of an ethnographic analysis would neither draw attention to these questions, nor provide their answers. Rather, in an ethnographic analysis, first other reading and writing samples of Daniel's would be examined.

Sample #2 is a page from a social studies report Daniel wrote about Japan, the topic country assigned to him by his teacher. Daniel wrote 17 lined, loose-leaf pages, almost all with traced illustrations, a few with no text other than labels. The first page of "Japan" offered a map of the country marked with six major cities. The second page, headed "Weather," had one line of text—"Here is the weather in Japan."—and was divided in quarters, each containing an outline map color coded to illustrate "Average precipitation in August," "Average Yearly Precipitation," "Average temperatures in August," and "Average Precipitation in Feb."

The more extended written text appeared on pages separated by topic and labeled with headings "People," "Lands," "Work," "Education," "Minerals and Energy," and so forth. The page called "Education" read as follows:

Nearly all of Japans school-age children attend school regularly. Attendance is compulsory through the lower level of secondary school. Children begin nursery school when they are about 3. At 6, they begin elementary school; at 12, lower-secondary school.

Any student who has completed lower-secondary school may enroll in an upper-secondary school. The Japanese upper-secondary school is comparable to the United States high school. It offers either a technical or a college preparatory course of instruction.

Japanese students, especially those who plan to attend college, strongly compete with each other for grades and honors.

Sample #3 is a composition Daniel wrote about his pet in response to his teacher's directive to write three paragraphs describing the animal, giving its good and bad habits, and "telling what its future is." Daniel wrote about his horse, Rex.

Rex

He is brown and black mixed. He is about six feet tall. I have him around half a year.

His good habits are he doesn't kick and his bad habits are he tries to bite you. He doesn't follow me around. I din't have him long enough to see how he got along with other horses.

The future of him is Rex and I are going to live together in an old shack.

Sample #4 is a letter Daniel wrote to me when I was a participant-observer in his school and asked all the students to write, telling me what they thought I ought to know. Daniel wrote:

Dear Andy,

We play kickball at recess. The name of the ball is "Big Kick" it is very light. Today, March 31, 1983, we played Amish against the Mennonite. I don't know who won yet because we didn't have last recess yet.

We give a newspaper out every first of the month. The name of the newspaper is "Meadow Brook Gazette." We each had to give a title to Verna Z. Burkholder. She looked over each one to see which one was the best. A sixth grader won, Marlin Martin. And whoever had something to do with Meadow Brook got a prize.

There are two first graders, five second graders, one third grader, three fourth graders, five fifth graders, two sixth graders, two seventh graders, and three eighth graders. They average up to about twenty with the teacher. We have about four weeks of school left. And I'm the happiest boy alive!

By looking at these samples of Daniel's work, can Daniel's literacy now be described, analyzed, and assessed? More information about his reading and writing can be obtained from all these samples than from a single test, and the range of skills and strategies evident in these samples is considerable, from the three-word answer to the opening reading comprehension question to the apparent plagiarism of the Japan report to the voiceless composition about Rex to the not-so-voiceless letter to me. So what conclusions can be drawn about Daniel and his literacy from all these samples? None yet, ethnographers would reply. Although a portfolio of Daniel's work has been examined, the context—the culture—that called forth these pieces has not been considered.

Daniel is Daniel Fisher, and he is the oldest of five children in an Old Order Amish family. His school, Meadow Brook, is operated by Pennsylvania's Old Order Amish community for the purpose of educating only Old Order Amish and Old Order Mennonite children. Daniel was one of three children in the eighth grade that year; they were the three oldest of 27 children enrolled in this first-through-eighth-grade one-room school.

As an ethnographer, I was a participant-observer in Meadow Brook school almost daily for six months. A few of the many things I learned about the Amish through these experiences include the following:

1. All texts are read as true, beginning with the Bible and extending to all others. The Amish have no concept of fiction, even though what is known in American literature as fiction is read.

2. The dominant mode of instruction is modeling—teacher for students, older students for younger ones. Children do what they see others doing.

3. Accuracy matters; appearance does not.

4. Time is valuable and not to be wasted.

5. The group is more important than any individual, whether self or other.

What do these five observations have to do with understanding Daniel's literacy? A great deal. Daniel, like his classmates, answers questions as asked and does work as assigned. He states facts as accurately and as briefly as possible, not wasting time explaining, supporting, or rewording information that is perfectly clear as stated. His reading textbook may want "evidence," but he knows his culture does not require any. Plagiarism also is not a problem with which his culture is concerned. Plagiarism is not an Amish concept. No Amish writers would ever attempt to claim another's words as their own, for they have no reason to. Neither fresh style nor original ideas are valued by this culture; getting work done as effectively, efficiently, and accurately as possible is. No Amish want to stand out from the group; they want only to be a part of it.

So is Daniel lazy, unoriginal, less than bright, or dishonest? Not at all. Is he literate according to the definition of his school? Most definitely. He is even sophisticated enough to adjust his literacy to his audience as he did in his letter to me. Does he work hard? Absolutely. He does all his work in precisely the fashion demanded. Does he need remediation, tutoring, or a resource room to bring him up to grade level or help him cope? No. Daniel was looked up to and emulated by all the younger boys at Meadow Brook because he was such a good Amishman.

CASE STUDY #2: MITCH

To test his reading comprehension, Mitch also was asked to answer questions about a story he had read. Mitch's story was called "On The Run." It was about Duke, a boy who was sent to a court-operated residential facility, Highland Hills, for stealing a car. Again, the questions (Q) are from the test; the answers (A) are the student's.

Q: How does Duke feel about himself at the beginning? What clues tell you this?

A: Duke feelt not sure about himself. He try to blam pass times on his actions.

Q: How do Duke's feelings about himself influence the decisions he makes?

A: He was blamming his pass on his crime the he did.

Q: What is the idea behind a place like Highland Hills?

A: To help you find yourself.

Q: Why is it important to know who you are? What should you do with this knowledge?

A: So you can take full responsablity for your actions.

Q: If you met Duke, how would you feel about him?

A: I will feel like he is learning his leson and is brave.

The curriculum at Mitch's school does not include report writing, so sample #2 of Mitch's literacy cannot parallel Daniel's. Instead, sample #2 for Mitch consists of his responses to arguments put forth by the reading comprehension testmaker with which he was to agree or disagree. Mitch was presented with three "arguments in favor of teenagers" and three "arguments in favor of adult authorities."

When presented with the statement, "Teenagers who have been in trouble understand each other's problems," Mitch was given three lines on which to respond. He wrote, "Yes becous thay been throw the same thing. Plus they know what's going on at the time," taking up all three lines. When presented with the statement, "People need to be educated to understand teenage problems" and given three more lines on which to respond, Mitch filled all three, writing, "Yes, thay wear teenage befor, but this time is changing faster than ever."

Sample #3 comes from the reading

workshop in which Mitch participates each Friday in English class. There students choose their own texts from a classroom library of books, magazines, and newspapers, and they write about what they have read in black-and-white composition books they call their reading logs.

The teacher's instructions for keeping the log say,

Tell me what you have read. . . . you must write something even if it is only a couple of words. Try to tell me what you thought about what you read and why. Tell me if you liked or didn't like it and why. Tell me if it meant anything to you or if it stunk and why . . . share your experiences, ideas or questions.

The log entries are often addressed to the teacher directly.

In reading workshop, Mitch can pursue his own interests, raise his own issues, and has unlimited space in his log and fewer constraints on what he may say.

One day Mitch wrote:

I just read a short articol from Yo magazin. It was about my budy Ice Cube [a currently popular rap musician]. He was tell Yo about the death threats. He say rapper live day by day with them. But he not sceared. In fact he named his new LP Kill at Will. I think the people that give these threat are just shoud jump off a brig, becose they are just jeleas.

Sample #4 for Mitch is also a letter. Through his English teacher, Mitch became pen pals with a student at an all-girls private Catholic school, Our Lady Academy. The Our Lady girls initiated the exchange, and Mitch received a letter from Andrea, who began their correspondence writing about her favorite and least favorite sports. Andrea then asked Mitch about his taste in sports and music. Mitch wrote back:

Dear Andrea
My name is Mitchell thay call me the godfather. Im 17 years old but I still look a little younger than that. I like sports to, the sport I like is football. Im one of the best player in Brighton school. But the only sports that Brighton have is basketball, baseball, sofball, and track.

My favorite music is rap and hip hop on the R&B tip. My favorite rappers are Big Daddy Kane, Eric B and Hakim, LL Cool J, Ice Cube, N.W.A., EPMD, Public Enemy, 3rd Base, Special Ed and MC Lite. That should tell you something about me. ((I'm live as shit))

Im very wild out in the world but when Im in school I play the game. I do what thay want me to do when thay want me to do it. Im a very good student thay think. But when Im out Im another person. I make that change so I can be someone in life. I hope you understan this letter so far becous it hard putting things in words.

It aright up here its just like collage. Yes you have to do a crime to get up here. I hop nobody told you otherwise. Becous it would'nt be fair to you if you had the wrong idea that this is a regular school. We only go home every other weekend.
P.S Wright back and send me a picher of you.
Im 5000 Jee
Stay safe
Godfather

By reading these samples of Mitch's work, some idea of the context in which he reads and writes can be appreciated, but, ethnographically, that is not quite enough. Instead of assessing, analyzing, or describing Mitch's literacy on this basis, an ethnographic analysis would focus more directly on the context of Mitch's learning, which is Brighton School.

Brighton is a residential school for adjudged and adjudicated juveniles, a school one hour and light-years away from Meadow Brook. Mitch is African American and from Philadelphia. He was sent to Brighton for breaking his probation on an assault charge for stealing cars. He had drugs in his possession when he was arrested, but his judge did not know he was also selling crack cocaine. Mitch's race, hometown, and drug and theft connections are shared by more than 95% of his schoolmates.

The differences between Brighton's culture and Meadow Brook's culture are as fascinating as the similarities between Brighton's literacy and Meadow Brook's literacy. Once again, these differences and similarities are accessible only through ethnography. Whereas Meadow Brook students do their work because their culture values inclusion, cooperation, and shared responsibility, Brighton students do their work because they will "lose points" if they do not, and enough points lost means no "home pass" on the next home pass weekend. The Brighton culture, in other words, values material reward and fears material punishment, neither of which are operative features of Meadow Brook School.

Similarly, whereas Meadow Brook students work diligently to avoid being singled out—to be as much like their peers as possible—Brighton students work so they can stand out from the rest. They love to compete—and to win—not as a team but as individuals. Much, if not most, of the work in Mitch's English class is cast as contests—to guess endings, to write the best ending, to read the most books—with winners receiving gum, M&M's, candy bars, or cola.

The environments of the two schools are notably different as well. Though both are rural, Meadow Brook is a stable, consistent, predictable environment in which people are quiet, respectful, and orderly at all times. Not only is there only one day off in the entire school calendar, but everyone is present and prompt nearly every day. School is work for these students, and work is of value, worthy of everyone's best efforts.

Brighton, on the other hand, is constantly in flux. Not only are there students new to the school and to Mitch's English class nearly every week, but class members are often absent—called to see their social workers or judges, having run away or not returned from home pass or having been discharged or "shipped" (i.e., sent to more secure facilities). Unpredictability and instability are the rule at Brighton, not the exception. No matter who is present or absent, teasing, punching, threatening, and "going off" are daily occurrences in the classroom and in the halls. These students may be there together and may share an "us–them" mentality in relation to their teachers and society in general, but on a day-to-day, hour-to-hour basis, it is every individual for himself or herself.

Just as these contextual differences are marked and affect the ways literacy is used and defined, however, the same may be said of the similarities. The students at both Meadow Brook and Brighton do as much as necessary to meet assignment requirements and as little as they can to achieve the same ends. When asked through the use of textbook questions to use textual evidence to support their answers, whether that evidence is called "parts of the story" (Meadow Brook) or "clues" (Brighton), none feel compelled to comply. In other words, all these students "read" their assignments, their teachers, and their cultures perfectly. They know what is actually required, and they know what really is not necessary or valued. In the case samples cited, none of the writers lost credit for omitting specific evidence as requested by the text. None were penalized for omitting information, and none were penalized for the mechanical or grammatical errors in their work. Neither teacher corrected mistakes that did not interfere with meaning. Daniel's teacher, Verna Burkholder, represents a culture that values efficiency more than perfection; Mitch's teacher, Eileen Larkin, represents a culture that values communication and participation most. Verna avoids wasting time on perceived frills; Eileen avoids being perceived as caring more about punctuation errors than about people's honest efforts.

For Mitch, Daniel, and their classmates, self-selected reading is somehow different from the assigned variety. Just as the Meadow Brook students eagerly read and swap books during their spare time in school, Brighton students look forward to Fridays and object loudly if for some reason reading workshop is skipped. Just as reading for their own reasons is more enthusiastically pursued than other varieties, writing for their own reasons calls for more personal investment as well. Daniel could be more himself writing a letter to me than a composition for Verna; Mitch was certainly more concerned about impressing Andrea than Eileen.

•   •   •

The question, "What's in it for me?", is one both Daniel and Mitch implicitly ask as they learn to read and write. It is also the question practitioners implicitly, or explicitly, must ask when confronted by a new way of seeing the world, in this case, ethnographically. "What's in it for me?" is not the negative, selfish, cynical query it

may appear to be at first glance. Rather, it is the operative logical question all people tacitly ask as they make choices and decisions throughout their lives. As pointed out in the introduction, ethnographers assume that people act rationally to make sense of the world they experience; they choose their actions on the basis of what makes sense, "what's in it" for them.

That is why ethnography makes so much sense as a way of understanding and assessing literacy development. Seeing students' reading and writing as ways they have chosen to deal with their worlds helps practitioners realize that not only might degrees of intelligence or ability explain differences in literacy behavior, but differences in context might, too. If students cannot answer the question, "What's in it for me?" in some positive way, they have no reason to become literately different from the way they are, even if they have the ability to do just that.

Daniel and Mitch are cases in point. Clearly, both boys can understand what they read, can write at length, and can invest themselves in literacy activities. Why should they do so beyond the demands of the situations in which they find themselves? Both seem to have the necessary intelligence to standardize their language, their spelling, and their control of conventions, but why should they? Neither their schools nor their lives require such changes. It makes no sense for them to change from their perspectives at least; theirs are the perspectives that matter when literacy behavior is at issue.

Ethnography brings five questions to literacy assessment, questions that go beyond samples, tests, and scores to the context of literacy learning itself.

1. Is what the student has been taught important? What has he or she learned to value as personal qualities and markers of success? Does humility matter or saving face? Are passivity and conformity marks of a "good" student or do people need to stand out and distinguish themselves in any ways they can?

2. What has the student been taught to do socially? What kinds of social activities and relations has he or she learned to manage successfully? Only small group activities; only with people like himself or herself? Are different people and different settings perceived as "not mine" or as irrelevant or even dangerous?

3. What has the student been taught to do academically? What sorts of activities has the school provided? Drill and repetition? Worksheets and kits? Formulaic essays? Basal readers?

4. What has the student been taught is possible? What does he or she see as his or her future in life? Exactly what family members have always done? Exactly what peers are doing? Whatever he or she dreams for himself or herself?

5. What kinds of experiences has the child had? That is, has he or she consistently experienced learning as positive or negative?

Clearly, these questions cannot be answered through test scores, profiles, or through anything else a cumulative record may contain. These are questions of context, questions for ethnographic consideration, questions to help design literacy intervention and instruction. What students know about the world, what they believe is possible, what they consider useful and important, and how they have experienced learning and literacy in the past bears directly on how they will grow as literate individuals in the future. These factors also bear directly on how clinicians and teachers can help them become those individuals.

REFERENCES

Bissex, G. (1980). *GNYS AT WRK: A child learns to write and read.* Cambridge, MA: Harvard University Press.

Calkins, L. (1983). *Lessons from a child.* Portsmouth, NH: Heinemann.

Cazden, C., & John, V. (1971). Learning in American Indian children. In M. Wax, S. Diamond, & F. Gearing (Eds.), *Anthropological perspectives in education.* New York, NY: Basic Books.

Cole, M. (1981). *The zone of proximal development: Where culture and cognition create each other.* Unpublished manuscript.

Fishman, A. (1988). *Amish literacy: What and how it means.* Portsmouth, NH: Heinemann.

Heath, S.B. (1983). *Ways with words: Language, life, and work in communities and classrooms.* New York, NY: Cambridge University Press.

Mehan, H. (1979). *Learning lessons: Social organization in the classroom.* Cambridge, MA: Harvard University Press.

Michaels, S. (1983). Teacher/child collaboration as oral preparation for literacy. In B. Schieffelin (Ed.), *Acquiring literacy: Ethnographic perspectives.* Norwood, NJ: Ablex.

Mischler, E. (1979). Meaning in context: Is there any other kind? *Harvard Educational Review, 49,* 1–19.

Perl, S., & Wilson, N. (1986). *Through teachers' eyes: Portraits of writing teachers at work.* Portsmouth, NH: Heinemann.

Taylor, D., & Dorsey-Gaines, C. (1988). *Growing up literate: Learning from inner city families.* Portsmouth, NH: Heinemann.

Wagner, D. (1983). Rediscovering "rote": Some cognitive and pedagogical preliminaries. In S. Irvine & J.W. Berry (Eds.), *Human assessment and cultural factors.* New York, NY: Plenum.

Part II
Assessment Problems: Procedures and Protocols

Assessing children with limited English proficiency: Current perspectives

Deena K. Bernstein, PhD
Associate Professor
Department of Speech and Theatre
Lehman College/City University of New York
New York, New York

FOR A NUMBER of years educators and speech–language pathologists have been concerned about identifying appropriate assessment techniques for evaluating minority children who may possess language disorders. Assessing a minority child in order to ascertain a language disorder is not an easy task. It is possible to err in two different directions during the assessment process. Most frequently limited-English-proficient (LEP) students who are not handicapped may be incorrectly identified as handicapped, often as learning-disabled or mentally retarded, merely because they are linguistically or culturally different. In Texas, for example, it is estimated that Hispanics are vastly overrepresented in special education programs. The other direction in which educators may err is failing to identify LEP students who are indeed language-disordered and in need of special education services. This occurs because evaluators erroneously assume that the LEP student's *only* difficulty is his or her

Top Lang Disord, 1989, 9(3), 15–20
© 1989 Aspen Publishers, Inc.

deficiency in learning the English language. Appropriate identification and assessment of bilingual/bicultural children require (1) the use of appropriate assessment instruments and techniques, and (2) the use of appropriate personnel in the assessment process.

ASSESSMENT INSTRUMENTS

Standardized tests

The instruments that should be used for assessing the communication skills of bilingual/bicultural children must possess certain characteristics. However, these characteristics should not differ from those we look for in instruments with which to assess the communication skills of monolingual children. Tests must possess a solid theoretical underpinning and must be valid and reliable. Furthermore, standardization must be based on the population for which it is to be used.

While a variety of published tests in many languages are available, most are fraught with problems. Some tests have not been standardized properly, others are direct translations from English, while still others may be culturally biased. While the area of standardized language testing has certainly grown within the last decade, there are few if any standardized tests that provide a complete, valid, and nonbiased evaluation of a handicapping condition (specifically, a language disorder) for bilingual/bicultural children.

Nonstandardized assessment: An alternative

Many communication specialists advocate the use of naturalistic assessment with monolingual English-speaking children (Lund & Duchan, 1988; Miller, 1981; James, 1988). This approach focuses on assessing language within a pragmatic framework. It allows the clinician to observe children in a variety of settings in order to describe the content of their language, the forms they use, and the uses to which they put their language skills. Using the naturalistic approach, the speech–language pathologist can describe how well a child communicates with speakers of different ages, during a variety of activities, and in diverse communication settings. While this form of assessment in evaluating the communication skills of monolingual children is relatively new, and often only complements the use of standardized tests within the school setting, its use when assessing LEP students is almost mandatory, as reliable, valid, standardized tests in most foreign languages are not available.

An analysis of the communication between the child and the clinician, peers, and parents and siblings is often the only form of data that a clinician may have in determining a child's communicative level. In a seminal work regarding the assessment of the communication skills of Asian children, Cheng (1987) provides an assessment checklist that speech–language pathologists can use when observing a child (in a variety of settings) and assessing his or her communication skills. It requires the practitioner to note the child's linguistic skills on a variety of tasks, such as relating past experiences, describing objects, and describing pictures. With its emphasis on pragmatics, this instrument can be used to evaluate children who speak a variety of different languages and come from diverse cultural backgrounds. For example, the author has found this instrument to be useful with Hispanic as well as Yiddish-speaking children. The naturalistic approach offers the depth of information needed to evaluate a bilingual/bicultural child clinically. It has the advantage of exploring language function as well as linguistic form and content, and it should provide the clinician with information regarding the child's pragmatic social skills, discourse abilities, and use of appropriate syntax and vocabulary.

PERSONNEL ISSUES

Most professionals responsible for assessing bilingual/bicultural children are not from the same linguistic and cultural background as their clients. The statistics concerning minority representation in the profession of speech–language pathology indicate that there is a profound shortage of professionals who are qualified to assess the language skills of LEP children. Because the federal mandate requires that the abilities of LEP children be assessed in their native tongue, speech–language pathologists need to develop certain foreign language competencies before assessing these students. Such competencies include, but are not limited to: second-language proficiency (i.e., accuracy in lexicon, semantics, phonology, syntax, and pragmatics) in order to communicate effectively on practical and professional topics during clinical management, and cultural knowledge (ASHA, 1988). Ideally, specialists assessing bilingual/bicultural children should provide services to their students in their native language. However, in the case where second-

language competencies are unattainable and professionals who speak the child's language are unavailable, speech–language pathologists must take the responsibility of finding suitable personnel to assist them in the assessment process.

The American Speech–Language–Hearing Association (1988) recommends the use of interpreters when assessing the language skills of minority language speakers if: (1) the certified speech-language pathologist on the staff does not meet the recommended competencies for providing services to speakers of limited English proficiency; (2) the child speaks an uncommon language; or (3) there are no trained professionals readily available with proficiency in that language. Individuals who can serve as interpreters (or translators) include professional interpreters or translators from language banks or services, bilingual professional staff from education disciplines other than communicative disorders, members of the child's community who have been trained to translate or interpret, and family members or friends. Even when the decision to use an interpreter or translator is made, the speech–language pathologist should still make every effort to acquire knowledge about the cultural background of the child being tested and some minimal knowledge of the native language system that the child possesses.

Using an interpreter/native speaker during assessment

If standardized tests are to be administered, interpreters must be present during the administration and interpretation of these tests. Care must be taken that the interpreter is informed about the purpose of the testing and the specific test(s) to be used. This means that the interpreter must be involved with the assessment team from the beginning and should feel free to ask questions about the planned testing process. It is particularly important that

---

The interpreter must be involved with the assessment team from the beginning and should feel free to ask questions about the planned testing process.

---

the interpreter understand the kinds and forms of information being sought from the child, including the conceptual areas to be explored and the expected response form. For example, if the child is expected to elaborate upon the content of a picture, the interpreter has to know how to probe for further details. The interpreter should go through the assessment procedure with the speech–language pathologist beforehand and be encouraged to question different assessment approaches. This process will help to clarify the purpose(s) of testing and the information being sought.

It is very important that the interpreter provide feedback to the speech–language pathologist about forms of testing that may be culturally inappropriate. For example, in some cultures children are taught not to comment on facts that are perfectly obvious to adults. Hence showing a child a picture or object and asking the child to describe it may produce no response, because to make one would be impolite. For persons of other cultures certain pictures about objects or events

might represent inappropriate test stimuli. The trained interpreter can aid the examiner in making the assessment materials and procedures as culturally relevant as possible.

To decide when an interpreter has been sufficiently trained and is performing adequately, the examiner can use a methodology often used in anthropological studies. When working in the field with an unfamiliar culture, the anthropologist frequently employs two informants from the same culture to ensure that a description of the culture being studied is not idiosyncratic to a single informant. When giving a Western-style test in another language to a culturally different child, the test can be translated by one informant and then translated back into English by a different informant. Observations should be made as to how closely the translated test resembles the original. Similarly, the practitioner in the schools can have the interpreter translate test instructions to another bilingual individual, who could then perform the requested actions and/or respond in English. Thus the examiner can determine where errors may be occurring in the testing process. In addition, the second bilingual individual can comment on instructions that were unclear or test items that might be inappropriate. Because it is so difficult to cross linguistic and cultural boundaries with test materials, the extra time taken initially in training and working with interpreters will be time well spent (Watson, Omark, Grouell, & Heller, 1986).

The examiner must also control the ways in which the interpreter interacts with the child in the testing situation. For example, probes and feedback during testing are appropriate in some instances. However, the interpreter must be made to appreciate those situations when such support is unacceptable. The interpreter must not help the child by providing answers or communicating false information to the practitioner about the child's performance. Such actions might be revealed during the training/checking process described above, or by having a second bilingual individual observe and comment about the interpreter's behaviors during initial testing sessions. I have found that interpreters begin to appreciate the intricacies of the assessment process when they have spent time observing monolingual children being evaluated. In addition to other procedures I have incorporated assessment observation into the training of interpreters.

During the testing session accurate translations of the child's responses, free of personal evaluation by the interpreter, must be obtained. If test questions and possible answers have been developed and translated prior to testing the child, then more control can be maintained, since the practitioner can listen to what the interpreter and child are saying and identify gross deviations that occur. Deviations from the expected in the child's answers should be noted and examined with regard to cultural appropriateness. General and specific observations by the interpreter about the child's behavior should be recorded; they may be useful in determining the student's needs.

Bilingual teacher aides

Bilingual teacher aides constitute a growing group of professionals who are an important resource within many school districts. They are both familiar to the children and familiar with the mixing of languages that is produced by bilingual children. They frequently come from the local community and are thus cognizant of local cultural rules. In order to assist with the assessment process, bilingual teacher aides, like interpreters, must be trained with regard to tests and the assessment process and must observe the same standards of confidentiality that apply to other assessment team members.

There are advantages and disadvantages to using bilingual teacher aides. Familiarity with the children and with their culture are definite assets. Training aides to recognize and understand exceptionalities can enhance the prescreening of bilingual children in ways that are not possible for the teacher who speaks only English—for example, Does that child sound strange in relation to his Hispanic peers? Is that child more awkward than her Laotian peers? A disadvantage of using bilingual teacher aides is that the aides are usually engaged in developing materials and providing instruction; using them for the assessment process takes time away from their instructional tasks. In addition, aides may find the shift between the teaching and testing roles to be difficult. The change from "helping" the child in the instructional setting to "not helping" the child in the testing situation may not only be difficult for the aide but confusing to the child. Finally, when the aide comes from the local community, confidentiality may be more difficult to maintain. A trained interpreter would thus appear to be preferable to the use of a trained bilingual teacher aide. However, aides have been used successfully when they have been adequately trained. Through inservice training, clinicians may provide bilingual aides with sufficient information regarding normal language development, techniques of collecting and analyzing language samples, and describing children's behavior in multiple contexts.

Use of alternative testers

In an extremely isolated situation where neither agencies nor the community can provide interpreters and where bilingual aides are unavailable, it may be necessary to use the child's parents or older siblings as interpreters. Prior to the initiation of assessment, parents or siblings must be trained with regard to the nature of the assessment process and informed about available services and benefits. While parents or siblings can serve as interpreters when both standardized and nonstandardized procedures are used, experience has shown that they can contribute more meaningfully during nonstandardized testing. In addition, family members and friends can be helpful when creating assessment procedures that are culturally and pragmatically appropriate. These may include:
- asking the child to relate an event;
- asking the child to describe a culturally appropriate picture;
- asking the child to talk about something that he or she has brought from home; and
- asking the child to discuss how he or she spent a (culturally relevant) holiday.

When parents or family members serve as the only cultural and linguistic informants, they must be used for all phases of assessment, including information gathering (medical, social, and educational) and the systematic observation and analysis of the child's linguistic and nonlinguistic behaviors.

•   •   •

Until such time as skilled speech–language pathologists and audiologists who are competent foreign language users become available, the needs of the estimated 3.5 million linguistic minority persons in the United States who have speech, language, and hearing disorders must be met by culturally sensitive professionals who can train and integrate others into the assessment process. Quite simply, the needs of communicatively handicapped linguistic minority populations must be addressed immediately, and with all of the resourcefulness that our profession can discover within its members.

REFERENCES

American Speech–Language–Hearing Association. (1988). Definition: Bilingual speech–language pathologists and audiologists (Draft). Rockville, MD: Author.

Cheng, L. (1987). Assessing Asian language performance. Rockville, MD: Aspen Publishers.

James, S. (1988). Assessing children with language disorders. In D. Bernstein & E. Tiegerman (Eds.), Language and communication disorders in children. Columbus, OH: Merrill.

Lund, N., & Duchan, J. (1988). Assessing children's language in naturalistic contexts (2nd ed.). Englewood Cliffs, NJ: Prentice-Hall.

Miller, J. (1981). Assessing language production in children. Baltimore, MD: University Park Press.

Watson, D., Omark, D., Grouell, S., & Heller, B. (1986). Nondiscriminatory assessment: A practitioner's handbook. Sacramento, CA: California State Department of Education.

Culturally valid testing: a proactive approach

Orlando L. Taylor, PhD
Graduate Professor
Department of Communication Arts
and Sciences
Howard University
Washington, DC

Kay T. Payne, PhD
Research Associate
Department of Communication Arts
and Sciences
Howard University
Washington, DC

SINCE THE enactment of Public Law (PL) 94–142, the Education for All Handicapped Children Act of 1975, it has been federally mandated that all test materials and procedures used for the evaluation of handicapped children be selected and administered in such a manner that they are not racially or culturally discriminatory. If this stipulation were enforced today to its fullest intent, most school systems in the United States would be in violation of the law. Eight years after PL 94-142 promised to be the salvation for all handicapped children, little has been done to improve tests and other evaluation procedures for handicapped children, especially those with communicative handicaps, to make the tests linguistically and culturally valid.

RESULTS OF DISCRIMINATORY TESTING

One of the results of the use of discriminatory tests in the school setting, including

Top Lang Disord, 1983, 3(3), 8-20
© 1983 Aspen Publishers, Inc.

tests of speech and language function, is the disproportionate and inappropriate placement of many children from culturally and linguistically diverse populations in special education classes. Many of these children do not suffer from permanent handicaps; rather, their performance on standardized tests is related to differences in language and dialect, values, outlook, world view, aspirations, and rules of social behavior. Once improperly identified as handicapped, these children are typically not afforded their full educational opportunities.

Discriminatory testing, of course, is not just a school issue. Faulty assessments of a person's communicative behavior at any age level and in any type of a clinical situation can lead to faulty management. In some cases, persons are inappropriately placed in therapy. In other cases, incorrect judgments are made with respect to the setting of priorities for clinical goals and objectives. Also, persons may be denied therapy by a well-meaning clinician who mistakenly interprets a mild communication disorder as a communication difference largely because available assessment procedures are not sufficiently sensitive to cultural and linguistic differences.

RESEARCH AND RULINGS ON NONDISCRIMINATORY TESTING

Nondiscriminatory testing has been a topic of interest to speech and language professionals since the late 1960s, when Taylor, Stround, Moore, Hurst, and Williams (1969), among others, argued that clinical judgments should not be based on linguistic norms and instruments that are inappropriate for the cultural group of a given client. The notion that tests and other assessment procedures should not be linguistically or culturally discriminatory was subsequently upheld by several important court decisions, including *Larry P. v. Riles*,[1] *Diana v. California State Board of Education*,[2] and *Mattie T. v. Holladay*,[3] and by PL 94-142.

To ensure that tests and evaluation procedures used to identify handicapped students are neither culturally nor linguistically biased, PL 94-142 includes the following stipulations, among others:

- Testing and evaluation materials and procedures must be selected and administered so that they are not racially or culturally discriminatory.
- Testing and evaluation materials and procedures must be provided and administered in the language or other mode of communication in which the child is most proficient.
- The tests administered to a child with motor, speech, hearing, visual, or other communication disability, or to a bilingual child, must accurately reflect the child's ability in the area tested, rather than the child's impaired communication skill or limited English language skill.
- Tests and other materials must be properly and professionally evaluated for the specific purpose for which they are used and administered by qualified personnel in conformance with instructions provided by the producers of the tests.

Given the present state of the art in speech and language tests, it can be concluded that there are few, if any, standardized measures that can provide a completely valid and nonbiased evalua-

There are few, if any, standardized measures that can provide a completely valid and nonbiased evaluation of handicapping conditions for linguistically and culturally diverse populations.

tion of handicapping conditions for linguistically and culturally diverse populations. For example, most standardized tests, if used in accordance with the publisher's instructions, would be culturally discriminatory because no specific norms have been established for various cultural groups and because representatives of diverse cultural groups were not used in the standardization sample. In addition, language tests are typically designed to measure facility with standard English, which makes it difficult to accurately identify language disorders in those students whose major mode of communication is a non-standard-English dialect.

Much of the literature concerning the issue of test bias has been concerned with the identification of sources of cultural and linguistic bias in specific tests (Hoover, Politzer, & Taylor, 1974; Roberts, 1970; Wolfram, 1974). Many authors have suggested ways in which sources of bias in standardized tests may be eliminated, but relatively few have outlined specific means by which clinicians can provide nondiscriminatory assessments as required by law in the absence of nonbiased or culturally valid instruments and procedures. (A major exception to this trend is the work of Seymour & Miller-Jones, 1981.)

KEY DEFINITIONS AND CONCEPTS

At this juncture, it is appropriate to define some basic concepts pertaining to the issue of nonbiased or culturally valid testing. For purposes of this article, *culture* is defined as the set of institutions, rituals, values, world views, artifacts, and rules of behavior (including language) used by a group of people for the purpose of relating to their environment. The concept of culture is not isomorphic with race, although members of a given culture are often of the same race. In fact, members of the same race need not share the same culture.

Variations typically exist within a culture. They are usually associated with factors such as age roles, region of settlement, gender roles, social status, economic status, and amount of formal education. Given this framework, it is reasonable to assert that cultural bias in testing is not just a race, class, or minority group issue. Tests might well be biased in the United States, for example, against the majority middle-class white population in a rural southern state if the linguistic and cultural presuppositions of the test are based on an urban, northern model.

It is also necessary to differentiate between *assessment, testing,* and *measurement,* since all three terms are typically used in speech–language evaluations and diagnostic processes. *Assessment* usually refers to the process by which data about a person are gathered and critically evaluated in an attempt to obtain an accurate view of the person and his or her adaptation to the environment. *Testing,* one of several approaches to assessment, is the use of specific tests or defined test procedures for the purpose of generating a score or rating for an individual. *Measurement* is the process of generating objective scores, subjective ratings, or other quantitative values or information that can be used in the assessment process.

In the ideal case, the clinical process for treating speech and language disorders begins with an assessment of communicative behaviors. This assessment may include test and nontest procedures that attempt to determine deviations of the client's communicative performance from the expectations of factors, such as age, gender, education, socioeconomic class, region, cultural or racial group, and external factors, such as audience, topic, situation, and context. *Culturally valid*, or *nonbiased, assessment* is a data collection process wherein testing, measurement, and evaluation are conducted using instruments and procedures that discriminate only in those areas for which they were designed (i.e., normal versus pathological behavior) and do not discriminate unfairly either for or against a client for cultural reasons or because of social variations within a culture based on such factors as age, gender, socioeconomic class, and dialect.

TYPES OF BIAS IN SPEECH AND LANGUAGE ASSESSMENTS

Bias in the collection of clinical data of any type may take many forms. In addition, bias can exist even in procedures that are thought to be objective, such as observation and collection of spontaneous language samples. The principal forms of bias are

- situational bias;
- bias in directions or format;
- value bias; and
- linguistic bias.

Situational bias

As far back as 1938, Morris discussed the pragmatic or functional dimension of language as a social device. Interest in the interactional dimension of language has escalated considerably in the past decade, as demonstrated by the work of Searle (1969), Dore (1974), Halliday (1975), and Bates (1976). This dimension of language has been incorporated into clinical models of communicative disorders (cf. Bloom & Lahey, 1978; Lucas, 1980).

The pragmatic dimension of language embraces the notion that language, whether verbal or nonverbal, is always generated within the framework of intentions and semantic references of speakers and the interpretations of listeners. The encoding process of the speaker and the decoding process of the listener are both based on culturally specific linguistic and communicative rules deemed to be appropriate for the topic, audience, situation, and intention (or perceived intention) of the communicative event.

In this context, then, one could view all assessments of communicative behavior as social occasions, even those in which an individual is observed in self-play or self-communication. Thus, the clinician is placed in the position of eliciting, recording, and evaluating language produced by the client in the framework of some set of communication rules.

Mismatches can occur between the clinician and the client with respect to the social rules of language interaction. Some of the major areas of mismatching include rules of who may speak to whom, appropriate elicitation procedures, appropriate language behaviors, what behavior serves as communication, and rules of production and interpretation.

Because of these interactional rules, silence—which may be a communicative device—may be misinterpreted as a sign of a disorder when it is actually considered appropriate by the speaker. When given a standardized test in which an examiner from another cultural group or gender seeks responses to obvious questions, the respondent may choose to give no

> *Familiarity with the framework of the assessment procedures is an advantage for children who find the testing framework consistent with their educational or leisure-time routines.*

response or an incorrect answer that is perceived to be what the examiner wants to hear. In any case, the respondent will probably produce what is perceived as appropriate within the framework of the topic, situation, and audience. Examiner misinterpretation, misunderstanding, or rejection of the individual's output can lead to faulty assessment of language growth and development.

Directions or format bias

Tests and other assessment procedures are frequently conducted in much the same manner as play or classroom activi-

ties. Familiarity with the framework of the assessment procedures is an advantage for children who find the testing framework consistent with their educational or leisure-time routines. Unfamiliarity with the testing framework can be a serious detriment.

Because different cultural groups have different child-rearing practices, it is reasonable to suspect that some tests are biased against some groups of children because the tests contain faulty presuppositions about the appropriateness of certain directions or assessment formats. For example, a test that requires children to tell stories about abstract or imaginary topics that have little or no relationship to their everyday lives may discriminate against many Chicano children, who operate with a more field-dependent orientation to cognition than other children do (Ramirez & Castaneda, 1974). These children might remain silent or produce very little language or atypically short sentences in the test situation, which could cause the examiner to underestimate their linguistic skills.

The issue of bias in test directions is a more complex matter, since in addition to unfamiliarity with the testing situation, directions involve such linguistic factors as content, length, and syntactic complexity. Syntactic complexity is frequently observed in multiple-choice questions. Consider for example, the following direction: "None of the following is true, except. . . ." Many test takers can be confused by the syntactic construction of this direction because it requires decoding of a sentence containing an exception to a negative case. The result is that the test taker is unsure whether the direction requires the selection of an alternative that is true or one that is false.

Value bias

Value bias can occur when a respondent is required to indicate a preference for a set of stimuli or is requested to indicate what a person should do in certain situations. For example, in the Weschler Intelligence Scale for Children–Revised, one item requires the subject to indicate what should be done if one finds a stamped, sealed, and addressed letter in the street. This item reflects an assessment of knowledge of or belief in a certain ethic, rather than an assessment of cognitive growth.

Even if presumed to be culturally fair, timed tests may discriminate unfairly against children of cultures that emphasize contemplation as a preferred mode of thinking such as many Native American cultures. Or a group play activity that involves friendly individual competition may discriminate against field-dependent children, who typically prefer noncompetitive group activity. In general, it can be asserted that test items are discriminatory when a correct response requires knowledge or acceptance of a value that may be unfamiliar or unacceptable to a respondent.

Linguistic bias

The best literature on test bias focuses on measures that discriminate in the area of speech and language function. Bias is most obvious in tests that purport to assess linguistic development but, in reality, assess knowledge of the phonological, semantic, syntactic, or pragmatic rules of a given language. Thus, the examination of a child for proficiency in English when his or her first or preferred language is Vietnamese or Spanish is obviously discriminatory.

A more complicated problem is presented when the respondent speaks a dialect of English that is reflective of his or her native geographic region, cultural group, or home language. Because dialects are often associated with identifiable racial, cultural, or social groups, it is sometimes mistakenly presumed that a client who is a member of any one of these groups communicates only according to the rules of the group. For example, it is often presumed that a black American from a black inner city community speaks what is commonly known as Black Vernacular English. This presumption may or may not be true. In fact, the subject may speak one of the many variations of languages spoken within the black American community.

Thus, bias can occur when the examiner thinks that the assessment procedure has to be altered to take into account the *presumed* dialect of the client. Notwithstanding individual differences, there are many social dialects spoken in the United States. Taylor (1982) reports that these dialects are associated with a number of cultural and historical factors, and that some variations within dialects are associated with such social factors as region, gender, socioeconomic class, education, and peer group associations. Dialects are *not* isomorphic with race; rather, they emerge as a result of an intricate interplay among political, social, cultural, historical, economic, and educational factors, even within races.

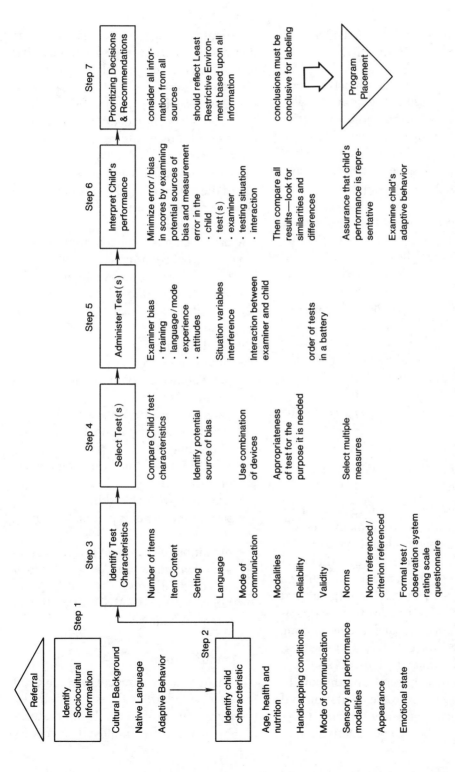

Figure 1. Model for identifying and minimizing potential sources of child evaluation bias. Reprinted with permission from G. Harbin & J. Brantley, *Model for identifying and minimizing potential sources of child evaluation bias.* Chapel Hill, N.C.: University of North Carolina, 1978.

MINIMIZING CULTURAL BIAS IN ASSESSMENT PROCEDURES

Harbin and Brantley (1978) have developed a comprehensive model for identifying and minimizing potential sources of child evaluation bias. This model is presented in Figure 1. Although this model was designed for general education and clinical evaluations, it is appropriate for speech and language evaluation.

The model is especially useful because it focuses on every phase of the evaluation process that might be subject to bias: (a) the referral source, (b) the examiner, (c) the tests and other assessment procedures, (d) the interpretation of the child's performance, and (e) the placement decision. The reader is encouraged to carefully examine each of the issues presented in the seven steps of the Harbin and Brantley model to determine if cultural biases are present in any of his or her evaluation procedures.

EXAMINATION OF CULTURAL VARIATIONS

An effort to reduce cultural bias in tests must begin with the examiner, irrespective of the subject's cultural group membership and even when the examiner and child are of the same general cultural group because there may be intracultural variations that are due to such factors as age, gender, region, and socioeconomic class. Saville-Troike (1977) and Watson, Omark, Grovell, and Heller (1980) are among those who support an ethnomethodological approach to the elicitation and interpretation of language samples. Relying heavily on theory and data from cultural anthropology, these authors assert that as a prerequisite for addressing human needs, the speech–language pathologists must become familiar with many aspects of the culture of the populations they serve. Indeed, clinicians should examine their own cultures with respect to their expectations.

The following is a list of some of the topics the clinician might seek knowledge about for a given cultural group:

- cultural values;
- preferred modes of communication;
- nonverbal communication rules;
- rules of communication interaction;
- Who communicates with whom? when? under what conditions? for what purposes?;
- child-rearing practices;
- rituals and traditions;
- perceptions of punishment and reward;
- What is play? fun? humorous?;
- social stratification and homogeneity of the culture;
- rules of interaction with nonmembers of the culture;
- preferred forms of address;
- preferred teaching and learning styles;
- definitions of *handicapped* in general and *communicatively handicapped* in particular; and
- taboo topics and activities, insults, and offensive behavior.

Test modification

Although many clinicians are reluctant to alter standardized test procedures, there are some professionally ethical techniques that can be employed to modify

Although many clinicians are reluctant to alter standarized test procedures, there are some professionally ethical techniques that can be employed to modify these procedures so as to minimize bias.

these procedures to minimize bias. Before any test is administered, the clinician might complete a checklist similar to the one presented in the boxed material to determine whether an assessment instrument is potentially biased against persons from a specific cultural group. If the answer to any question in the checklist is no, appropriate corrective remedies should be instituted prior to the administration of the test.

The clinician should also determine the average mental or chronological age equivalency for each test item for subsequent use in determining the likely effect of potentially biased items on a respondent's total and subtest scores. For example, if the score on a vocabulary test increases by approximately 3 months for each correct response, eight potentially biased items might reduce a respondent's score by 24 months.

In conducting item analyses, the clinician should also consider the appropriate language or dialect for the cultural group in question. One way to determine whether a test is biased against dialect speakers is to conduct an item analysis of the instrument in which the phonological, semantic, syntactic, and pragmatic as-

Checklist for Determination of Potential Discrimination of an Assessment Instrument

1. Do I know the specific purpose for which this test was designed?
2. Has the test been validated for this purpose?
3. Are any limitations of the test described in the manual?
4. Do I know the specific information about the group on whom the test was standardized (sociocultural, sex, age, etc.)?
5. Are the characteristics of the student being tested comparable to those in the standardization sample?
6. Does the test manual or research literature (or my own experience) indicate any differences in test performance across cultural groups?
7. Do test items take into account differences in values or adaptive behaviors?
8. Does the test use vocabulary that is cultural, regional, colloquial, or archaic?
9. Does the test rely heavily on receptive and expressive standard English language to measure abilities *other than* language?
10. Is an equivalent form of the test available in any other language?
11. Am I aware of what the test demands of (or assumes about) the students in terms of:
    *   reading level of questions or directions;
    *   speed of response;
    *   style of problem solving;
    *   "test-taking" behavior; and
    *   format?
12. Will students with specific physical or sensory handicaps be penalized by this test or by certain items?
13. Has an item-by-item analysis been made of the test from the framework of the linguistic and communicative features of the group for which it is to be used?

sumptions of normalcy are compared with the linguistic assumptions of the client's home community.

Wolfram, Williams, and Taylor (1972) and Wolfram (1979) have offered a model for conducing item analysis of these types. Using Black Vernacular English and Appalachian English as a base, Wolfram analyzed items from the Illinois Test of Psycholinguistic Abilities (ITPA) Grammatical Closure subtest to demonstrate differences between the correct response for each item and the alternate correct response for speakers from each of these dialect communities (See Wolfram, 1979, Table 1, p. 11). Wolfram et al. (1972) did a similar analysis for several other frequently given tests of articulation, auditory discrimination, and grammatical acquisition.

Once potential sources of bias have been identified, the clinician has four alternatives: (a) Change the stimuli into a parallel form that is likely to be appropriate for the cultural or linguistic group; (b) change the scoring to permit dialect alternatives to be considered correct; (c) multiply the number of potentially biased items by the average age equivalency of the items and add the product to the score obtained by persons from the cultural group; or (d) establish new test norms for the targeted population by obtaining typical response profiles and scores from random samples of normal persons of various age groups in the targeted population. Alternatives a and b are perhaps the easiest and most feasible choices for the clinician; however, Alternatives c and especially d offer the most dramatic opportunities for effecting change.

Naturalistic observations

Perhaps the best alternative to standardized tests as an approach to collecting speech and language data from an individual is the use of focal child assessment techniques with individual children and scan sampling techniques with groups of children (Watson et al., 1980). The advantage of these techniques is obvious: They offer opportunities for collecting data with fewer presuppositional constraints. They also permit the demonstration of code-switching behavior (i.e., the conscious or unconscious art of using different rules of language behavior as appropriate for specific roles, contexts, or audiences). These approaches have become increasingly popular with the escalation of interest in pragmatic and semantic analyses.

In conducting naturalistic observations, the clinician should take steps to ensure that the settings, tasks, protocol, participants, and so forth, used in the observational situation are compatible with the communicative and interactional rules of the person being observed. Also, and perhaps most important, naturalistic settings, which may include participants, must be sufficiently varied to permit the individual to use the widest possible range of his or her communicative repertoire. Analysis of data derived from these samples should include linguistic, pragmatic, and contextual parameters and, where possible, be corroborated by members of the respondent's speech community.

Payne (1982) has conducted some preliminary research in the Virgin Islands that demonstrates the advantage of using parents and other members of the speech community to corroborate diagnostic judgments of professional speech–language pathologists. In addition, her findings suggest that speech-community members are a valuable source of information on communicative norms and perceptions of disordered communication.

Payne states that the clinician should visit the client's speech community to acquire information that would be helpful in the diagnosis and treatment of speech and language disorders. The objectives of this visit should include

- gaining a deeper insight into dialectal and stylistic patterns of variation that are within the range of acceptable speech and language behavior;
- finding differences in speech-community norms that may foster different perceptions of speech and language disorders from those held by the clinician; and
- discovering language functions and language uses that may be useful as elicitation techniques in assessment as well as in therapy.

Other assessment procedures

Seymour and Miller-Jones (1981) have offered some additional considerations for resolving bias problems in assessment. From the reference point of black-English-speaking children, the authors cite a large and impressive body of literature to support the notions that (a) a bidialectal referent should be used as the standard with which the language of these children is evaluated; (b) the children's cognitive styles and orientations should be considered in the assessment of language; and (c) standardized tests should *not* be used for diagnostic purposes in the assessment of language and cognition.

As an alternative assessment strategy, obtaining language samples in naturalistic settings is supported by Seymour and Miller-Jones (1981). In addition, the authors make a strong case for the use of criterion-referenced tests that use no psychometric norms. According to Glaser (1963), a criterion-referenced test translates the test score into a statement about the behavior of an individual. For example, a content-reference scale, which is a type of criterion reference, summarizes the areas of the examination in which the subject showed strengths and weaknesses. Seymour and Miller-Jones state that the criterion of language tests of this kind should be the sequential order of language and cognitive development within the subject's own culture and linguistic group.

To date, there are no commercially developed criterion-referenced language tests available to speech–language pathologists; however, a strong case can be made that none are necessary, given the wide range of linguistic and communicative behavior that exists in the United States as well as within many ethnic and cultural groups. For example, a criterion-referenced test for black children that uses the linguistic behaviors of inner-city Washington, D.C., children as a point of reference may discriminate against black children from another part of the country or from another social class.

An individual clinician might use the criterion-referenced approach to assessment by developing his or her own in-house instrument. To do this, the clinician might conduct a survey of the linguistic behaviors of normal individuals at a number of age levels, including adults, from the region or cultural groups that represent the clinical population. These behaviors could then be used as the point of reference for assessing the clinical population through the use of tasks designed to elicit these behaviors. Or the clinician might use the client who is receiving treatment as his or her own point of reference by comparing the client's periodic performance on tasks that reflect the linguistic and communicative behaviors of the client's community.

•   •   •

Many of the approaches advanced to resolve the problem of test bias involve compensatory strategies within the total assessment situation. These strategies have been called "proactive" because they propose constructive solutions to a real clinical problem. These strategies are just first steps that have been proposed to stimulate more thinking and research on the topics discussed.

FOOTNOTES

1. Larry P. v. Riles, 495 F. Supp. 926 (N. D. Cal., 1979).
2. Diana v. California State Board of Education, C-70 37 RFP (N. D. Cal., Jan. 7, 1979, and June 18, 1973).
3. Mattie T. v. Holladay, 522 F. Supp. 72 (N. D. Miss., July 28, 1977).

REFERENCES

Bates, E. *Language, thought and culture.* New York: Academic Press, 1976.

Bloom, L., & Lahey, M. *Language development and language disorders.* New York: Wiley, 1978.

Dore, J. A pragmatic description of early language development. *Journal of Psycholinguistic Research*, 1974, *3*, 343–350.

Glaser, R. Instructional technology and the measurement of learning outcomes. *American Psychologist*, 1963, *18*, 510–522.

Halliday, M.A. Learning how to mean. In E.H. Lenneberg & E. Lenneberg (Eds.), *Foundations of language development* (Vol. 1). New York: Academic Press, 1975.

Harbin G., & Brantley, J. *Model for identifying and minimizing potential sources of child evaluation bias.* Chapel Hill: University of North Carolina, 1978.

Hoover, M.R., Politzer, R. & Taylor, O. *Bias in achievement and diagnostic reading tests: A linguistically oriented view.* Unpublished paper, National Institute of Education, National Conference on Test Bias, 1974.

Lucas, E.V. *Semantic and pragmatic language disorders: Assessment and procedures.* Rockville, Md.: Aspen Systems Corp., 1980.

Morris, C.W. Foundation of the theory of signs. In O. Nurath (Ed.), *International encyclopedia of unified science.* Chicago: University of Chicago Press, 1938.

Payne, K. *Perceptions of speech disorders by speech pathologist and speech community: A case study in the U.S. Virgin Islands.* Unpublished doctoral dissertation, Howard University, 1982.

Ramirez, M., & Castaneda, A. *Cultural democracy, bicognitive development, and education.* New York: Academic Press, 1974.

Roberts, E. *An evaluation of standardized tests as tools of language development* (Language Research Report No. 1). Cambridge, Mass.: Language Research Foundation, 1970.

Searle, J.R. *Speech acts.* London: Cambridge University Press, 1969.

Saville-Troike, M. *Culture in the classroom.* Arlington, Va.: National Clearinghouse for Bilingual Education, 1977.

Seymour, H., & Miller-Jones, D. Language and cognitive assessment of black children. *Speech and language: Advances in basic research and practice.* New York: Academic Press, 1981.

Taylor, O.L. The sociolinguistic dimension of standardized testing. In M. Saville-Troike (Ed.), *Linguistics and anthropology*. Washington, D.C.: Georgetown University Press, 1977.

Taylor, O.L. Language differences. In G. Shames & E. Wiig (Eds.), *Human communication disorders: An introduction*. Columbus, Ohio: Merrill, 1982.

Taylor, O., Stround, V., Moore, E., Hurst, C., & Williams, R. Philosophies and goals of ASHA Black Caucus. *ASHA*, 1969, *11*, 216–218.

Watson D., Grovell, S., Heller, B., & Omark, D. *Nondiscriminatory assessment test matrix*. Sacramento: California Association of School Psychologists and Psychometrists, 1980.

Wolfram, W. Levels of sociolinguistic bias in testing. In D. Harrison & T. Trabasso (Eds.), *Black English: A seminar*. Hillsdale, N.J.: Lawrence Erlbaum Associates, 1974.

Wolfram, W. *Speech pathology and dialect differences*. Arlington, Va.: Center for Applied Linguistics, 1979.

Wolfram, W., Williams, R., & Taylor, O. *Some predicted dialect interference in select language development tests*. Short course presented at the annual meeting of the American Speech-Hearing Association, Rockville, Maryland, 1972.

Test interpretation and sociolinguistic differences

Walt Wolfram, PhD
Professor of Communication Sciences
University of the District of Columbia
Director of Research
Center for Applied Linguistics
Washington, DC

THE USE OF formal testing instruments in speech and language pathology derives from a simple concern within the profession—to provide an orderly, systematic, and convenient basis for tapping the language capabilities of a population of speakers. Objectifiable, formal measurement is a token of definitiveness that is difficult to resist. Thus, the central component of speech and language evaluation often relies on standardized assessment instruments of one type or another.

Despite the traditional rationale for applying formal assessment instruments, there is a growing feeling that some speakers are done a disservice when they are classified on the basis of the results of these tests. Obviously, when a test reveals significant differences among groups of individuals, something has been demonstrated. But the recurring concern is whether these instruments actually reveal what they are designed to measure. Although various questions of validity

Top Lang Disord, 1983, 3(3), 21–34
© 1983 Aspen Publishers, Inc.

have been raised with respect to standardized tests, one of the most persistent issues concerns their application across different cultural groups. For which groups of the American population are such tests applicable? Are they applicable across a range of social and ethnic groups or are they limited in their application only to those populations on which they have been developed? And how must results be interpreted for speakers who do not come from the specific norm population? These are essential questions that cannot be ignored as language variation in American English becomes a recognized fact of life within the profession.

Some of the critical dimensions of testing from a sociolinguistic perspective follow. In particular, there is concern with the application of formalized testing instruments to those who do not speak the variety of "Standard American English" that is assumed for most tests. The concern here is with establishing a sociolinguistic framework for examining language diversity and testing that in turn can be used as a basis for setting forth practical principles to guide practitioners as consumers of information from these tests. The emphasis is on the general framework of application and practical principles that derive from this framework rather than specific non-Standard English dialects. Specific reference to dialects such as Vernacular Black English or Appalachian English is meant to be illustrative rather than inclusive of the range of non-Standard English varieties. The general principles should apply regardless of the regional or social community in which a variety is found, although the descriptive details obviously will differ.

THE LINGUISTIC DIMENSION

It stands without question that language is an exceedingly complex phenomenon, simultaneously organized on a number of different but interrelated levels. Although the normal adult language user taps this resource with little apparent effort, the accurate description of language organization remains an imposing and sometimes elusive task for the descriptive linguist. Given the enormous complexity of language organization, one can hardly fault language assessment instruments that focus on a particular level of language rather than the entire system. Traditionally, the practical consequence of this selectivity has resulted in the construction of separate tests for phonological, morphological, syntactic, and lexical forms. Furthermore, most of the traditional instruments focus on language form as opposed to language function, although more recent assessment instruments have turned to pragmatics, including the examination of language functions and speech acts.

Two observations can be made with respect to the way in which traditional assessment instruments tap language ability. To a certain extent, these observations bear on the content validity of these instruments regardless of the dialect of the test taker, but we shall see how they are particularly significant for those speakers who do not speak a standard variety of English. As noted previously, the typical standardized testing instrument focuses on a restricted aspect of a given domain or level of language. That is, given a particular level of language organization, only a subset of language capability within the level may be tapped. For example, consider what "word knowledge" implies from the standpoint of a total language organization and how such knowledge is typically tapped in a testing instrument. In terms of language organization in the real world, "knowing a word" includes at least (a) syntactic constraints—knowing appropriate sentence structures for the word; (b) semantic constraints—knowing appropriate ideas for its use; (c) stylistic constraints—knowing appropriate settings and styles of speaking for its use; (d) morphological information—knowing what words it is related to and how it attaches to other items; (e) pragmatic constraints—knowing what it entails, presupposes, and implies; and (f) phonological information—knowing how it is produced. With these aspects of word knowledge in mind, consider how word knowledge is tapped in vocabulary tests. Typically, vocabulary is measured through a test taker's association of a label with a pictorial representation falling within the semantic territory of that label, for example, the Peabody Picture Vocabulary Test (PPVT). In terms of the dimensions of word knowledge specified earlier, this is only a limited subset of what "knowing a word" entails. Thus, the demands of inferencing about word knowledge are heightened accordingly with the reduction of the domain of knowledge tapped. It is not disputed here that passive semantic association with a pictorial image is a part of knowing a word, only that it is a restricted subset of information relating to word knowledge in the overall framework of language organization.

A second observation about the construction of tests concerns the kinds of language knowledge that are tapped. Many traditional instruments tap only the more superficial aspects of language organization rather than the underlying categories and relationships. That is, the most readily apparent or superficial realizations of language are examined rather than the deeper conceptual bases of language capability. For example, given the example of word knowledge in the PPVT, one must conclude that passive labeling association of a pictorial representation is a more superficial aspect of word knowledge than evidence of an underlying conceptual unit covering a particular semantic domain. Attaching words to concepts of knowledge already acquired is a far quicker and easier task than forming a new concept to go with a novel word (Nelson, 1981). Similarly, knowledge of grammatical relationships and categories exists at a level of language organization considerably deeper than the production of particular surface morphemes (Chomsky, 1965), and phonological systems reveal organization deeper than that of surface production indicated in traditional phonemic inventories (Chomsky & Halle, 1968).

The limitations of traditional tests have led to reservations about using such instruments as the sole basis of evaluation for any speaker, but their impact is even more significant given the ways in which the dialects of English typically differ from each other. Studies of non-Standard English varieties indicate that the majority of differences exist on the more superficial levels of language organization (Labov, 1972; Wolfram & Fasold, 1974). In fact, it can be concluded that the deeper the language level, the more similar the different dialects of English are apt to become. Unfortunately, it is the level of maximum differentiation, the "surface level," that is usually in focus in the kinds of speech and language instruments that have been described previously. The more superficial the level of language organization tapped in a testing instrument, the greater the likelihood that it will be inappropriate across a range of dialects.

It is also reasonable to suggest that a test which taps a restricted domain of language organization will be less amenable to cross-dialectal application than one representing a broader range of language capability. It may be the case that the limited domain of the language that is tapped coincides with an area in which dialect differences are prominent, as with lexical labeling or surface phonetic productions. Tapping a wider range of semantic or phonological ability might compensate for or neutralize the effect of selective dialect differentiation. As the burden on inferences about language capability is heightened because of selectivity, the general applicability of the instrument becomes more suspect. Naturally, this can only serve as a disadvantage to those who do not use the language variety assumed in the assessment instrument. The following hypothesis is, therefore, offered: *The more superficial and limited the scope of language capability tapped in a testing instrument, the greater the likelihood that the instrument will be inappropriate for speakers beyond the immediate population on which it was normed.* Usually, of course, the immediate population represents only those who speak the standard varieties of English.

In a recent discussion of language assessment tools, Vaughn-Cooke (1980) has set forth a number of linguistic guidelines on which these instruments may be evaluated. Table 1 provides a summary of Vaughn-Cooke's proposed guidelines and her rating of a number of prominent language assessment tools in terms of these guidelines. In addition to traditional elicitation instruments, several procedures that go beyond formal tests are included (e.g., Bloom & Lahey's, 1978, "content, form, and use analysis").

The relationship of Vaughn-Cooke's guidelines to the previous discussion of selectivity and superficiality should be obvious. Virtually all of the proposed guidelines are concerned with tapping a representative or appropriate aspect of language capability. It is indeed striking that a number of the widely used instruments do not meet these guidelines. However, although none of the assessment instruments surveyed by Vaughn-Cooke has been constructed to deal with language variation per se, several hold the potential to be adapted to accommodate linguistic diversity.

THE SOCIOLINGUISTIC DIMENSION

In the previous section, concern for language variation derived by extension from more general concerns about the ability of formal instruments to tap representative language capability was expressed. Issues more directly related to sociolinguistic variation are discussed here. In previous explorations of tests (Wolfram, 1976), the following three sociolinguistic levels related to testing considerations were delineated: (a) differ-

Table 1. Results of the evaluation of seven assessment tools according to some proposed guidelines based on linguistic research

Guideline	Language assessment tools						
	UTLD	HTLD	PPVT	BLST	GCS	DSS	CFUA
The procedure can account for language variation.	−	−	−	+	+	⊕	⊕
The assumptions about language that underlie the procedure are valid.	−	−	−	− +	+	+	+
The procedure includes an analysis of a spontaneous speech sample (when an oral system is used to communicate).	−	−	−	−	−	+	+
The procedure reliably indicates whether a system is developing normally.	−	−	−	−	−	+	+ −
The results of the procedure provide principled guidelines for language intervention.	−	−	−	−	−	− +	+
The procedure can provide an adequate description of some aspect of the child's knowledge of language.	−	−	−	−	+	+	+

UTLD = Utah Test of Language Development; HTLD = Houston Test of Language Development; BLST = Bankson Language Screening Test; PPVT = Peabody Picture Vocabulary Test; DSS = Developmental Sentence Scoring; CFUA = Content, Form and Use Analysis; GCS = Grammatic Closure subtest of the Illinois Test of Psycholinguistic Abilities; + − means some aspects of the test can meet the guideline, others do not; ⊕ means the procedure can be adapted to meet this guideline; − means the procedure cannot meet the guideline; + means the procedure can meet the guideline. Reprinted with permission from Vaughn-Cooke (1980), Table 2, p. 41.

ences in linguistic forms per se; (b) differences in how language is used to tap information, or what has been called *task orientation;* and (c) differences in the social occasions that relate to language use in testing. For convenience, this format has been adopted for the discussion, although the actual testing situation obviously does not break down into discrete, neatly defined sociolinguistic levels.

DIFFERENCES IN LINGUISTIC FORM

A number of assessment tools used in speech and language pathology and allied fields are designed to elicit particular language forms as an index of language development or capability. Articulation tests focused on particular phonemic realizations, syntactic or morphological tests focused on select morphemes or syntactic constructions, and vocabulary tests focused on specific lexical items all fit this characterization. In these assessment instruments, structural variation among the dialects of English becomes an important

A linguistically appropriate, or "correct," form may differ from community to community depending on the particular dialect norm.

variable if they are applied outside of the specific populations on which they are normed. A linguistically appropriate, or "correct," form may differ from community to community depending on the particular dialect norm. Practically, this calls for an understanding of how various non-standard English varieties are systematically different from their standard counterparts. The model typically used to determine the points at which a test must contend with dialect diversity in linguistic structure generally follows that set up in the field of *contrastive linguistics*. In brief, contrastive linguistics places the rules of language variety X and language variety Y side by side, and, on the basis of comparing similarities and differences in the systems, points out areas of potential conflict for a speaker of X confronted with the norms of Y. Procedurally, we can set up the responses of a test considered correct on the basis of a Standard English variety, compare them with the rules of non-Standard English varieties, and determine where the alternate responses might be expected due to potential conflicts between systems. For example, if a test normed on a middle-class Standard English-speaking population determines that a form such as *any* is the correct response to fill the blank in a construction such as "They didn't have _____ cookies," there is a point of conflict where a variety of English uses multiple negatives as in "They didn't have no cookies." Given the potential point of conflict, traditional contrastive linguistics would then predict that *no* is an alternate form for speakers from the non-Standard English variety. This form would be appropriate in terms of the rules of the indigenous variety, notwith-

standing its social evaluation as a socially stigmatized form. A classic case of the application of such analysis is offered later for the Grammatic Closure subtest of the Illinois Test of Psycholinguistic Abilities (ITPA). Table 2 shows the difference between what has been designated the "correct" response in the test manual and the systematically different responses that would be predicted for speakers of Appalachian English (as described in Feagin, 1979; and Wolfram & Christian, 1976) and Vernacular Black English (as described in works such as Fasold & Wolfram, 1970; Labov, 1972). Alternate forms here are defined as those considered "incorrect" given the Standard English model adopted in the test but linguistically appropriate given the rules of a non-Standard English variety. Each structure is fully documented in an empirically based descriptive analysis.

When alternate responses are set up on the basis of predictions drawn from a contrastive analysis of the structures of different varieties, we must be realistic in interpreting the significance of this kind of analysis. In many instances, we are still limited to prediction rather than observation of alternate responses. Limited empirical studies (e.g., Cole, 1979; King, 1972) document the incidence of a number of predicted forms, but we still must contend with differences between predicted and observed responses. On a theoretical level, the adoption of the contrastive base in text examination is subject to the same limitations that have been suggested for the predictive hypothesis in the field of contrastive language studies (Corder, 1967; Wardhaugh, 1970).

There are several reasons why we would

Table 2. ITPA Grammatical Closure subtest with comparison of correct responses and Appalachian and Vernacular Black English alternant forms

Stimulus with correct item according to ITPA test manual	Alternant	
	Appalachian English	Vernacular Black English
1. Here is a dog. Here are two *dogs/doggies*.		dog
2. This cat is under the chair. Where is the cat? She is *on*/(any preposition—other than "under"—indicating location).		
3. Each child has a ball. This is hers, and this is *his*.	his'n	
4. This dog likes to bark. Here he is *barking*.		
5. Here is a dress. Here are two *dresses*.		dress
6. The boy is opening the gate. Here the gate has been *opened*.		open
7. There is milk in this glass. It is a glass *of/with/ for/o'/lots of milk*.		
8. This bicycle belongs to John. Whose bicycle is it? It is *John's*.		John
9. This boy is writing something. This is what he *wrote/has written/did write*.	writed/writ has wrote	writed/wrote
10. This is the man's home, and this is where he works. Here he is going to work, and here he is going *home/back home*/to *his home*.	at home	
11. Here it is night, and here it is morning. He goes to work first thing in the morning, and he goes home first thing *at night*.	of the night	
12. This man is painting. He is a *painter/fence painter*.	a-paintin'	
13. The boy is going to eat all the cookies. Now all the cookies have been *eaten*.	eat/ate/eated/et	ate
14. He wanted another cookie, but there weren't *any/any more*.	none/no more	none/no more
15. This horse is not big. This horse is big. This horse is even *bigger*.	more bigger	more bigger
16. And this horse is the very *biggest*.	most biggest	most biggest
17. Here is a man. Here are two *men/gentlemen*.	mans/mens	mans/mens
18. This man is planting a tree. Here the tree has been *planted*.		
19. This is soap, and these are *soap/bars of soap/ more soap*.	soaps	soaps
20. This child has lots of blocks. This child has even *more*.		
21. And this child has the *most*.	mostest	mostest
22. Here is a foot. Here are two *feet*.	foots/feets	foots/feets
23. Here is a sheep. Here are lots of *sheep*.	sheeps	sheeps
24. This cookie is not very good. This cookie is good. This cookie is even *better*.	gooder	gooder
25. And this cookie is the very *best*.	bestest	

Table 2. continued

Stimulus with correct item according to ITPA test manual	Alternant	
	Appalachian English	Vernacular Black English
26. This man is hanging the picture. Here the picture has been *hung*.	hanged	hanged
27. The thief is stealing the jewels. These are the jewels that he *stole*.	stoled/stealed	stoled/stealed
28. Here is a woman. Here are two *women*.	womans/womens	womans/womens
29. The boy had two bananas. He gave one away and he kept one for *himself*.	hisself	hisself
30. Here is a leaf. Here are two *leaves*.	leafs	leafs
31. Here is a child. Here are three *children*.	childrens	childrens
32. Here is a mouse. Here are two *mice*.	mouses	mouses
33. These children all fell down. He hurt himself, and she hurt herself. They all hurt *themselves*.	theirselves/theirself	theirselves/theyselves theirself/theyself

Note: Items considered to be correct according to the procedures for scoring are italicized. Reprinted with permission from Wolfram (1980), Table 1, p. 21.

not expect all of the predictions to be realized by speakers of the non-Standard English varieties. These are related in part to the nature of dialect diversity and in part to the integration of sociolinguistic considerations beyond differences in linguistic form. For one, many of the structures predicted as alternate forms are inherently variable (cf. Labov, 1969) rather than categorical in their occurrence. In the ideal predictions, however, alternate forms may have been set forth as though they were categorical. Thus, for example, predictions for plural absence in Vernacular Black English specify plural absence for regular plural markers (e.g., Items 1 and 5), but plural absence of −z is a variable feature, and its incidence for speakers of the dialect is not typically higher than 10%–20% out of all potential cases in which it might be absent. Predictions as they are currently specified for

tests have not taken this inherent variability into account, but any realistic predictive base would have to recognize it, just as it has been recognized in some descriptive studies (e.g., Fasold, 1972; Labov, 1969; Wolfram, 1969).

Another reason that predicted items might not be realized in the actual testing situation relates to the speech style appropriate for the testing situation. In virtually all situations of direct elicitation, the speech style is geared toward the more formal styles or registers available to the subject. In this context, forms that might be constrained stylistically would not realistically constitute alternate forms. For example, the contrastive analysis in Table 2 predicts *a*-prefixing as a legitimate alternate test response (cf. Item 12). There is reason to doubt that it would actually be produced by speakers of the dialect in question in such a situation, however, even though it is certainly an intrinsic structural unit in the variety, since *a*-prefixing seems to be stylistically excluded from the more formal styles of language usage in the variety.

Given the qualifications that must be made about contrastive analysis based solely on prediction, it becomes imperative to broaden the empirical base for establishing alternate forms. Ultimately, contrastive analysis is more adequately applied as an explanation for observed language performance rather than a prediction of possible occurrence, although predicting the possible range of dialect alternates may be a reasonable starting point.

TASK CHARACTERISTICS

Aspects of sociolinguistic differences are not limited to the structural differences in language forms. Test considerations must also examine the operations involved in obtaining information as well as the diagnostic linguistic forms within the test. These operations include strategies for giving directions and tapping information about language. Directions call for the establishment of a frame of reference so that there is a common baseline that can be assumed for all test takers. Obviously, the desired goal of directions is clarity for the test taker so that directions can be eliminated as a variable affecting success. Unfortunately, the negotiated meaning of the directions cannot be assumed despite traditional methods for their standardization, and even the most "simple" and "obvious" directions may be laden with potential for misinterpretation. This potential misinterpretation may involve a particular item or discourse structure of the directions. It has been pointed out elsewhere (Wolfram, 1976) that the simple interpretation of an instruction to "repeat" as paraphrase repetition rather than as verbatim repetition may have had a significant impact on the scores of working-class black children who were administered a "simple" and "obvious" repetition task.

Typically, there are many ways of getting at the bits of information desired in a test, and many formal instruments use specialized methods for tapping such information. In fact, the close examination of language structure used in testing tasks suggests that tests have established their own style or register, if not dialect. For example, the notion of a question frame as an incomplete declarative (e.g., "Here is a dog. Here are two _____."), or the specialized use of verb *-ing* forms as truncated relative clauses (e.g., "Show me, digging" for "Show me someone who is digging") involve a specialized use of language conventionalized for testing purposes. Examples of conventionalized styles in test tasks accumulate fairly rapidly when actual language usage is surveyed in tests. Given that specialized uses of language in tests are different from everyday language uses of *all* test takers to some extent and not unique to the non-Standard English speaker, we may still hypothesize that *the more distant an individual's everyday speaking style is from the style of testing tasks, the greater the potential for task interference.* At least we cannot ignore the specialized methods of task orientation as a variable that may potentially affect performance for different social and ethnic groups of test takers.

TESTING AS A SOCIAL OCCASION

Finally, something should be said about the social occasion of testing and how language use may be affected by this context. Tests do not take place in a contextually neutral social setting with a non-contextual orientation, although many tests implicitly make this assumption, or at least assume that it is possible to control the occasion so tightly that unwanted background factors do not influence performance in a significant way. Unfortunately, these assumptions can be challenged on the basis of probing the underlying orientations that motivate test takers to respond in the way that they do. In this regard, ethnomethodological investigations that examine the particular rationale leading test takers to particular "correct" and "incorrect" answers have provided helpful evidence for recognizing the social occasion surrounding testing (Cicourel, et al., 1974).

Testing calls for the test taker to enter the experimental frame created by the test constructor and administrator, and if the test taker is unable or unwilling to "play the experimental game," the resulting measurements cannot be accurate. Among other things, values and assumptions about language within the experimental frame may be guided by status relationships between test administrators and test takers. Thus, one ethnographic study of a rural black southern community concludes that "experience in interacting with adults has taught him [the child] the values of silence and withdrawal" (Ward, 1971, p. 88). The common working-class dictum that "children should be seen, not heard" may thus be the appro-

priate orientation for children to enter the adult-dominated social situation. In a social situation that directly or indirectly rewards verbosity and speaking about "obvious" information, children from such backgrounds may be at a serious disadvantage. As Labov (1976) has pointed out, even some of the most innocuous-appearing procedures for eliciting language data (e.g., obtaining a "spontaneous speech sample") may be frought with sociocultural values and attitudes. Values about language use are particularly difficult to suspend or reorient upon entering the experimental frame. And, although such value orientations may not be as readily objectifiable as differences in linguistic form, their potential impact is not lessened by their quantitative unwieldiness.

Different groups may also enter the experimental frame with different orientations in terms of background experience, which may be manifested in what they talk about and how they talk about it. In the parlance of current educational psychologists, some groups, in particular experimental settings, reveal "relatively context independent text, in the sense that the text was not imbedded in a local context/practice," whereas others show "relatively context dependent text in that it was more imbedded in a local context/practice and assumed knowledge of the context/practice" (Bernstein, 1981, p. 361). Although the possible reasons for observed differences and the significance of the differences certainly may be disputed (see Dittmar, 1976, for a critique of such studies), the differences in language use in particular experimental frames seem real, and thus must be considered as a potential variable affecting language assessment.

Interpreting test results

As the preceding discussion has indicated, there is no unidimensional axis along which sociolinguistic information can be applied to the results of standardized assessment instruments. The linguistic and sociolinguistic considerations inherent in the design of the instrument must be reviewed along with the data from actual test performance. Given the potential for sociolinguistic bias of one type or another, a number of different philosophical posi-

---

There is no unidimensional axis along which sociological information can be applied to the results of standardized assessment instruments.

---

tions about the application of tests to sociolinguistically diverse populations have been advocated. Rather than advocate a particular sociopolitical stance on test application here, the consideration of a series of principles is stressed to guide those confronted with results from assessment instruments for whatever reason. Given the current state of affairs in assessment, this is considered to be an expedient approach, but it should not be taken to mean advocating the continuing, indiscriminate application of many of these instruments across diverse populations.

For the most part, the practical principles derive from the earlier discussion of a linguistic and sociolinguistic framework for testing. From a practical perspective, they are presented as a series of questions that have to be asked about the application of a test or the interpretation of results from that test. Some of these questions are appropriate regardless of the sociolinguistic background of the test taker; others are specific to those who speak one of the non-Standard English varieties.

As a preliminary, we must ask, *What kind of assumptions about language organization underlie the construction of the test?* The discussion of the linguistic dimensions of testing has shown that many formal testing instruments are superficial and selective in the domain of language organization tapped, thus placing a heavy burden on inferencing about language capability. The precise aspect of speech and language capability tapped in a test must be understood if results are to be interpreted adequately. Unfortunately, claims about what a test measures and what it actually measures are not always isomorphic. Thus, the test user must determine *what the test actually measures in terms of speech and language capability in relation to what it claims to be measuring.* To a large extent, this question is pertinent to all test takers, but there is an added dimension to be considered when dealing with speakers of different dialects. As mentioned previously, the PPVT may be an adequate instrument for measuring the passive recognition of culturally specific lexical items. However, the claim that this "hearing vocabulary" translates into "verbal intelligence" is based on inferences about vocabulary, language facility, and cognitive skills that are not warranted by an examination of overall language organization, to say nothing of the sociolinguistic dimension of language.

Similarly, the Grammatic Closure subtest of the Illinois Test of Psycholinguistic Abilities (ITPA) may be appropriate in measuring a child's paradigmatic ability based on a subset of Standard English suffixes, verb forms, and selected superficial details of syntax (e.g., negative indefinites, surface prepositions), but this is considerably more modest than its claim to assess "the child's ability to make use of the redundancies of oral language in acquiring automatic habits for handling syntax and grammatic inflections" (ITPA, 1968, p. 7). As stated earlier, so many of the items in this test are focused on differences between Standard English and non-Standard English varieties that it functions mainly as an index of productive knowledge of Standard English forms.

Given the kinds of dialect differences that might turn up in the performance of a non-Standard English speaker, it becomes important to know *which structural forms produced by speakers of non-Standard English dialects may be attributable to dialect differences.* Application of the contrastive linguistic method should be able to indicate many of the structural details that differ in systematic ways from the correct responses that are assumed on the basis of a Standard English model. Such responses become important in determining whether nonnormative responses on the test are simply a function of test bias against non-Standard English speakers or indicative of a pathology when judged in terms of the norms of the community. In this regard we want to know *if the results from the test can be adjusted*

in some way to accommodate dialect differences. For example, if the test were scored in such a way to give speakers credit for appropriate community forms, *Would the test be able to distinguish those speakers from a non-Standard English-speaking community who indicate an authentic pathology within the context of the indigenous community from those that simply use indigenous community norms?* If results from a test are amenable to this kind of adaptation, then it may be worth the clinician's time to set up alternate community norms, as has been done in the previous presentation of the ITPA Grammatic Closure subtest. Although the clinician must realize the limitations of alternate norming, which does not adopt conventional standardization procedures, such an accommodation might provide a stopgap basis for using results from traditional instruments. As indicated in Vaughn-Cooke's analysis, some assessment instruments can be adopted to accommodate language variation, but others cannot. Such potential may be an important consideration in selecting assessment instruments, given the paucity of tests that have been specifically designed and adequately normed to include language variation.

The focus on differences in language items specifically included in assessment tests should not be taken to minimize the importance of considering the ways in which speech and language information is tapped and the social occasion of testing. Thus, we must consider *the sociolinguistic assumptions that underlie the social occasion of testing* and *how particular elicitation techniques might influence the results of the test.* The discussion about values governing language use or background information orientation may be essential in considering the quantity and the quality of the language obtained in a testing situation. Similarly, the particularized convention for eliciting information must be considered as a potential influence on the assessment of language capabilities. And, if the clinical setting with an adult interviewer/administrator prohibits collecting an adequate language sample, alternatives that integrate the most conducive community environments and interlocutors for obtaining speech samples must be considered. The inconvenience to the clinician in altering the place and interlocutors for obtaining a language sample may not be nearly as severe as the harm done to clients who have not had an adequate opportunity to demonstrate their genuine language capability.

Admittedly, the kinds of principles explicated earlier make demands not always included within the traditional speech and language training program. For one, it presupposes a more sophisticated understanding of language organization so that practitioners are in a position to evaluate for themselves the linguistic basis of instruments they use. Such is hardly an extravagant demand, however, given the complexity of language and the integral way in which linguistic organization plays a role in considerations of diagnosis and remediation.

It seems further necessary for practitioners to gain familiarity with the structural details of the non-Standard English varieties represented by their clientele. Such information is a basis for observing

performance in terms of community norms with or without formalized test instruments, and, ultimately, judgments differentiating "difference" from "disorder" are premised on such knowledge.

The knowledge base presumed in this discussion extends beyond simple structural knowledge of different dialects. It includes sociolinguistic understanding of language use and the values and attitudes about language that reflect a community perspective. The sociocultural dimensions of language are critical as a base for understanding underlying orientations to the language event and the social interactions that may govern it.

Finally, there is a presumed familiarity with the experimental base of standardized testing instruments. Introductory information in testing manuals that details the method of sampling, the norming populations, and other experimental details of test development and construction should be more than extraneous material to be disregarded as irrelevant to the test giver. Instead, the practical consequences of particular assumptions and methods of experimental design may become important variables in evaluating the potential for sociolinguistic bias. Also, an understanding of acceptable experimental design standards for tests (e.g., *Standards for Educational & Psychological Tests*, 1974) must be obtained to guard against the misuse of test application and results across populations.

The challenge to apply appropriate information from standardized assessment instruments is a formidable one but one well within the scope of what we might reasonably demand for practitioners within our profession. Ultimately, our charge is to assist those with genuine speech pathologies regardless of the indigeneous population, and an understanding of the testing dimension is just a small, preliminary step in that direction. Without taking such a step, our approach to serving diverse populations within our society continues to hold more potential for disservice than service.

REFERENCES

Bernstein, B. Codes, modalities, and the process of cultural reproduction: A model. *Language in Society*, 1981, *10*, 327–364.

Bloom, L., & Lahey, M. *Language development and language disorders*. New York: Wiley, 1978.

Chomsky, N. *Aspects of the theory of syntax*. Cambridge, Mass.: MIT Press, 1965.

Chomsky, N., & Halle, M. *The sound pattern of English*. New York: Harper & Row, 1968.

Cicourel, A.V., et al. *Language use and school performance*. New York: Academic Press, 1974.

Cole, L. *Developmental analysis of social dialect features in the spontaneous language of preschool black children*. Unpublished doctoral dissertation, Northwestern University, 1979.

Corder, S.P. The significance of learner's errors. *International Review of Applied Linguistics*, 1967, *4*, 161–169.

Dittmar, N. *A critical survey of sociolinguistics: Theory and application*. New York: St. Martin's Press, 1976.

Fasold, R. *Tense marking in Black English: A linguistic and social analysis*. Arlington, Va.: Center for Applied Linguistics, 1972.

Fasold, R.W., & Wolfram, W. Some linguistic features of Negro dialect. In R.W. Fasold & R.W. Shuy (Eds.), *Teaching Standard English in the inner city*. Washington, D.C.: Center for Applied Linguistics, 1970.

Feagin, C. *Variation and change in Alabama English: A sociolinguistic study of the white community*. Washington, D.C.: Georgetown University Press, 1979.

Illinois Test of Psycholinguistic Abilities. Urbana: University of Illinois Press, 1968.

King, P. *An analysis of the Northwestern Syntax Screening Test for lower class black children in Prince George's County*. Unpublished master's thesis, Howard University, 1972.

Labov, W. Contraction, deletion, and inherent variability of the English copula. *Language*, 1969, *45*, 715–762.

Labov, W. *Language in the inner city: Studies in the Black English vernacular*. Philadelphia: University of Pennsylvania Press, 1972.

Labov, W. Systematically misleading data from test questions. *Urban Review*, 1976, *9*, 146–169.

Nelson, K. Acquisition of words by first language learners, In H. Winitz (Ed.), *Native language and foreign language acquisition*. New York: New York Academy of Sciences, 1981.

Standards for educational & psychological tests. Washington, D.C.: American Psychological Association, 1974.

Vaughn-Cooke, F.B. Evaluating the language of Black English speakers: Implications of the Ann Arbor decision. In M.F. Whiteman (Ed.), *Reactions to Ann Arbor: Vernacular Black English and education*. Washington, D.C.: Center for Applied Linguistics, 1980.

Ward, M.C. *Them children: a study in language learning*. New York: Holt, Rinehart & Winston, 1971.

Wardhaugh, R. The contrastive analysis hypothesis. *TESOL Quarterly*, 1970, *4*, 123–129.

Wolfram, W.A. *A sociolinguistic description of Detroit Negro speech*. Washington, D.C.: Center for Applied Linguistics, 1969.

Wolfram, W. Levels of sociolinguistic bias in testing. In D.S. Harrison & T. Trabasso (Eds.), *Seminar in Black English*. Hillsdale, N.J.: Erlbaum, 1976.

Wolfram, W. Beyond Black English: Implications of the Ann Arbor decision for other non-mainstream varieties. In M.F. Whiteman (Ed.), *Reactions to Ann Arbor: Vernacular Black English and Education*. Washington, D.C.: Center for Applied Linguistics, 1980.

Wolfram, W. & Christian, D. *Appalachian Speech*. Arlington: Center for Applied Linguistics, 1976.

Wolfram, W., & Fasold, R.W. *The study of social dialects in American English*. Englewood Cliffs, N.J.: Prentice-Hall, 1974.

Application of nonstandardized assessment procedures to diverse linguistic populations

Laurence B. Leonard, PhD
Professor
Department of Audiology and
*   Speech Sciences*
Purdue University
West Lafayette, Indiana

Amy L. Weiss, MA
Doctoral Candidate
Department of Audiology and
*   Speech Sciences*
Purdue University
West Lafayette, Indiana

THERE IS AMPLE evidence in the literature which supports the notion that most of the available standardized tests of children's language ability require knowledge of standard English and thus may penalize the child who speaks a non-standard-English dialect (e.g., Arnold & Reed, 1976; Duchan & Baskerville, 1977; Johnson, 1974). This state of affairs presents a significant obstacle to the clinical assessment of children who experience language learning deficits in their own nonstandard dialect. Some proposed solutions to this problem have been scoring the child's responses to dialect-biased items correct if the responses are consistent with his or her own dialect, developing non-standard-English norms for these tests, and avoiding the use of such tests altogether and using nonstandardized procedures for language assessment.

The solution with the fewest drawbacks seems to be the use of nonstandardized assessment procedures (see Seymour & Miller-Jones, 1981). To date, however,

Top Lang Disord, 1983, 3(3), 35-45
© 1983 Aspen Publishers, Inc.

more has been written about the need for a nonstandardized approach to assessment than about the manner in which nonstandardized assessment might be carried out. This article presents a set of guidelines for the use of nonstandardized language assessment procedures with children who speak nonstandard dialects of English. Special reference is made to black English; however, the guidelines presented are equally applicable to other non-standard-English dialects.

THE ASSESSMENT PROCESS

This article focuses on the language assessment phase of a diagnostic session and therefore does not address other aspects of the evaluation process. Implicit in this discussion, however, is the assumption that the child's hearing, oral structure and function, neurological functioning, emotional development, and, where appropriate, nonverbal intellectual abilities have been evaluated. In addition, it is assumed that the language specialist has spoken with the child's parents or guardians and that reports of the child's developmental and medical history have been obtained. These steps in the evaluation process, of course, apply to all children regardless of their particular dialects.

Spontaneous speech samples

As a first step in nonstandardized assessment, the collection of a spontaneous speech sample is recommended. This involves the collection and transcription of a corpus of utterances spontaneously produced by a child in one or more conversational settings in which the nature and

scope of the child's discourse is only minimally directed by the child's coconversationalist. The goal of speech sample collection is to amass a selection of utterances representative of the child's speech to gain an accurate impression of the characteristics of his or her expressive language.

There is a growing literature involved with identifying variables that affect speech sample collection. Studies have addressed elicitor effects (Johnston, Trainor, Casey, & Hagler, 1981; Olswang & Carpenter, 1978), materials used (James & Button, 1978; Longhurst & File, 1977), and the optimal settings for sample collection (Kramer, James, & Saxman, 1979; Scott & Taylor, 1978), among others.

There are a variety of language functions and conversational behaviors that cannot be readily assessed through formal testing and are best observed in a spontaneous interchange.

Because a concise review of the rationales supporting oral language sampling as a useful clinical tool is available elsewhere (Barrie-Blackley, Musselwhite, & Rogister, 1978), as are descriptions of various methods for sample analysis (Lee, 1974; Miller, 1981; Tyack & Gottsleben, 1974), only those dealing with issues that are perceived as closely aligned with nonstandardized assessment for speakers of nonstandard-English dialects are addressed.

There are several reasons why spontaneous speech samples can be valuable. First, there are a variety of language functions (e.g., see Dore, 1974, 1977; Halliday,

1975) and conversational behaviors (e.g., see Bloom, Rocissano, & Hood, 1976; Garvey, 1981) that cannot be readily assessed through formal testing and are best observed in a spontaneous interchange. Shuy and Staton (1982) recently described several such behaviors observed in the speech of black-English-speaking children.

A second reason why spontaneous speech samples are useful is that comparisons of the speech that children produce spontaneously in naturalistic settings with that formally elicited from standardized tests have yielded differences in linguistic complexity. For example, Prutting, Gallagher, and Mulac (1975) found that the expressive language performance of many of their subjects was underestimated when results from the administration of the Northwestern Syntax Screening Test (Expressive subtest) were compared with data gleaned from the same children's speech samples. If these difficulties in interpretation of formal test results exist for children who speak standard English, it can be assumed that they are at least as troublesome for the accurate assessment of the language skills of non-standard-English speakers.

A third reason for using spontaneous speech samples with children who may speak a non-standard-English dialect is that such children are often particularly sensitive to the speaking context and their interactant. Seymour and Miller-Jones (1981) noted that black-English-speaking children, for example, may view their dialect as substandard. As a result, these children may significantly reduce their verbal output when interacting with a standard-English speaker or may attempt to switch styles. For children with limited proficiency in standard English, style switching may result in hypercorrection, that is, the inappropriate application of standard English features (e.g., "they walks").

The speaking setting, too, might have an influence on the verbal behavior of non-standard-English-speaking children. For example, Hall and Nagy (1981) observed that even when interacting with other black-English speakers, a group of black children exhibited differences between their verbal behavior in the home and that in the school setting; such differences were not found for a group of white children (however, the dialects spoken by the children were not specified).

The nature of spontaneous speech samples makes it possible to incorporate culture-appropriate materials and topics into the procedure and enlist the participation of family members and peers by instructing them to interact with the child and materials in any manner they see fit. Although these factors may not eliminate all of the child's apprehension or all of the artificiality of the evaluation setting, they should permit a more representative sample of the child's speech than would be possible if they were not considered. Because such factors as the inclusion or exclusion of the mother can also influence the sampled verbal behavior of children experiencing genuine language learning difficulties (e.g., see Olswang & Carpenter, 1978) is an additional reason for considering these factors.

Analysis considerations

Speech sample data can be put to use in several ways. Certain communicative behaviors, or at least appropriate contexts for these behaviors, may occur frequently enough in the sample to permit direct analysis of the sample so that a conclusion concerning the child's linguistic and communicative status can be made. Other behaviors may not occur with sufficient frequency to permit conclusions to be drawn, but may serve as the basis for more detailed probing.

It is suggested, however, that clinicians first examine the child's speech sample to determine the general appropriateness of assessing his or her communicative skills in relation to standard-English expectations. That is, the first step in assessment would be to look for evidence of non-standard-English usage in the child's speech sample.

The value of first examining the child's speech for instances of non-standard-English usage is that there are a number of standard-English features that would be inappropriate to assess in a non-standard-English-speaking child. To determine only later that certain analyses already performed on the sample data should be discounted would represent inefficient use of the clinician's time.

A different approach might be to make the a priori decision on the basis of certain presenting characteristics that a child's speech will not be analyzed for features that are exclusively characteristic of standard English. For example, it might be decided at the outset that certain aspects of the speech of a black child from an urban or rural southern environment will not be examined. The risk involved in this approach is that if the child's dominant (or only) dialect is standard English, a number of assessable and potentially important features of his or her speech will go unattended.

How should a clinician go about examining a child's speech sample for instances of non-standard-English usage? Certainly inventories of features of several non-standard-English dialects are available (e.g., see Williams & Wolfram, 1977; Wolfram & Fasold, 1974), and it would be possible to search through a child's speech sample for instances of these features.

This procedure could be problematic if certain precautions are not taken, however. For example, a number of features of black English are marked by null (ϕ) relative to standard English. For example, plural -*s* for words preceded by a quantifier (e.g., *three pig*), possessive '*s* when the name of the possessor precedes the name of the item possessed (e.g., *John pen*), and third-person singular -*s* (e.g., *he walk*) are often not used in black English.

These features are also absent from the speech of both young, normally developing children and language-disordered children from standard-English-speaking environments. Thus, interpreting the absence of these elements as evidence that a child speaks black English could lead to a failure to identify language learning problems in black children who speak standard English.

The most appropriate means of identifying children's use of nonstandard English on the basis of a speech sample is to look for features with surface realizations that differ from those exhibited at any point in the development of standard-English usage. That is, the presence of these features in a child's speech would make it unlikely that the child's dialect is standard English. There are a number of such features in black English (some of these are evident in other non-standard-English dialects as well), for example:

- distributive *be* (e.g., black English: *I be good;* standard English: *I am good sometimes.*);
- remote time *been* (e.g., black English: *I been walked;* standard English: *I already walked, some time ago.*);
- completive aspect *done* (e.g., black English: *I done went fishing;* standard English: *I already went fishing.*);
- inflectional marking following consonant-cluster simplification (e.g., black English: *desses, tessing;* standard English: *desks, testing*);
- embedded *do* inversion (e.g., black English: *He wants to know did she go;* standard English: *He wants to know if she went.*);
- specific consonant clusters (e.g., black English: *skreet, aks;* standard English: *street, ask*);
- preposed negative auxiliary (e.g., black English: *Couldn't nobody do it;* standard English: *Nobody could do it.*); and
- existential *it* (e.g., black English: *It's a new kid on the block;* standard English: *There's a new kid on the block.*).

There are certain limitations to this approach. Although the features listed seem to be present in the speech of many black-English-speaking children by age 4 or 5 (Cole, 1980; Ramer & Rees, 1973; Stephens, 1976), normative information is limited, and it is not known precisely when these features emerge. Thus, it is possible that for children of developmental levels of approximately 24 months

(when children's utterances begin to exceed two words in length and dialect considerations become pertinent) to 4 years, surface markings of nonstandard English may be too few in number to serve a useful purpose.

A related limitation to this approach is that the use of black English, like any dialect, operates on a continuum not only in terms of the degree to which a black-English feature is used but also in terms of the number of different black-English features used. Thus, some black-English-speaking children may not use some or any of the features listed for reasons that have nothing to do with ability.

If an examination of a child's speech reveals the presence of surface features of nonstandard English, what is the next course of action? One possibility is to gain information concerning the degree of the child's ability with the observed non-standard-English forms. That is, since some of these features do not occur frequently in general usage and thus may not have been observed more than one or two times in a sample, it might be necessary to assess the child's use of these features more thoroughly.

The clinical utility of an in-depth assessment of a child's use of non-standard-English features is questionable, however, for two reasons. First, as noted earlier, the normative information concerning these features is limited, and it is unknown just when non-standard-English-speaking children show their first use of these forms, use them in alternation with other forms, or show mastery of these forms. Second, there is insufficient information concerning the forms that might be used in alternation with these non-standard-

English forms as the child is in the process of acquiring them. Without such information, it would be difficult to determine whether a child's use of alternate forms reflects developmental errors or evidence of style switching.

If a child is observed to use surface features of nonstandard English during the speech sample, it would be more appropriate to devote the time set aside for language assessment to an evaluation of the child's use of features shared by standard English and the nonstandard dialect reflected in the child's speech. For the child whose speech is limited to single- or two-word utterances, of course, relatively few aspects of the child's linguistic usage are likely to be dialect specific.

For children who are operating at higher levels of linguistic development, however, there are many language features that cut across dialects. These shared features include not only those from the semantic and pragmatic realms of language but also those from the phonological, morphological, and syntactic realms. They range from features as basic as the subject + verb + object construction and the phoneme [*sh*] to embedded clauses and the issuing of warnings.

Use of probes

How might the features shared by standard English and the nonstandard dialect reflected in a child's speech be assessed? The use (or absence) of features that are generally frequent in their occurrence can be assessed directly using the speech sample. For example, in a 100-utterance sample in which the child is describing a number of ongoing activities, it is possible

that as many as 20 obligatory contexts for the inflection -*ing* might be identified. In a similar-size sample involving a storytelling format with animate characters, numerous obligatory contexts for personal pronoun usage should be evident. It is unlikely, however, that an adequate assessment of a child's use of the many shared features of standard and nonstandard English will be possible from speech sample data alone. In these cases, specific probes appear necessary.

The chief advantage of probes is that they allow for a detailed assessment of the child's use of the communicative feature under examination. Such an assessment

> *The chief advantage of probes is that they allow for a detailed assessment of the child's use of the communicative feature under examination.*

can provide information concerning the consistency with which the child uses a feature and the contexts that might influence this usage.

The chief drawback of probes is that they place some structure on the speaking situation at best and can resemble a formal testing situation at worst. Thus they may prove problematic for some non-standard-English-speaking children. To reduce this negative aspect of probes, it is recommended that materials and topics appropriate to the child's culture be used and that, where possible, persons with whom the child is familiar be enlisted to assist in the activities.

Production tasks

There are many tasks that the clinician can use in probes (Leonard, Prutting, Perozzi, & Berkley, 1978). A number of these are production tasks that were developed by researchers interested in examining various aspects of children's language. Many have since appeared in a variety of standardized language tests. One of the most common is the immediate imitation task. For example, if the clinician wishes to determine a child's use of the conjunction construction with forward deletion of redundant elements, he or she might construct 10 to 15 sentences of the form *Ray and Leroy like football* and ask the child to repeat each of them after him or her.

A related task is the delayed imitation task. To assess a child's use of sentences with participial complements, for example, the clinician might select sentence pairs and present the sentences in each pair in succession, such as *The men like swimming* and *The men like fishing*. Then the clinician can show the child a particular picture and ask, "Which one is this?" In this task, the stimulus utterance is further removed in time from the child's response than it is in the immediate imitation task. In addition, however, the child must comprehend the utterances well enough to select the utterance that best matches the picture.

Another task that the clinician might use is to present a carrier phrase and ask the child to complete the sentence. Contained in the carrier phrase is sufficient information to suggest the use of a specific word or structure in the response. For example, to assess a child's anaphoric use of the pronoun *she*, the clinician might present pairs of pictures, such as a pair in which in the first picture a girl is riding a bicycle and in the second the same girl is throwing a ball. The clinician might point to each picture in succession, saying "Here the girl is riding a bike, and here _____."

The parallel sentence procedure is another task that can be used in probes. In this procedure, the clinician describes some stimulus picture, object, or enactment with a particular sentence form, and the child is encouraged to describe a second stimulus using the same form. For example, if the clinician wants to test in detail his or her impression that a child produces words with regressive velar assimilation in phrases containing other words with word-final *k* or *g*, he or she might make a toy horse "walk" across the table, saying "Walk the horse," and then ask the child to perform the identical task with a toy dog in an attempt to evoke the phrase "Walk the dog." The use of a number of items of this type should enable the clinician to gain valuable information concerning evidence of velar assimilation in these linguistic contexts.

A paraphrase task can also be employed to assess a child's use of particular linguistic features. If the clinician wants to assess a child's use of the definite article *the* and the indefinite article *a*, for example, he or she can construct two or three brief age- and culture-appropriate stories that contain a substantial number of occurrences of *the* and *a*. After telling the stories to the child, the clinician can ask the child to tell the stories to a friend who was not present when the stories were first told. The assumption behind the use of this task is that although the child will only be able to paraphrase the stories at best, collectively, the stories will contain enough instances of *the* and *a* that the child will be confronted with a number of obligatory contexts for these articles even if he or she only approximates the stories.

The form of assessment that bears the greatest similarity to a naturalistic speech situation is one in which the clinician interacts with the child in an informal setting but structures the materials or his or her comments in a way that increases the likelihood that the child will produce a particular linguistic or communicative behavior. For example, assume that a child was referred to a clinician with the parental concern that when the child is not understood by others, he or she rebuffs their requests for a repetition or rephrasing of the message. Following Gallagher (1977), the clinician might interact with the child in a play session and respond to a predetermined number (e.g., 12) of the child's utterances with a comment which indicates that the utterance was not heard or understood (e.g., "What?" "I didn't understand you."). The frequency with which the child repeats, revises, and abandons his or her communicative attempts can then be noted.

Comprehension tasks

Detailed probing using any of the tasks mentioned earlier might reveal that the child has considerable difficulty producing the feature under examination. If so, it is important to assess the child's ability to comprehend the feature. There are at least three comprehension tasks that can be employed.

The most widely used comprehension task is the identification task. In this task the child is asked to select from an array of pictures or objects the one that best corresponds to the verbal stimulus presented by the clinician. If the clinician is concerned about a child's comprehension of mental verbs such as *think*, for example, a number of items could be constructed. The clinician might show the child a picture in which a football player is carrying a ball and is being pursued by opponents, with a teammate in the background. The clinician might describe the picture with the utterance "They know John has the ball." Then the child might be presented with an array of four pictures, including one identical to the picture first presented, except that the teammate in the background is holding the ball. The clinician might then ask "Show me 'They think John has the ball.'"

An acting-out task can also be used to assess a child's comprehension of a linguistic feature. In this task, a spoken stimulus is presented, and the child must respond in an active manner, rather than rely solely on a recognition level of understanding, as in the identification task. For example, the child's comprehension of *behind* might be assessed by constructing a number of items in which the child is asked to manipulate toys to reflect the requested relationship (e.g., "Put the ball behind the block.").

A child's understanding of a linguistic feature can also be examined by means of a judgment task. In this task, the child is asked to make a formal judgment of the suitability of a spoken stimulus or to select which of two spoken stimuli is more appropriate. To assess a child's understanding of adjective-order rules, for example, the clinician might select a dozen pairs of sentences in which the order of the adjectives in the sentences of each pair is different (e.g., "I have the big green truck." "I have the green big truck."). The clinician might present each pair and ask the child which of the two sentences of the pair "sounds better."

The judgment task is a rather difficult task because it often requires the child to evaluate the form or the situational appropriateness of an utterance apart from its meaning. For the assessment of certain linguistic features, such as adjective ordering, however, this task may be preferable to the other two comprehension tasks.

Selection of probes

The production and comprehension tasks described earlier can be used to assess features of nonstandard English as well as those shared by standard and nonstandard English. Most instances of detailed probing should probably focus on features of the latter type when a child who speaks a nonstandard dialect of English is being evaluated.

There are circumstances in which systematic testing of nonstandard features might be appropriate, however. In particular, such testing might be conducted if the initial speech sample and parental interview did not provide sufficient information to determine a child's dialect. For example, a black child whose mean length of utterance suggests a level of linguistic development of approximately 4 years (at least according to standard-English norms) may not have produced any of the surface features of black English (e.g., distributive *be*, completive aspect *done*,

existential *it*) during the speech sample, either because of sampling limitations or because these features are not part of his or her dialect. By presenting the child with a number of items that make use of these features, this determination might be possible. For example, the clinician might present stories that include instances of distributive *be* and then ask the child to tell the stories to his or her sister when she enters the room. Or the child might be asked to play a game in which he or she imitates sentences containing lexical items such as *street* or *ask* (pronounced [skrit] and [æks], respectively) by telling them to a friend whose ears were covered when the sentences were first produced by the clinician.

If a child shows evidence of producing these surface features of black English, it would probably be most appropriate to devote the remainder of the assessment session to an examination of the child's use of features shared by black and standard English. On the other hand, if the child responds with utterances containing neither the black-English feature nor its standard-English equivalent, it would probably be necessary to systematically test for his or her use of the standard-English equivalents of these features (e.g., by presenting sentences containing *ask* pronounced as [æsk].

If the child is able to produce the standard-English equivalents, and particularly if he or she also showed evidence during the initial speech sample of producing features of standard English (e.g., contractible copula, third-person singular -*s*) that are often not evident in black English, it would be appropriate to assess the child's linguistic ability using standard

English as the target dialect. On the other hand, if the child does not produce the standard-English features, the determination of the child's dominant dialect must be made by using probes that assess the child's comprehension of the nonstandard and standard features.

•   •   •

The value of nonstandardized assessment should not be considered restricted to cases in which there is no alternative form of assessment. Nonstandardized procedures are also frequently used with children from standard-English-speaking environments. In fact, clinicians often administer standardized language tests to standard-English-speaking children only to document the existence of a language problem for administrative or legal purposes. To obtain the type of information

useful in planning the course of language intervention with these children, clinicians often rely on nonstandardized forms of assessment.

Similarly, the recommendation of nonstandardized assessment procedures for use with children who speak nonstandard English is not based solely on the need to avoid an unjustified label of "language disordered" that might result from the application of existing standardized tests to the assessment of these children. The use of nonstandardized procedures is also vital for making appropriate decisions for management even if the child's communicative behavior reflects limitations unrelated to dialect. Thus, although the development of suitable standardized tests for non-standard-English-speaking children is welcomed, nonstandardized assessment for these children, as for other children, is also needed.

REFERENCES

Arnold, K., & Reed, L. The grammatic closure subtest of the ITPA: A comparative study of black and white children. *Journal of Speech and Hearing Disorders,* 1976, *41,* 477–485.

Barrie-Blackley, S., Musselwhite, C., & Rogister, S. *Clinical oral language sampling.* Danville, Ill.: Interstate, 1978.

Bloom, L., Rocissano, L., & Hood, L. Adult–child discourse: Developmental interaction between information processing and linguistic knowledge. *Cognitive Psychology,* 1976, *8,* 521–552.

Cole, L. *A developmental analysis of social dialect features in the spontaneous language of black preschool children.* Unpublished doctoral dissertation, Northwestern University, 1980.

Dore, J. A pragmatic description of early language development. *Journal of Psycholinguistic Research,* 1974, *3,* 343–350.

Dore, J. Children's illocutionary acts. In R. Freedle (Ed.), *Discourse production and comprehension.* Norwood, NJ: ABLEX, 1977.

Duchan, J., & Baskerville, R. Responses of black and white children to the grammatic closure subtest of the ITPA. *Language, Speech, and Hearing Services in Schools,* 1977, *8,* 126–132.

Gallagher, T. Revision behaviors in the speech of normal children developing language. *Journal of Speech and Hearing Research,* 1977, *20,* 303–318.

Garvey, C., & Berninger, G. Timing and turn taking in children's conversations. *Discourse Processes,* 1981, *4,* 27–58.

Hall, W., & Nagy, W. Cultural differences in communication. *New York University Education Quarterly,* 1981, *13,* 16–22.

Halliday, M. *Learning how to mean.* London: Edward Arnold, 1975.

James, S., & Button, M. Choosing stimulus materials for eliciting language samples from children with language disorders. *Language, Speech, and Hearing Services in Schools,* 1978, *9,* 91–97.

Johnson, D. The influence of social class and race on language test performance and spontaneous speech of preschool children. *Child Development*, 1974, *45*, 517–521.

Johnston, J., Trainor, M., Casey, P., & Hagler, P. *Effect of interviewer style and materials on language samples.* Paper presented at the meeting of the American Speech-Language-Hearing Association, Los Angeles, November 1981.

Kramer, C., James, S., & Saxman, J. A comparison of language samples elicited at home and in the clinic. *Journal of Speech and Hearing Disorders*, 1979, *44*, 321–330.

Lee, L. *Developmental sentence analysis.* Evanston, Ill.: Northwestern University Press, 1974.

Leonard, L., Prutting, C., Perozzi, J., & Berkley, R. Nonstandardized approaches to the assessment of language behaviors. *ASHA*, 1978, *20*, 371–379.

Longhurst, T., & File, J. A comparison of developmental sentence scores from Head Start children in four conditions. *Language, Speech, and Hearing Services in Schools*, 1977, *8*, 54–64.

Miller, J. *Assessing language production in children.* Baltimore, Md.: University Park Press, 1981.

Olswang, L., & Carpenter, R. Elicitor effects on the language obtained from young language-impaired children. *Journal of Speech and Hearing Disorders*, 1978, *43*, 76–88.

Prutting, C., Gallagher, T., & Mulac, A. The expressive portion of the NSST compared to a spontaneous language sample. *Journal of Speech and Hearing Disorders*, 1975, *40*, 40–48.

Ramer, A., & Rees, N. Selected aspects of the development of English morphology in black American children of low socioeconomic background. *Journal of Speech and Hearing Research*, 1973, *16*, 569–577.

Scott, C., & Taylor, A. A comparison of home and clinic gathered language samples. *Journal of Speech and Hearing Disorders*, 1978, *43*, 482–495.

Seymour, H., & Miller-Jones, D. Language and cognitive assessment of black children. In N. Lass (Ed.), *Speech and language: Advances in basic research and practice* (Vol. 4). New York: Academic Press, 1981.

Shuy, R., & Staton, J. Assessing oral language ability in children. In L. Feagans & D. Farran (Eds.), *The language of children reared in poverty.* New York: Academic Press, 1982.

Stephens, M.I. Elicited imitation of selected features of two American English dialects in Head Start children. *Journal of Speech and Hearing Disorders*, 1976, *19*, 493–508.

Tyack, D., & Gottsleben, R. *Language sampling, analysis, and training.* Palo Alto, Calif.: Consulting Psychologists Press, 1974.

Williams, R., & Wolfram, W. *Social dialects: Differences versus disorders.* Rockville, Md.: American Speech and Hearing Association, 1977.

Wolfram, W., & Fasold, R. *The study of social dialects in American English.* Englewood Cliffs, NJ: Prentice-Hall, 1974.

Second language learners' use of requests and responses in elementary classrooms

Louise Cherry Wilkinson, PhD
Professor and Executive Officer
Ph.D. Program in Educational
  Psychology
City Univesity of New York
Graduate School
New York, New York

Linda M. Milosky, PhD
Assistant Professor
Department of Speech-Language
  Pathology and Audiology
University of Utah
Salt Lake City, Utah

Celia Genishi, PhD
Associate Professor
Department of Curriculum and
  Instruction
University of Texas-Austin
Austin, Texas

WITHIN THE PAST decade, a new approach to research on language and education has developed. The sociolinguistic approach focuses on descriptions of teachers' and students' use of language in classrooms (Wilkinson, 1982). These descriptions provide a rich understanding of life in real classrooms and reveal the diversity of students' skills and the complexity of their communication with teachers and each other. Such descriptions can serve as reference points for the assessment and diagnosis of children's specific communication problems. These descriptions can also serve as sources for ideas about programs that help children adjust to school. Furthermore, comparing findings of studies of children of different linguistic and cultural backgrounds allows researchers and clinicians to better differentiate between cultural differences and communication disorders.

ASSUMPTIONS

The sociolinguistic approach to classroom language is guided by the assump-

Top Lang Disord, 1986, 6(2), 57-70
© 1986 Aspen Publishers, Inc.

tion that interaction in classrooms requires competence in both structural and functional aspects of language. *Structural aspects* include grammatical, phonological, and lexical skills. *Functional aspects* of language refer to the actual use of language appropriately and effectively in real situations. Knowledge of functional language is required to meet the cognitive and social aims of the classroom.

The second assumption underlying this approach is that the classroom is a unique situation for communication. Although language use here may share some general characteristics with other situations such as the home, the kinds of skills that are necessary for using language in the classroom are specific to the ongoing teaching and learning. For example, many conversations between teachers and students concern the exchange, evaluation, and acquisition of information, as noted by Blank and White (this issue). Thus students' contributions to these conversations may be more restricted and more likely to be critically evaluated than at home.

A third assumption is that children demonstrate individual proficiency differences in the skills that are required for language comprehension and production in the classroom. It cannot be assumed that these special aspects of communicative competence have been previously taught or learned. Certainly, some children come to classrooms with a greater knowledge than others of what is required to be proficient.

THE EFFECTIVE SPEAKER IN ALL-STUDENT INSTRUCTIONAL GROUPS

Wilkinson and her colleagues (Wilkinson & Calculator, 1982; Wilkinson & Spinelli, 1983) have studied the interactions of all-student instructional groups. These groups are common in elementary school classrooms and are used for teaching reading and mathematics. Students in these groups work individually and together on "seatwork" assignments, with cooperation often encouraged. The ability to make requests and receive adequate responses is essential to the teaching and learning processes in all-student groups. Wilkinson's prior research on elementary students' small groups focused on request-response sequences, in which information or materials may be exchanged. This research has provided a test of a model that predicts the characteristics of the requests of effective speakers.

In general, an effective speaker is successful in communication. Specifically, such a speaker receives appropriate responses to requests. The boxed material identifies and gives examples of the request characteristics of an effective speaker's interactions. In short, the model predicts that an effective speaker's requests are *direct, designated, on-task,* and *sincere,* and they are *revised* if they are initially unsuccessful. Studies conducted with monolingual, English-speaking students in first, second, and third grades provide support for the model of

The ability to make requests and receive adequate responses is essential to the teaching and learning processes in all-student groups.

Request Characteristics of the Effective Speaker

A successful request is likely to be:

1. *Direct:* Use of linguistic forms that directly signal the speaker's needs. For requests for action, the imperative or *I want/I need* statements; for requests for information, the *Wh-*, *yes–no*, or tag question.

   Direct requests: *How do you do this one?*, *I need a pencil;*
   Indirect requests: *I don't get this, Anybody have a pencil?*

2. *Designated to a listener:* Unambiguously indicates the intended listener through verbal or nonverbal means:

   C: Sally, where do you put the dollar sign? *or*
   C: (*looking at P*) Did you get that one?

3. *Sincere:* According to Labov and Fanshel (1978), a request is sincere if (a) the action, purpose, and need for the request are clear; for example, in a request for information, the listener believes that the speaker really wants the information and does not already know the information; (b) there is both an ability and an obligation of the listener to respond to the request; and (c) the speaker has a right to make the request.

   Sincere: "John, I can't find the price for hamburger."

   Insincere: "Well, slow-poke, what one are you finally up to now?"

4. *Revised if unsuccessful:* A restatement of a request previously made by the same speaker to the same listener who had not responded appropriately:

   A. "Bob, I need a pencil;"
   B. "Uh;"
   A. "Bob, can I borrow a pencil?"

5. *On task:* Related to the academic content or procedures and materials of the assignment.

   On task: "Is this one add or subtract?"
   Off task: "Whaddya gonna do at recess?"

6. *Responded to appropriately:* The requested action or information was given or else a reason was given why the action and/or information could not be given.

   Appropriate response: C: "Alice, what's five?"
                                A: "I got 22 for that one."
   Inappropriate response: C: "Alice, what's five?"
                                A: "What did you get for it?"

---

the effective speaker's use of requests. Furthermore, these studies have found positive correlations between successful requests and achievement in reading or math.

ELEMENTARY SCHOOL SECOND LANGUAGE LEARNERS

A study of elementary school second language learners was conducted to determine how well the Wilkinson model described the interactions of students who were not from monolingual English-speaking homes. One question is whether Hispanic children from bilingual homes differ in their requests. This information is important when teachers instruct children how to interact in peer-instructional groups; it is also necessary to delineate cultural differences before assessing children with disordered language. Another question involves the significance of such group interactions. Specifically, is there a relationship between students' skill at obtaining responses to requests and their academic achievement?

Two third-grade classrooms in an elementary school in a Chicano neighborhood in San Antonio, Texas, were selected for this study. Forty-eight of the 50 subjects were of Mexican-American descent and demonstrated the phonological and prosodic features characteristic of Chicano English. Two black children in the class were included in the analysis because their interactions in the groups could not be separated out without disrupting the integrity of the interactional analysis. Of the 48 Hispanic students, 34 reported that both Spanish and English were spoken in the home, 5 said that Spanish was spoken in the home, and 9 said that English only was spoken in the home. The children, on entering school, had been given the Bilingual Syntax Measure (Burt, Dulay, & Hernandaz, 1975), and 43 were found to be sufficiently proficient in English so as not to qualify for bilingual education.

The students comprised 10 heterogeneous reading groups, assigned by the teacher at the beginning of the school year. According to the teachers, although there were differences in reading achievement within groups, average achievement from group to group was the same. The ages of the students ranged from 8 years, 3 months to 10 years, 3 months, with a mean age of 9 years, 1 month. No students were diagnosed as having learning disabilities or any language problems. There were 25 males and 25 females. Parental permission was obtained for the students' participation in the study.

Individual assessment

The students' English language ability was screened to rule out gross comprehension or production deficits. Screenings typically lasted 20 minutes each and were conducted by a member of the research staff.

An expressive language sample was obtained by informally interviewing each student for approximately 10 minutes. The interviewer posed open-ended questions regarding topics that were presumed to be of interest to the students, such as television, friends, movies, and games. For the purposes of analysis, the first 3 minutes of conversation were excluded, since many of the students were shy and only became comfortable with the researcher during this period.

These samples were analyzed using the method suggested by Loban (1976). Transcripts were first segmented into communication units (C-units), e.g., an independent clause plus all of its dependent clauses. The average number of words per C-unit and the average number of dependent clauses per C-unit were calculated using samples of 30 C-units. The Peabody Picture Vocabulary Test-Revised (Dunn & Dunn, 1981) was also administered. Finally, at the investigators' request, the teachers administered the Metropolitan Reading Achievement Test (Prescott, Balow, Hogan, & Farr, 1978) to ensure a current measure of students' reading achievement.

Recording the reading activities

The primary data for the present study consisted of recordings of reading activities in the classrooms. Reading as a formal classroom activity typically began at 9:30 or 10:00 a.m. and lasted for approximately 40 minutes in each classroom. When teachers announced the beginning of the activity, students moved to specific tables, and the teachers provided instructions for the reading groups. These reading activities were audio- and videotaped on four typical days over a two-week period. According to the teacher and principal, audio- and videotaping of both teachers and students were routine in these classrooms, and the students were used to the presence of adults other than teachers. Before, during, and after the recording, a member of the research staff prepared descriptions of the ongoing events in the reading group, including the behavior of the students. These descriptions supplemented the recordings with relevant contextual information that may not have been apparent on the tapes.

Reading groups were established by the teachers before the study, with five students in each group. Groups were similar in the way in which reading activity was initiated, maintained, and terminated. Initially, teachers gave instructions about the assignment for that day. The teacher then left, and the students worked in their groups on the individual tasks that had been assigned. In all cases, the tasks were the same for all of the students for that period of reading activity (e.g., a particular worksheet or workbook page). The reading groups were organized around tasks to be completed by individual students; children were encouraged, however, to cooperate with other students in their group in the completion of a task. The dominant activity during the reading period was reading, either silently or aloud. During the final phase of the activity, the teachers collected the assignments, and the students returned to their regular seats.

Coding of the videotapes

Following transcription, speech and gestural communication that occurred during the student interactions was analyzed according to a procedure described in Wilkinson and Calculator (1982). The first part of the analysis consisted of identifying requests and responses, including requests for information such as, *Did you write "girl" here?* and, *What is the second one?*; requests for action, as in *Underline that one* and *Stop that or you're gonna miss recess;* or requests for materials such as *I need a pencil.* The second part of analysis consisted of describing the students' requests and responses according to the categories presented in the box.

From this analysis, six measures were computed for each student: (a) the proportion of utterances that were requests; (b) the proportion of requests that elicited appropriate responses; (c) the proportion of unsuccessful requests that were revised; (d) the proportion of requests that took a direct form; (e) the proportion of requests that were on task; and (f) the proportion of requests that were sincere.

RESULTS AND DISCUSSION

There were no differences among the reading groups in mean reading achievement scores or in knowledge of English as measured by the Loban scores and the performance on the Peabody Picture Vocabulary Test. Means for the entire sample are presented in Table 1.

The students produced 1,910 requests, comprising 783 requests for action and 1,127 requests for information. Analysis showed that these second language learners almost always spoke English and that they were effective in obtaining responses to requests for action or information about 60% of the time.

An analysis was then conducted to determine how well the request characteristics in the proposed model predicted receiving an appropriate response. Requests were classified in a multidimensional contingency table, which was defined by the following dimensions: appropriate response, direct form, designated listener, on task, sincere, revised, and request for action or information. Log-linear models were fitted to this table

to find the simplest model that adequately predicted the frequencies observed in the table (Bishop, Fienberg, & Holland, 1975; see Wilkinson & Spinelli, 1983, for further explanation of analysis). This analysis revealed that receiving an appropriate response depended on other request characteristics; requests were more likely to obtain appropriate responses if they were of a direct form and if they were not revised.

The typical third-grader in these groups usually produced requests that were *direct, sincere,* and *on task.* However, the speaker specifically designated the intended respondent only one in five times, and revised requests for a "second try" only one in three times. Thus the data on second language learners from the present study essentially confirm the model of the effective speakers' use of requests and responses in all-student instructional groups. The exception was that designation of listeners and use of revisions were infrequent.

Although there were no statistically significant differences among the groups on mean reading achievement, analyses were conducted to explore any relationships between reading achievement and obtaining appropriate responses. In the present

Table 1. Descriptive data for Hispanic subjects

	n	Mean	SD
PPVT–R			
Raw score	48	89.809	10.846
Loban's analysis			
Mean length of C-Unit (in words)	50	5.861	1.228
Metropolitan Reading Achievement Test			
Number of items correct	48	44.937	7.042

study, as in previous studies, reading achievement was positively related to obtaining appropriate responses to requests (Kendall's *tau* = 0.36, *p* < .02). This relationship held when individual students' achievement scores were correlated with the proportion of appropriate responses and when the performance of groups was examined by correlating means of group scores on both variables. Thus both groups and individual students who obtained more appropriate responses to their requests were also those with higher reading achievement.

The positive relationship between using requests and achievement in reading may reflect true causal associations between them. These causal associations may be either direct or indirect. In the direct case, students who obtain appropriate responses to their requests may learn reading content as a consequence. In the indirect case, some other intellectual ability promotes both effective requests and the development of reading skills. Further research is being conducted to examine these relationships, the sources of individual differences in language usage, and their consequences for achievement.

Figure 1 displays the range of performance observed for requests and responses. Each characteristic of requests is listed on the *x* axis: *sincere, on task, designate, direct, response,* and *revise*. On the *y* axis is the proportion of requests that showed each characteristic. The performance levels of the individual children are distributed vertically for each characteristic. For each subject, the proportion of requests having the characteristic was calculated. For the purpose of illustrating the amount of variability among subjects and

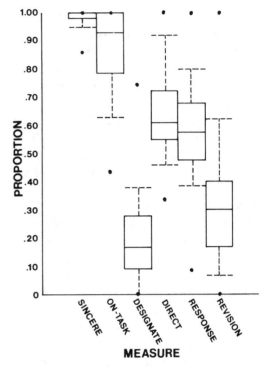

Figure 1. Distribution in characteristics of requests for the 50 children.

the range of scores for each characteristic, the figure symbols summarize these distributions as follows: the black circles indicate the lowest and highest proportions obtained among the 50 subjects for a given request characteristic; the dashed bar indicates the proportional values corresponding to the 10th and 90th percentiles of the sample (e.g., 10% of the children used direct forms 46% of the time or less; 10% used them 92% of the time or more); and the box indicates the interquartile range, with the median the solid bar in the middle (e.g., half of the sample used direct forms between 55% and 72% of the time, with a median value of 61%.)

Some interesting patterns in this figure can be noted. Scores for sincerity and task relevance were generally high and of limited variability. Thus there seems to be a common competence among children in these aspects of producing requests. The remaining four characteristics show much greater variability in scores and a generally lower average performance. The variability suggests genuine individual differences in the degree to which requests are *direct, designated, revised,* and *effective.*

In this study, the highest-achieving students worked cooperatively and acknowledged the need for all group members to stay on task with the same focus. Members of this group (Group A), which ranked highest in reading achievement (mean Metropolitan Test score of 49.8), received appropriate responses to their requests 64% of the time. Their mean proportions for each characteristic of requests are superimposed on the proportions for the entire sample in Figure 2. This figure illustrates Group A's relatively high proportion of direct requests (83%) and success in getting appropriate responses (64%).

The following excerpt from Group A illustrates the high-achieving students' group interaction. (*Gregorio, Raul, Sonia, and Esteban are engaged in completing part of a reading worksheet.*)

G: Which ones have y'all done? You're skipping me. You're not even letting me catch up to you. (*looks at S*)

S: Okay, we did five; this one. (*points to sheet*)

E: Down.

G: Five, what is that?

S: Crossly. (*points on sheet*)

G: Oh, okay. What's, what's the other one, brake?

R: Right.

S: Brake is seven down.

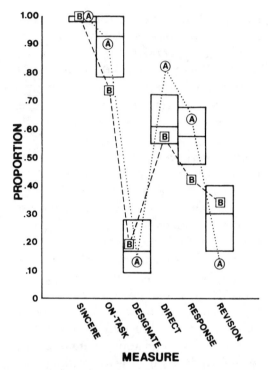

Figure 2. Differences among selected reading groups in characteristics of requests (A ranked highest and B lowest in mean reading achievement).

R: What's a route? (*looks at G*)

G: Huh?

R: What's a route?

G: A path that you always go on when you go home if you walk.

Gregorio, in using both a request for information (*Which ones have y'all done?*) and a request for action (*You're skipping me*), reminds the other students in the group that they have an obligation to be cooperative. Gregorio is an effective speaker, obtaining appropriate responses to his requests 64% of the time. This is evidenced by his success at temporarily changing the focus of the group discussion to allow him to catch up. After Gregorio's problem is resolved, another student, Raul, easily claims the floor to obtain a definition.

In contrast, students in the lowest achieving group (Group B; with a mean score on the Metropolitan Test of 43.2) seemed unable to interact with each other in a smooth, orderly, and productive way. They had difficulty coordinating the use of materials, and they seemed concerned with "copying" rather than cooperation. On the average, students in this group received appropriate responses to their requests only 42% of the time, as can be seen in Figure 2. The following excerpt illustrates the ineffectiveness of the students (Christina, Felisa, Karin, Julio, Manuela) in this group in doing the task at hand.

C: I read these three, you read these three. (*points to sheet*)
J: Remember we could help, each other? (*to M & K*)
F: Let's do it.
C: (*reading*) Anna sat down.
F: (*taps table in front of M*) Hey, look. Look, look, you're (*pointing at M*) look, look, look, look, look. You're one, she's two, three, four, five, six (*points around table as she counts*).
M: I'm one.
J: All up. (*gestures around table*)
M: You're two (*points at C*) three, (*points at F*) I'm four.
C: Five. (*holds five fingers up*)
E: I'm five. (*points to self*)
K: I'm five. (*points to self*)
M: See, see.
F: One, two, three, four, five, six. (*points around table*)
K: I'm five.
C: You're not, you haven't even started reading yet.

M: (*reading*) Christina sat down and . . . Christina.
J: All of us read it.
M: No.
F: No.

In the following excerpt, some of the students have created barricades with their folders. The students have difficulty managing both the physical space and the arrangement of their group, and in the following discussion, they are not able to discuss how best to communicate in order to cooperate.

K: (*to C*) Put your folder down.
F: (*to C*) You said you . . .
C: Yeah, but . . .
K: Christina.
F: Christina.
K: Christina, you're supposed to put your folder down they want to see what you're doin.
F: You liar.
K: Ms. Morton said.
F: To help each other, to help each other.
K: We're not talking about that.
F: I know, but she said to help each other.
F: I know but she said put the folder down. Felisa doesn't even know . . . she being so . . . I was talking about putting your folders down 'cause Ms. Morton (told) wanted to see that you were doing.

The next example demonstrates the interactions of a particular student who is regarded as an effective speaker. That is, her use of requests conforms to the present model. Figure 3 displays Juanita's profile of requests and response characteristics. She obtains appropriate responses to her requests 78% of the time. She designates many more requests than other students, uses direct forms frequently, and her

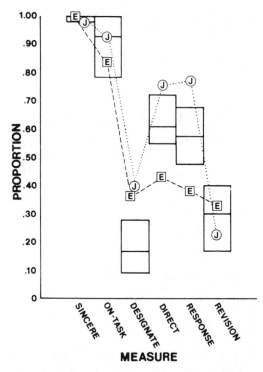

Figure 3. Individual differences in characteristics of requests for an effective speaker (J) and an ineffective speaker (E).

requests are generally on task and sincere. Juanita assumes the role of the leader of the group and taskmaster, pacing the other students and allotting tasks for each to do. Juanita is in the top half of her class in reading achievement, and her Peabody Picture Vocabulary Test performance is in the 90th percentile for her class. All the other students in her group (Carmen, Pablo, and Gloria) scored substantially

---

Juanita assumes the role of the leader of the group and taskmaster, pacing the other students and allotting tasks for each to do.

---

lower than she did on both reading achievement and language measures.

In the following excerpt, Juanita's effectiveness as a speaker is apparent as she allocates turns to read aloud, confirms responses, and restrains the other students in the group until all are ready to proceed:

C: (*reading*) On what page does Chapter Three begin and end?
J: (*to C*) Wait, wait, wait.
P: Chapter Four. (*writes down*)
G: Chapter Four.
J: Wait (*points to P*) he's still on Chapter Four.
P: How do you spell four?
C: (*erases*) Oh.
J: You put f-o-u-r.
P: (*reading*) Number four; on what page?
J: Hey, No, no, no (*points to C*) She does it.
C: (*begins reading turn that was allotted by J*)

Enrique's profile in Figure 3 suggests a markedly different quality in interaction. He is an ineffective speaker, since he obtains appropriate responses only 40% of the time. Although the profile shows that he does designate his requests, a close examination of his individual conversations reveals that almost all of his designated requests are directed to one other student, Paula. Enrique is more often indirect that direct. As the following excerpt shows, Enrique's revisions are not more direct than his initial requests, and he does not specify why or where he is having a problem. In this conversation, Enrique receives only the answer to the problem, with no explanation or elaboration:

P: Let's do this, you start. (*points to E's paper*)

E: This is hard.

P: Write number five. (*turns to E*) Number five is. (*turns back to her own work, erases*) Oh, I know which one it is. I'm finished, now I have to do the next page.

E: I don't understand this one. This one's hard. (*taps P's arm*) Paula, this one's tricky. (*points to his page*)

P: No it's not.

E: It says . . . Yes it is.

P: I already got it. It's this one. (*shows E answer on her paper*).

Two minor findings in the present study differed from findings in the previous studies. In the studies of monolingual speakers of standard English (Wilkinson & Calculator, 1982; Wilkinson & Spinelli, 1983), students who revised an initial unsuccessful request were likely to obtain an appropriate response with a "second try," as in the following example:

C: How do you do this one?

T: Uh, wait a minute.

C: Can you help me with this one please?

T: Oh, on that one you gotta add the rabbits and pigs.

In the present study, however, when students followed an inappropriate or nonresponse with a revision, they were still unlikely to be successful in obtaining an appropriate response. Occasionally, some of the students indicated that a revised request was counterproductive to the group effort of "moving along," as in the following example:

C: Wait for me then.

D: (*reads*) Read the . . .

C: Wait.

D: No, I'm gonna read.

C: Don't read it. You just get me confused with my name.

D: Read.

C: Wait.

Another difference between the second language learners in the present study and the monolingual, first language learners of English studied previously is that directness of request forms were not uniquely associated with achievement in reading for these students. Production of indirect forms was just as likely to be associated with higher reading achievement. However, directness was associated with receiving an appropriate response.

In addition, the second language learners very rarely designated their requests to specific students in their reading groups (20% of the time), in sharp contrast to the first language learners (83% of the time). These two findings, taken together, suggest a cultural style on the part of the Hispanic children of using requests that are less verbally direct but focus on group interaction. During the group interactions, students often spoke while their heads were down, presumably directing their gaze to their work, with the communicative focus of the request often not specifically designated, but perhaps addressed to the group in general. This behavior also may indicate that designation by either verbal or nonverbal means may be considered too personal and therefore impolite.

In summary, the results of this work have shown that these second language learners are, on the whole, using language effectively to obtain responses in their all-student reading groups. Typical students examined in all of these studies used language in very similar ways; their requests were directly and clearly stated, interpreted sincerely, and concerned the teaching and learning task. Thus the language usage of these elementary school children places a premium on explicitness, directness, and assertiveness. A similar pattern was found for monolingual elementary school students' use of language in their all-student mathematics groups (Wilkinson & Spinelli, 1983).

CLINICAL IMPLICATIONS

In planning intervention strategies, clinicians may wish to identify patterns of interaction appropriate to language-impaired students' cultural and linguistic environment in school. Equipped with such knowledge, clinicians can be more assured that they will not inadvertently violate cultural norms. For example, as part of a program designed to improve a language-impaired child's use of yes–no questions, a clinician might set up a group interaction situation that simulates classroom interaction. Knowledge of typical requesting patterns in such groups will help the clinician instruct the client in the pragmatically appropriate use of certain yes–no question forms. Since comparable studies have not been conducted with language-impaired children, it is not yet known how the requesting patterns of such children would compare. However, knowledge of the similarities and differences between monolingual and bilingual children does allow the clinician to evaluate and plan therapy in a way that respects cultural differences.

The findings from this series of studies suggest that both monolingual English-speaking and bilingual Hispanic students who receive responses to their requests during small-group instructional interaction generally use requests that are direct, on task, and sincere. Examination of the relationship between classroom achievement in reading and mathematics and obtaining appropriate responses to requests reveals a positive correlation for both monolingual and bilingual speakers of English. However, differences between these studies suggest that there may be some culturally distinct styles of communication. Directness of the request form may be useful for the leader or taskmaster of the group, who may also be the highest achiever in the group; however, this strategy may not be useful for all students in all of their classroom interactions. In therapy, clinicians have typically taught a child to look at the intended listener, address the listener by name, and wait to begin speaking until the child is sure attention is secured. The findings from the present study suggest that this pattern may not represent that of all speakers or all groups. Furthermore, intervention strategies must be sensitive, in general, to the degree of shared background knowledge and social relations among interactants. It may sometimes be unnecessary or even inappropriate for speakers to designate their requests.

A reexamination of assumptions about group interaction and types of interaction to be modeled in therapy may be called for. Perhaps clinicians have assumed an ideal situation that affords each student equal time to talk and assigns each student equal responsibility for group leadership. The research studies reported suggest that groups often have a self-selected "taskmaster" who paces interaction to meet group needs, and all students may not readily take on this role. The sociolinguistic analyses presented here may be adapted for clinical diagnosis and for intervention purposes.

In applying a sociolinguistic analysis, clinicians may find it useful to observe the conditions under which the child is successful in obtaining appropriate responses to requests, the variety of patterns of requests that the child produces, and the nature of the child's behavior following the failure to obtain an appropriate response. After obtaining such a profile, the clinician may examine which differences may be cultural, situational, or individual. No one factor may necessarily be attributed to a cultural, individual, or situational source. However, identifying patterns of request and response production may help indicate when change is desirable. For example, if a child consistently produces indirect requests when other group members are mainly using direct requests, the clinician may want to assess the child's ability to differentiate the two types of requests.

Furthermore, the clinician may decide to ensure that the child can use the syntactic forms that are available in his or her repertoire to produce both kinds of request and to teach the child how such usage may change according to the demands of the situation. For example, direct imperative requests for materials, which may be accepted in the situation of all-student instructional groups, may not be accepted by a teacher leading an instructional group. If a student receives

> *If a student receives no response to a request, repeats it without revising, and continues to receive no response, the clinician may need to help the child evaluate why.*

no response to a request, repeats it without revising, and continues to receive no response, the clinician may need to help the child evaluate why. Is it because the group perceives the request and its revisions as counterproductive to group goals? Is it because the child has not designated the listener as other members of the group typically do? The findings of Bryan, Donahue, and Pearl (1981) and Donahue and Bryan (1983) suggest that clinicians may need to teach language-impaired children conversational control strategies. These strategies include how to render their requests and statements more assertive and explicit, as well as how to soften them when appropriate.

• • •

The sociolinguistic analyses used in these studies provide a set of variables with which to characterize interaction. These variables also permit identification of interactional aspects that may differ across cultures, those that seem to be stable across certain cultures, and those that may be disadvantageous to the language user in the classroom.

REFERENCES

Bishop, T., Fienberg, S., & Holland, P. (1975). *Discrete multivariate analyses: Theory and practice.* Cambridge: MIT Press.

Bryan, T., Donahue, M., & Pearl, R. (1981). Learning disabled children's peer interactions during a small group problem solving task. *Learning Disability Quar-*

terly, 4, 13–22.

Burt, M., Dulay, H., & Hernandaz, E. (1975). *Bilingual syntax measure.* New York: Harcourt, Brace, Jovanovich.

Donahue, M., & Bryan, T. (1983). Conversational skills and modeling in learning disabled boys. *Applied Psycholinguistics, 4,* 251–278.

Dunn, L., & Dunn, L. (1981). *Peabody Picture Vocabulary Test-Revised.* Circle Pines, MN: American Guidance Service.

Labov, W., & Fanshel, R. (1978). *Therapeutic discourse.* New York: Academic Press.

Loban, W. (1976). *Language development.* Champaign,

IL: National Council of Teachers of English.

Prescott, G., Balow, I., Hogan, T., & Farr, R. (1978). *Metropolitan Reading Achievement Test.* New York: Harcourt, Brace, Jovanovich.

Wilkinson, L.C. (Ed.). (1982). *Communicating in the classroom.* New York: Academic Press.

Wilkinson, L.C., & Calculator, S. (1982). Requests and responses in peer-directed reading ability groups. *American Educational Research Journal, 19*(1), 107–120.

Wilkinson, L.C. & Spinelli, F. (1983). Using requests effectively in peer-directed instruction groups. *American Educational Research Journal, 20*(4), 479–501.

Part III
Intervention within a Multicultural Context

Intervention strategies: A multicultural approach

Li-Rong Lilly Cheng, PhD
Coordinator
Bilingual/Multicultural Program
Department of Communicative
*   Disorders*
San Diego State University
San Diego, California

THERE ARE two major aspects of intervention planning for limited-English-proficient (LEP) students. One aspect addresses the basic philosophy underpinning intervention, and the other addresses the actual development of intervention materials. Both components should support the students' background as well as ease their transition into U.S. culture. An experiential approach provides an opportunity for comparing and contrasting the students' home culture with mainstream U.S. culture.

GENERAL INTERVENTION PHILOSOPHY: THE EXPERIENTIAL APPROACH

The basic philosophy behind intervention strategies for a multicultural/multilingual population is expressed clearly in the following observation by Jordan (1980):

What is being advocated here is that the selection of teaching practices be informed by

Top Lang Disord, 1989, 9(3), 84–91
© 1989 Aspen Publishers, Inc.

knowledge of the children's cultural background. The process involved can be seen as selecting from a "library" of potentially available teaching strategies and practices those which are best suited to a particular population of children. (p. 7)

In the last ten years, various researchers in language research such as Berger and Kellner (1981), Duchan (1986), Gallagher and Dárnton (1978), Irwin (1982), Johnston (1981), Lund and Duchan (1988), Prutting and Kirchner (1983), Schiefelbusch (1986), Van Dongen and Westby (1986), Wallach and Butler (1984), and Wallach and Miller (1988) have contributed toward the building of a framework for language learning and intervention. Wallach and Miller (1988) introduce this framework:

Learning is a constant process of fitting incoming information into what one already knows . . . and language intervention is an ongoing process of discovering how best to facilitate the match-up between what the student already knows and the information we are trying to teach. (p. xiii)

The eight constructs outlined by Duchan (1986)—namely, overall sense-making, turn-taking, intents, agenda, topic, breakdowns and repairs, and scripts—can be adopted as constructs for providing intervention to the language-minority population. LEP children need to make sense of interactions in an American context. Therapy must be organized around naturalistic interaction, allowing the child to take the lead and building upon modeling and expansion of what the child says and does (Cheng, 1984). Examples are given in the sections that follow.

INCORPORATING STUDENT CULTURE IN INTERVENTION ACTIVITIES

Building a multicultural calendar

The clinician marks on the calendar significant personal days and holidays from different countries and cultures throughout the year; weekly or monthly themes can then be developed for language activities. Students are able not only to compare and contrast how similar special days are celebrated throughout the world (e.g., birthdays, countries' independence days) but also to learn about new holidays and traditions.

Halloween is an example of a holiday that is celebrated throughout the United States and in some parts of Europe. Therapy materials may include an explanation of the day as well as associated items, history, folk tales, myths, and so forth. Stories about Halloween can be shared. Attention should be paid to: special foods—candies, roasted pumpkin seeds, hot apple cider; special clothing—costumes; special activities—trick-or-treating, bobbing for apples, school parade, haunted houses; special decorations—carved pumpkins; special cards—Halloween design; symbols—ghosts, goblins, skeletons, black cats, monsters, spiders, spooky bats, witches on brooms.

A sample eventcast might be:

Halloween is a day when everyone dresses up in costumes. The costumes can be funny or scary. People carve faces on pumpkins, hollow them out, and put a candle inside; then they are called Jack-O-Lanterns. During the day children have parades at school to show their costumes. At night they go trick-or-treating, which means that they go to each house in the neighborhood, knock on the door, and say "Trick or treat!" Most neighbors will give the children candy (treat); if not, the children might play a trick on them. People try to scare each other on Halloween, so they often dress up as ghosts, witches, devils, and other spooky characters; also, they might make a haunted house out of their home that people can visit.

Another holiday that can be discussed is Chinese New Year: calendar—the lunar calendar; special foods—fish (meaning "plenty"), cake (meaning "prosperity"); special activity—red envelope with money for the young; special clothing—red, symbolizing prosperity; special greeting—*Kung-Hei-Fat-Choy* (good wishes and prosperity); animal symbol for each year of the 12-year cycle—rat (1984); ox (1985), tiger (1986), hare (1987), dragon (1988), snake (1989), horse (1990), ram (1991), monkey (1992), chicken (1993), dog (1994), pig (1995).

Study maps

Obtain maps of the world, the United States, North America, the city and state, the district, and/or the area of the student's home. The maps are studied and discussed, including each person's place of origin (city, village, country), the routes of trips that each person has taken, and the methods of transportation. Topics such as different ways of traveling and the cities, countries, and peoples of places one has seen can be used. Children are encouraged to share their personal life stories through looking at the maps and describing their personal journeys.

Narrative study through folk tales

Folk stories that have been handed down from one generation to the next teach children about human experiences (Van Dongen & Westby, 1986). Bettelheim (1977) submitted that myths, folk tales and fairy tales together formed the "literature" of preliterate societies:

[A] child's intellectual life, apart from immediate experiences within the family, depended on mythical and religious stories and on fairy tales. . . . Simultaneously, since these stories answered the child's most important questions, they were a major agent of his socialization. (p. 24)

The construction and discussion of narratives is a current popular methodology in language intervention. Dundes (1980) describes narratives as a culture's vision of the world; through them, children develop an understanding of their physical and social worlds. Thus stories and folk tales from the children's homelands can be used in therapy to enhance narrative competence; their familiarity may help students to feel less shy when talking about them. For example, the stories can be translated into English versions. The clinician then reads a story, explains its content, and asks questions. The LEP child is then encouraged to retell the story and ask questions. Stories familiar to American children can be introduced and discussed in the same manner. Folk tales from Asian cultures may be obtained from Children's Book Press, 1461 Ninth Avenue, San Francisco, CA 94122; and from the Evaluation and Dissemination Center at California State University, Los Angeles. (For additional resources, see Van Dongen & Westby, 1986).

Another method of storytelling is called a collective story. Take a shared experience, such as a birthday in school or a field trip, and have each student say or draw something about that experience. Collect everyone's input and combine it into a collective story. (Some students may contribute a lot, while others may be silent.) A copy of the collective story is given to everyone and reread or retold.

The method of cooperative learning can also be adapted for use with Asian/Pacific Islander children: each is assigned a piece of a story, and then all members of the group contribute toward the overall construction of the story. Furthermore, three other genres of narratives—accounting, recounting, and eventcasting (Heath, 1983)—can also be integrated into therapy activities.

Providing sharing time

Objects from the homeland of the students can be useful therapy materials. For example, the children can bring items of native clothing and explain how the items are worn and what they may symbolize. The class can take turns modeling and trying on the different clothes. Other items for sharing include recipes, games, jewelry, and artwork/crafts from the homeland.

Incorporating a cross-cultural perspective into general language intervention

The clinician should find out from the teacher which topics a child's class is cov-

---

The clinician should find out from the teacher which topics a child's class is covering and incorporate a cross-cultural perspective into therapy using such topics.

---

ering in social studies, science, geography, or other areas and incorporate a cross-cultural perspective into therapy using such topics. For example, if the class is studying weather, discuss types of storms that occur in different countries, such as typhoons in Southeast Asia versus hurricanes and tornados in the southern and midwestern United States.

Clinicians can also reinforce the core curriculum by enhancing the vocabulary and concepts of reading materials that the class is using. For example, the core curriculum in social studies may have the following themes:

- For kindergarten—knowledge of self, knowledge of others, community helpers, citizenship and value, everyday events (flag salute, calendar time, sequencing, seasons, climate), special occasions (holidays), and rules and why we need them;
- For first graders—all about me, about families, families need food, holidays, families need clothes, families need shelter, families live in neighborhoods, living in the United States;
- For second graders—global communities, map skills, living in the immediate community, holidays, winter holidays, workers in the community, careers, American heroes, community rules;
- For third graders—maps, communities, cities, heritage.

For some children the above topics help to structure and reinforce aspects of an already familiar culture. For others, especially those with multicultural backgrounds, these units provide a framework of characteristics and concepts that are inherent parts of a new culture. Use of the above themes as therapy materials can enhance communication and academic skills, paving the way for success in the classroom. In addition, a forum is created in which similarities and differences between cultures can be discussed. The units can be further expanded via the use of cultural capsules and cultural clusters.

Cultural capsules and clusters

Cultural capsules (first described by Taylor & Sorenson, 1961) refer to elements of one culture that may not be found in other cultures. For example, capsule elements found in the United States include cereal (breakfast food), hide-and-seek (children's game), and pets (animals that are considered to be pets differ among cultures). Cultural clusters (described by Meade & Morain, 1973) are activities or events that help to form a culture. Examples include activities and behavior at the dinner table, birthday celebrations, school field trips, and answering the telephone. Capsules and clusters are inherent within each culture; although they may appear to be obvious examples of familiar elements and events, by nature they constitute that which makes each of the world's cultures unique. These items can thus become useful instructional aids to help narrow cultural gaps.

FACILITATING THE TRANSITION INTO THE MAINSTREAM CULTURE

LEP populations need to be prepared to function in English within the mainstream American society. By contrasting and comparing the home culture of the students with that of the United States we are not only being supportive of students' backgrounds but also helping them to gain valuable insights and facilitating their transition into the mainstream. The following are general suggestions for clinical activities.

Role playing

The following roles are suggested, each of which might be tailored to reflect the mainstream culture of the United States or of other countries: teacher–student; salesperson–customer; father/mother–child; older brother/sister–younger brother/sister; restaurant waiter/waitress–customer; airline flight attendant–passenger; bus driver–passenger; mother–infant; physician–patient; grandparent–grandchild; principal–student; school nurse–student; cashier–customer; postal clerk–customer; ticket agent–customer.

Preparing scripts for commonly occurring activities

The following are suggestions for event scripts that can be used for therapy: shopping for groceries and finding items in department stores; going to church; going to a family gathering; cooking; going to school; storytelling; ordering in a fast-food outlet and in a restaurant; using utensils properly; asking for help; greeting; making apologies; accepting compliments; accepting criticism; paying compliments, making telephone calls; talking to a physician or nurse.

Using culturally unique items as topics of discussion

When working with children from different language backgrounds, care must be taken to ensure that instructional items used are familiar to the children. The following are some "culturally loaded" elements that may be unfamiliar to Southeast Asian and Pacific Islander children: stationery supplies—ruler, eraser, pencil sharpener, chalk, staplers, paper clips, clipboard, rubber band, labels; foods—hamburger, sandwich, cheese, chips, soft drinks, french fries; household objects—cooking utensils, linen, furniture items, tools, appliances; brand name items—Kleenex, Xerox, Sanka, Sony, IBM. (For more information, see Cheng, 1987.)

Conducting social/pragmatic activities

That which is socially appropriate in one culture may not be acceptable in another. For example, in many Asian cultures maintaining eye contact is considered to be impolite, and giggling is a sign of embarrassment. In the classroom, Asian children may look down when talking to the teacher or giggle if reprimanded; to Asian students, these are signs of respect and deference. Children from multicultural backgrounds need to learn which kinds of behaviors are expected and considered to be appropriate in various settings.

Johnston, Weinrich, and Johnson (1984) provide therapy guidelines for pragmatic activities that include conversation, use of a register, use of syntactic forms to convey pragmatic information, and effective nonverbal communication. These activities are useful for modeling and teaching LEP children about social behavior: For example, topicalization for K–3 includes describing objects, identifying foods by taste, and decorating a dollhouse, among other activities. The conversation module

for preschoolers includes telephone answering and polishing shoes.

Personal weather report

English has a wide variety of words that can be used to express feelings and emotions. Other languages may not have comparable counterparts, often because certain cultures discourage the open display and discussion of feelings. A chart that shows various facial expressions and the terms used to describe them can facilitate discussion of their appropriate English usage (see Appendix).

Language clinicians can start each session with a "personal weather report" by saying "I am feeling exhausted today" or "I am feeling very excited today." The students can also share their personal weather reports and thus begin to learn about expressive words. For example, feelings commonly expressed by preschool-aged English speakers include cold, hot, hurt, happy, sad, and surprised. "Cold" can refer to temperature, but it can also refer to a type of illness or an unfeeling person. "Hot" refers to temperature, but it is also a slang term used to describe something that we really like, as in "That car is hot!" Another slang meaning for "hot" is stolen. "Hurt" can refer to physical pain but can also express a mental state, as in "you hurt my feelings." "Happy" is a feeling of pleasure; "sad" is a feeling of sorrow or low spirits. "Surprised" is a reaction to something unexpected; it can be happy or sad.

•   •   •

Clinicians can adopt, adapt, and create therapy materials that are culturally sensitive, socially meaningful, linguistically comprehensible, and personally motivating for the populations they serve. Successful language intervention strategies require that they be developed by clinicians who have undertaken the task of identifying socially and culturally relevant materials and who have availed themselves of every opportunity to expand their knowledge of their clients' cultures, languages, and discourse styles. Becoming a cross-cultural communicator requires a commitment to the provision of quality services in an America that is fast becoming increasingly multicultural.

REFERENCES

Berger, P., & Kellner, H. (1981). *Sociology reinterpreted: An essay on methods and vocation*. Garden City, NJ: Doubleday.

Bettelheim, B. (1977). *The uses of enchantment*. New York: Vintage Books.

Cheng, L. (1984). The assessment of communicative competence using a naturalistic instrument. In *Claremont Reading Conference Yearbook*. Claremont, CA: Claremont Graduate School.

Cheng, L. (1987). *Assessing Asian language performance: Guidelines for evaluating limited-English-proficient students*. Rockville, MD: Aspen Publishers.

Duchan, J.F. (1986). Language intervention through sensemaking and fine tuning. In R. Schiefelbusch (Ed.), *Language competence: assessment and intervention* (pp. 187–212). San Diego, CA: College-Hill Press.

Dundes, A. (1980). *Interpreting folklore*. Bloomington, IN: University of Indiana Press.

Gallagher, T., & Darnton, B. (1978). Conversational aspects of the speech of language disordered children: Revision behaviors. *Journal of Speech and Hearing Research, 21*, 118–135.

Heath, S.B. (1983). *Ways with words*. Cambridge: Cambridge University Press.

Irwin, J. (1982). *Pragmatics: The role in language development*. La Verne, CA: Fox Point Publisher.

Johnston, J. (1981). On location: Thinking and talking about space. *Topics in Language Disorders, 2*(1), 17–31.

Johnston, E.B., Weinrich, B.D., & Johnson, A.R. (1984). A source book of pragmatic activities. Tucson, AZ: Communication Skill Builders.

Jordan, C. (1980). *The adaptation of educational practices to cultural differences: Configurations from the Hawaiian case*. Paper presented at the Conference on Culture and Education, Brigham Young University, Laie, Hawaii.

Lund, N.J., & Duchan, J.F. (1988). *Assessing children's language in naturalistic contexts*. Englewood Cliffs, NJ: Prentice-Hall.

Meade, B., & Morain, G. (1973). The culture cluster. *Foreign Language Annals, 6*, 331–338.

Prutting, C.A., & Kirchner, D.M. (1983). Applied pragmatics. In T.M. Gallagher & C.A. Prutting (Eds.), *Pragmatic assessment and intervention issues in language* (pp. 29–64). San Diego: College-Hill Press.

Schiefelbusch, R.L. (Ed.). (1986). *Language competence: Assessment and intervention*. San Diego: College-Hill Press.

Taylor, H.D., & Sorenson, J.L. (1961). Culture capsules. *Modern Language Journal, 45*, 350–354.

Van Dongen, R., & Westby, C. (1986). Building the narrative mode of thought through children's literature. *Topics in Language Disorders, 7*,(1), 70–83.

Wallach, G.P., & Butler, K.G. (1984). *Language learning disabilities in school-age children*. Baltimore, MD: Williams & Wilkins.

Wallach, G.P., & Miller, L. (1988). *Language intervention and academic success*. Boston: Little, Brown.

Appendix
Personal weather report

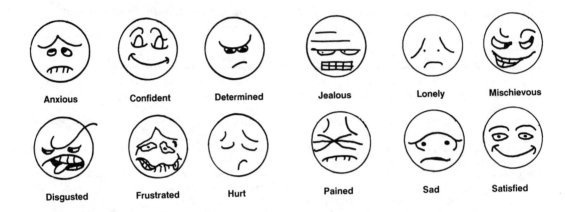

Anxious	Confident	Determined	Jealous	Lonely	Mischievous
Disgusted	Frustrated	Hurt	Pained	Sad	Satisfied

Culture in education and the instruction of language learning-disabled students

Carol E. Westby, PhD
Programs for Children
Albuquerque, New Mexico

Geraldine R. Rouse, MS
Albuquerque Public Schools
Albuquerque, New Mexico

Education is deeply rooted in culture. In the United States, whites are most typically brought up in some version of the northern European tradition. This makes problems for everyone else, because educators, like the missionaries of the past, practice an unconscious form of cultural imperialism which they impose indiscriminately on others. . . . I refer not so much to content as to how learning is organized, how it is presented, its setting, the language used, and the people who teach it, the rules by which they play as well as the institutions themselves (Hall, 1976, p. 205).

ANTHROPOLOGY IN EDUCATION

In order to succeed in a classroom, children must learn the content that is presented; but to learn this content, they must first learn the rules of the classroom game. Traditional classrooms have their own culture or patterns of interaction (Mehan, 1979); however, for many children the culture of the classroom is quite different from their home culture. Ethno-

Top Lang Disord, 1985, 5(4), 15-28
© 1985 Aspen Publishers, Inc.

graphy, a descriptive, qualitative methodology of anthropology, provides a way of discovering what the classroom game rules are and how learning is organized and presented in school. Through systematic observations and in-depth interviews, ethnographers can discover the rules children need to know to function effectively in school, as well as the rules teachers use to organize behaviors. Unlike psychologically oriented quantitative research, which isolates variables for analysis, ethnography uses a holistic analysis to identify and describe the interrelationships among variables (Rist, 1977). This article describes the organization of activities in an elementary classroom of language learning-disabled Hispanic children and demonstrates how the use of ethnographic research methods can contribute to understanding the culture of the school.

High- and low-context cultures

Hall (1959, 1976, 1983), an anthropologist who has used ethnographic methods to study many cultures, proposed a paradigm that can be used to compare and contrast cultures and to understand the nature of interactions occurring within a culture. He suggested that cultures vary along a continuum in the degree to which their communicative messages are contextualized. In high-context cultures, most of the communicative information is either in the physical context or internalized in the person, while very little is contained in the verbally transmitted part of the message. People are deeply involved with each other and able to anticipate each other's actions. In high-context cultures, individuals learn through observation of

unanalyzed routines. Such cultures are rooted in the past and are slow to change. For people within them, life is highly predictable.

Low-context cultures, on the other hand, are highly individualized with relatively little mutual involvement among people. An orientation to group solidarity does not exist. In a low-context culture, the mass of communicative information is conveyed through the verbal code. Many routines and behaviors are verbally taught and cannot be easily predicted for given members of the culture. While no culture is exclusively of one type or the other, some may be nearer one end of the continuum than the other. Within a culture, activities or behaviors may also vary along the continuum. For example, in mainstream American culture, face-to-face interactions between mother and child are generally high context, while writing a term paper for a college class or using a computer is low context.

According to Hall (1976), mainstream American culture is toward the lower end of the continuum. Spanish and Native American cultures, in relation to mainstream Anglo culture and particularly in relation to the culture of the U.S. school, are high context. (Of course, variation exists among members of any cultural group along this continuum.) When Hispanic and Native American children from relatively high-context cultures enter the relatively low-context culture of the school, the problems they may experience are only partly due to the language they speak; problems also stem from how information is organized and transmitted in the school setting. Conflicts may arise from several sources (Erickson & Mohatt, 1982;

Heath, 1983; Phillips, 1972; Wilcox, 1982).

Cultural conflicts in school

The group versus the individual

One source of conflict can arise from the different values that high- and low-context cultures place on the role of their members. High-context cultures emphasize the role of their members as part of the group, while low-context cultures stress the individual functioning of their members. High-context cultures lack participant structures in which one person attempts to control many of the activities of other people in a group. To stand out from one's peers is to be avoided at all costs (Erickson & Mohatt, 1982; Hall, 1976; Phillips, 1972). Consequently, children from high-context cultures may not respond to the teacher-controlled structure of the classroom and may seem unmotivated because they fail to bid when questions are asked, or they refuse to respond when called on.

Language structure and function

Differences in the structure and function of language in high- and low-context cultures is a second source of conflict. Language in high-context cultures is embedded within a context of immediate purposes (Donaldson, 1978). Communication derives from interpersonal involvement in a shared reality, which obviates the need for linguistic elaboration of the message (Bernstein, 1964). In a low-context culture, a shared reality cannot be assumed, and hence linguistic messages must be explicitly and precisely elaborated to minimize the risk of misinterpretation. Most of the language in school reflects a low-context culture. Many facts are learned apart from contexts, and meaning must be obtained from the words alone since minimal information is available from the context.

In high-context cultures, language accompanies action and is used to maintain interaction, common interests, and group solidarity. It is seldom used to predict and plan for the future (Scollon & Scollon, 1981; Tough, 1977). The sameness and predictability of high-context cultures require less planning. In fact, talk about the future may be discouraged. For example, in the Navajo culture, planning for the future is discouraged because it may affect destiny and limit possibilities for living a good life (Sorrell, Mike, Bidtah, & Thomas, n.d.). The low-context majority culture of schools encourages social advancement through education and employment. Thus schools emphasize long-term planning and expect students to sacrifice immediate pleasures and rewards. As a result, children must engage in activities that have no immediate payoff or observable purpose.

Use of time

A third source of cultural conflict may arise from a culture's use of time. High-context cultures tend to be more polychronic relative to low-context cultures. Polychronic time is characterized by situations in which several events happen at once. Polychronic time stresses completion of transactions rather than adherence to preset schedules (Hall, 1976). In polychronic-time cultures, no order exists as to who speaks first or is served first. Planning for the future may not be as common. Timelines or schedules for activities may be more flexible, or they may simply not exist.

Time in low-context cultures tends to be monochronic; that is, low-context cultures tend to be characterized by single events happening one at a time. Planning is critical because scheduling is required to complete all the activities. Actions are tightly scheduled throughout the day, week, and year, and people make plans and talk constantly about the future (Dundes, 1980). Schools adhere tightly to monochronic time. A lesson must be completed in a set time, and during the lesson the child should be doing nothing else. The teacher's time must become the child's time, and a task that is not completed within the school time frame may be considered a failure.

A PROGRAM FOR LANGUAGE LEARNING-DISABLED BICULTURAL CHILDREN

If, as Hall (1976) said, education is deeply rooted in culture, then the teacher of high-context children must be aware of possible sources of cultural conflict and help children make a transition to learning the culture of the school. Understanding cultural influences on learning is imperative in the education of those children who are language learning-disabled in their home culture because these children need help learning the cultures of both home and school.

Hall's concept of high- and low-context cultures and activities has helped to explain the activities and interactions that were studied in a classroom of eight Hispanic children, ages 6 to 9 years, who had been identified as language learning-disabled according to the New Mexico Standards for Special Education. The class was team taught by an Hispanic speech-language pathologist and an Anglo teacher assisted by an Anglo aide. Data were collected using a variety of field research techniques (Hall, 1959; Spradley, 1979). In addition, throughout the year videotapes were made of the children and teachers engaging in major classroom activities. Ethnographic interviews were conducted with the speech-language clinician, classroom teacher, and aide to determine their perceptions of what they did and why, and to validate observational data.

The children

The children's families were bilingual and bicultural. Many of their homes included extended family members such as aunts, uncles, and grandparents. Adults in the home often spoke to each other in New Mexican Spanish, an informal everyday Spanish, as contrasted with a formal educated Spanish (Ornstein-Galicia, 1981). Although some Spanish was directed to the children, in most families Chicano English, an ethnic variety of English, was used with the children and was the language used outside the home. Chicano English differs from Anglo English primarily in its phonology and intonation patterns, somewhat in its syntax and morphology, but not significantly in its lexicon (Penalosa, 1980).

The children enrolled in the class knew the Spanish words for common household items and some Spanish slang. They relied more on Chicano English for communication, but they were competent in neither English nor Spanish according to formal tests and interviews with their families, who viewed them as slower or less talkative than their other children. Performance on the Leiter International Performance Scale and the Wechsler Intelligence Scale for Children—Revised (WISC-R), interpreted with the System of Multicultural Pluralistic Assessment (SOMPA) (Mercer, 1979), placed these children in the low average range of cognitive abilities. None of the children possessed enough Spanish for the examiners to administer tests in Spanish. The children's performance on English language assessments was significantly depressed in relation to their nonverbal level of cognitive functioning. The children were enrolled in a school where 70% of the children were Hispanic, and they had spent a year or two in kindergarten with support from a bilingual, bicultural speech-language pathologist or Chapter I cognitive language development specialist before being placed in the special education classroom.

Classroom goals

The goals of the classroom, as described by the speech-language clinician and teacher, were to (a) increase the children's communicative competence both in informal social language and (b) increase the children's communicative competence in literate school language. These goals were consistent with what Cummins (1983) called basic interpersonal communicative skills (BISC) and cognitive/academic lin-

The goals of the classroom, as described by the speech-language clinician and teacher, were to (a) increase the children's communicative competence both in informal social language and (b) increase the children's communicative competence in literate school language.

guistic proficiency (CALP). Analyses of ethnographic data indicated that both the content of the activities taught and the teacher–child interaction strategies used in the activities were important in achieving the classroom goals. In addition, analyses of the videotapes and ethnographic interviews revealed that the activities could be placed along a continuum from high to low context and that the teacher–child interactions differed in the various activities.

Activity characteristics

High-context activities

The organization and the language used in some activities made them high context. High-context activities included field trips, cooking activities, weaving (and other art projects), construction of an adobe pueblo, and pretend play with realistic props. These activities were high context in several respects: (a) There was no competition among the children and no attempt by the teachers to determine correct and incorrect responses. (b) The activities were negotiated among the children and teachers; anyone could talk at any time. There was no calling on a specific child to perform, and the activity was not totally controlled by the teachers; (c) The activities were not strictly time bound. Thus an activity begun at 9:00 A.M. might continue all morning and could take several weeks to complete; (d) Language was context dependent. Thus a student could say, "Give me that thing there" and be understood, rather than having to say, "Give me the red spatula lying beside the sack of sugar."

Many of the activities, such as making tortillas or empanadas, were activities that the children had seen regularly at home, although they were limited in their ability to talk about them. These activities permitted the teacher to provide the children with comprehensible input (Krashen & Terrell, 1983); that is, language at a level they could understand and language that was just a little beyond their present stage of development. The teachers built situational frames for each activity by first displaying materials and discussing with the children what each item was, how it was used, and who used it. The children were not pressured to speak. The emphasis was on input. Although questions were often asked of the group, no one was required to answer. Anyone could respond, and they could respond with any words they had available (in Spanish or English) without threat of correction.

Pretend play differed from the other high-context activities in two ways: (a) it was distanced from the actual experience, that is, the materials used and the actions peformed were symbolic and not real; and (b) the children were required to talk to each other. As with the other high-context activities, the adult set the situational frame by discussing all the materials available and the sequence of events that would be used. For example, "We'll pretend to have a surprise birthday party for Tony. Someone will have to bake a cake and someone will need to go to the store to buy candles and a birthday present. Someone will also have to write and send the invitations."

When new pretend play themes were introduced (e.g., seeing a physician, going to the hospital), the adult actually entered into the play, taking a role and modeling verbal scripts for various situations. As the children became more verbal, the adult acted as a stage manager to the play, reminding the children to talk, telling them to listen to each other, or repeating what one child had said so another child would respond. The pretend play provided children with the opportunity to use verbal scripts they had heard, again without threat of correction.

Low-context, familiar-topic activities

Some activities contained both high- and low-context components. They were high context because of the nature of their organization and because the topic of the communication was familiar, but they were low context because contextual cues were lacking. The Brown Bear activity, adapted from the Think Aloud program (Camp & Bash, 1981), was one such activity. It served as a modified sharing time. Sharing time for children from minority cultures is often an unsuccessful activity because they cannot carry on a structured monologue that takes into account the needs of the listeners (Michaels, 1981). In the Brown Bear activity, children selected a paper peanut from a bowl that was attached to a large, brown cardboard bear. On the peanuts were written questions such as, "What would happen next if you invited someone to your home?" Unlike formal sharing time, no child was singled out to perform. Children could respond when they had an idea to share, and almost all contributions were acceptable. If no child offered a response, the adults engaged in informal discussion about a time when they had invited someone to their homes. This dialogue provided a model for the children on how to use explicit language to talk about such an experience. Children were permitted to interrupt the dialogue. For example, a child could respond with "My friend broke my bicycle" after the teacher mentioned that her visitor broke a glass. The situations were ones that all children had experienced, unlike some topics that might arise in a traditional sharing time. The Brown Bear activity appeared to function for the children as a transition between high- and low-context tasks.

Low-context, unfamiliar-topic activities

Activities such as calendar time, morning message, and book reports were at the low-context end of the continuum. These activities were similar to activities in traditional classrooms in content and organization. During calendar time, the children responded to questions about the month, day of the week, year, season, weather, what they did yesterday or the day before, and what they would do tomorrow. For the morning message activity, several sentences were written on the chalkboard. The children were asked to locate a letter, a word, or a sentence, or to correct a spelling, punctuation, semantic, or gram-

matical error. The teacher had total control of the calendar and morning message activities, and children were often called on or had to bid for a turn. Responses were judged as right or wrong. Language was not used to communicate a need-meeting message or share personal information, but was used to talk explicitly about language. Minimal or no contextual cues were available to assist the children's comprehension.

Incorporating low-context activities at home

At the same time that high-context activities were being included in school, low-context activities were being introduced into the children's homes. To familiarize the children with literate language and encourage its use at home, book reports were introduced. The children's families were invited to school, and the speech-language pathologist explained that the children would be taking home books, and asked that someone in the family read the books to the children. In the majority of families, at least one adult had sufficient literacy skills to read the books that the children selected. In one family, both parents were illiterate, but older sisters in the family were willing to read to the child. The speech-language pathologist demonstrated how to read to the children, ask questions, and talk about the stories. The adult could ask questions such as, "What's the story about?" "What is the boy doing?" "How did the boy feel when that happened?" "Why did the boy do that?" and "Remember when we saw something like that?"

The books available for the book reports were all familiar children's literature and included many books by authors from the Southwest. The books were displayed on a rack, and the children were free to select their own. Each day, the children who had had books read to them met with a teacher to discuss the books. Some children limited their reports to describing what happened on each page, while other children responded to questions about the characters' feelings and reasons for their behavior. If a student was unable to say anything about a book, and if it appeared that the book had not been read to the child or that the child had not understood the story, the child was sent home again with the same book and a note giving specific suggestions for ways to discuss the book. After every 10 book reports, a personal note was sent to the family thanking them for their support, describing what the child had learned, and giving a new suggestion as to what the reader could ask or say about the books.

TEACHER–CHILD INTERACTION STRATEGIES

Analysis of the ethnographic interview data revealed that the teacher-child interaction strategies differed in the high-context activities, the low-context, familiar-topic activities, and the low-context, unfamiliar-topic activities. The various types of teacher–child interaction strategies are explained and numbered for reference in Table 1. These interaction strategies had some similarities with those proposed by Blank, Rose, and Berlin (1978) and Tough (1977). The differences that appeared were probably the result of the language acquisition goals of this class-

room and the fact that these children were language learning disabled.

High-context activity strategies

In this classroom, two of the teachers' major goals were (a) to give the children significant amounts of comprehensive language input and (b) to encourage them to talk. These purposes differed somewhat from the purposes of teacher–child communication in more traditional classrooms (Mehan, 1979). In most traditional classrooms, the function of teacher–child discourse is for the children to display what they know. Teachers' strategies are generally to orient the children to the task and then attempt to simplify the task if the children fail. In field trips and art and cooking projects in this program, many of the teacher–child discourse strategies functioned to give the children information in a natural manner through modeling of activities and discourse (see Table 1, items 1a, 1d). Demands were seldom made on the child to display knowledge. Enabling strategies (1) were often used primarily to help the children comprehend and were less often used to help them perform by verbally displaying knowledge.

In pretend play, the children had to perform, but after the initial framing input and modeling by the adult (1a, 1b), the children related primarily to each other, not to the adult. The adult assisted the children only by modeling dialogue when taking a role in the play and by giving reminding cues (1c) that functioned to alert the children to reflect on what they knew about the task. From real experiences through field trips and class-

Table 1. Teacher–child interaction strategies

Teacher Strategy	Example
1. *Enabling:* Encourages student to reflect on or become aware of aspects of discussion or activity	
a. Modeling: Demonstrates desired activity or discourse	*Shows how to break an egg or to order pizza at restaurant.*
b. Directed action or attention to general task or salient characteristics: Orients child to task or focuses attention on specific components of task	"What do you think happened in this picture?" "How can you tell it's night?"
c. Reminding cues: Helps child to remember materials or actions	"Do you have everything you need to make the cake?"
d. Discourse cues: Adults engage in informal conversation to convey a concept or facilitate discussion	*Teacher talks with another adult about experience related to topic under discussion.*
e. Proposing novel situations: Introduces new idea into conversation	*Children talk about playing in the street. Teacher asks,* "What if a policeman came?"
f. Relating unknown to known: Relates new activity to previously experienced event	*Teacher relates Little Red Hen making tortillas to children making tortillas in class.*
2. *Responding to lack of information or misinformation:* Deals with incorrect or inadequate response	
a. Informing: Provides correct information if children lack information and have not responded to enabling strategies or if the response is incorrect	*Teacher explains about lighthouse after child calls lighthouse a motel.*
b. Monitoring questions: Asks child to judge response	"Does that make sense?"
3. *Sustaining:* Encourages child to expand appropriate response	
a. Acceptance: Indicates child's response was acceptable	"Good."
b. Request for more information: Usually follows acceptance response and requests additional information	"And what else happened?"
c. Acknowledgment: Accepts response that may not be correct in order to encourage participation	"Uh huh" *and repeats child's statement.*
4. *Encouraging peer conversation:* Stimulates talk among students and allows them to control conversation	
a. Branching: Allows associative responses to occur that stimulate group talk	T: "What happened (*pointing to policeman*)?" C: "I want to be a policeman." T: "What would you like to be (*looking at another child*)?"
b. Talking to/asking: Reminds children to talk to each other	"I want you to talk to each other."
5. *Requesting justification:* Requires child to explain response	"What made you think of that?"

(continues)

Table 1 *(continued)*

Teacher Strategy	Example
6. *Maintaining on-target behavior:* Refocuses student to topic or prompts student to take next step	
a. Directed action or attention to recognize salient characteristics: Alerts student to specific aspects of activity or conversation	"Look more closely at this part of the picture."
b. Repetition of teacher question: Acknowledges student's statement and repeats question with emphasis	"Yes, he hurt himself, but what happened first?"
c. Alerting to inappropriate or perseverative responses: Indicates child is off-target or repetitive	"I've already heard that. Tell me something different."
d. Checking: Requests clarification when teacher does not understand response	"What do you mean?"
e. Reprimand: Informs child of inappropriate response after five perseverative responses; refocusing has been unsuccessful; or the child monopolizes conversation	C: "My mommy bought me a ball." T: "We're not talking about that now."
f. Relating unknown to known: See 1f.	
g. Reinforcement of student actions: Specifies child must participate as directed by another member of the group	"You have to do what John said."
h. Restructures task to highlight specific components: Alters question or activity to alert child to particular features	T: "What do we need to add to the lemonade (*gestures toward salt, flour, sugar*)?" C: "Salt." T: "Let's taste these and see if we can find out."

room projects, the children had some knowledge of how to play store, make a cake, or organize a surprise birthday party. If the children did not play at the level desired, the teacher either entered the play and modeled naturalistic dialogue or decided the children needed additional input through field trips, classroom projects, or presentation of information in the

---

From real experiences through field trips and classroom projects, the children had some knowledge of how to play store, make a cake, or organize a surprise birthday party.

---

framing period at the beginning of the next pretend play session. Peer conversation and interaction were encouraged (4b, 6g) when the teacher told the children that they had to respond to each other. Otherwise, the play itself was not interrupted by the teacher. Because of the many contextual cues available to the children in the high-context activities, it was seldom necessary to reprimand or to use other strategies for maintaining on-target behavior (6a–6h). These strategies were needed primarily with the two most severely learning-disabled children, who were likely to make comments that had no apparent relation to the immediate activity.

Low-context, familiar-topic activity strategies

Enabling strategies (1) and strategies for maintaining on-target behavior (6) were used most frequently in the low-context, familiar-topic activities such as Brown Bear. The children were encouraged to talk with the teacher and each other. Because an emphasis was placed on making the children feel confident in their ability to communicate, the teachers used many enabling strategies (1b, 1d, 1e, 1f) and sustaining strategies (3) to help them respond and to keep them responding. Associative responses (that is, responses that might be only remotely related to the task) were allowed if they could be used to engage the other children in conversation (4a). The teachers responded to misinformation by providing the correct information or asking the children to think about their response (2a, 2b). Reprimands (6e) were rare, but they did occur, mainly with those children who were most communicatively disordered. They occurred, however, only after the teacher had used other enabling strategies and strategies for maintaining on-target behavior. Reprimands were not given for wrong responses, but for perseverative responses and responses that indicated that the child had not attended to the task.

Low-context, unfamiliar-activity strategies

In the calendar and morning message activities, the teachers made the least use of almost all strategies. This was initially surprising. It was expected that because these low-context activities lacked contextual cues, they would be more difficult for the children, and, consequently, the children would need and receive more assistance. In high-context activities, comprehension can be facilitated by the external materials and the immediate goals of the tasks. In low-context activities, comprehension depends on internal language sources. The task is presented through linguistic means, and the child must comprehend the task from what is said. No additional contextual cues are present to assist the child in comprehending. Comprehension is possible only by understanding the actual words spoken. Calendar time required memorization of abstract facts, and morning message was basically a metalinguistic task. In these tasks, few strategies could be used by the teacher to assist the children to discover the answer if they did not already have it.

Although the content and organization of the interaction in the book report activity was low context, it was possible to help the child negotiate meaning within the text by using enabling strategies (1b, 1f) and strategies for maintaining on-target behavior (6a, 6b, 6d). The stories dictated the topic of conversation. Hence, when children gave associative responses, their attention was directed to the book (6a), or they were reprimanded (6e). Although the justification strategy (5) that required the children to give reasons for their responses was used sometimes in the high-context activities, it was used extensively in all the low-context activities. This strategy served to orient the children to use language for talking about language and thought, which is essential for dealing with the low-context learning requirements of school.

What is startling about the use of these

strategies is that if children are minimally competent in language, they would not become competent from many low-context school activities because much of what facilitates language acquisition—the negotiation of meaning—is missing from them. Book reports provided the one exception. Although it was a low-context, unfamiliar-topic activity, book reports allowed for considerable negotiation of meaning in this program. Thus, while book reports had the linguistic content of low-context tasks and were teacher controlled, they permitted communicative interaction that was similar in many respects to the interaction in high-context activities.

PLANNING

The program allowed bicultural children to acquire, then maintain and use aspects of high-context culture in the low-context environment of the school. At the same time, however, the children had to acquire the ability to cope with the school culture. An overarching goal of all the activities in this program was that of developing language to be used for planning purposes. Planning requires knowing and thinking about the future and metacognition, or thinking about knowing and thinking. Children from high-context cultures are less likely to use language for metacognitive thought, and language learning-disabled children tend to exhibit metacognitive deficits (Wong, 1982). A person who is just about to do something, or who already knows what to do, does not need to plan. Hence minimal planning is required in cultures in which behavioral routines are well known. As tasks become

less familiar and more complicated, planning becomes more important (Pea, 1982). The children in this program had not acquired many familiar routines of their culture, and for them planning became especially important even in activities that might not have required planning by others.

To plan, a child must (a) determine what the task is, (b) reflect on what he or she knows or needs to know, (c) devise a plan for dealing with the task, (d) monitor progress, and (e) evaluate the outcome. In the high-context activities, the teachers demonstrated these stages by planning aloud. They described the task (e.g., making tortillas), what would be needed, the steps involved, and who would be responsible for each step. As they were doing the task, they talked about how it was going, and they judged the results by tasting the tortillas.

In the pretend play, after the adult set the situational frame and the theme was discussed (e.g., playing store), the children were asked to make a plan for the play. They were to decide who would take what roles, what they would need, what they would do, and when they would do it. At the end of the play time, the children were asked to evaluate whether they had followed their plan or made changes in it.

Planning is important not only for people to organize their own behavior in a low-context culture, but also to understand the behaviors of others in such a culture. Understanding that people's behavior is motivated and intentionally planned is critical to comprehending stories (Bruce, 1980). In book reports, the adult discussed with the child what happened in the stories, how the characters felt about what happened, how the characters planned to deal with what happened, and how the plan worked out. For example, in the *Three Little Pigs*, children may be asked, "What was the wolf's plan to get the pigs?" "What was the pigs' plan to take care of the wolf?" and "Whose plan worked and why?"

The orientation toward planning in all activities was designed to facilitate the children's abilities to understand how things were done in a low-context culture, which was essential if they were to function in that culture. The program permitted the children to use high-context learning styles in a low-context culture, and helped them learn how to learn and perform in a low-context culture.

•   •   •

As bilingual and bicultural special education programs develop, increasing attention is given to their evaluation. All too often, however, the success or failure of a program is judged solely on students' test performance on preselected variables (Tymitz, 1983). In contrast to such psychologically oriented quantitative methodology, the ethnographic qualitative methodology used in this project yielded an in-depth description of the program, and, consequently, provided a naturalistic basis for evaluating the interrelationships among many variables that contribute to a child's learning. Although quantitative data may be necessary in program evaluation, it must be preceded by qualitative data that can be used to propose ecologically valid hypotheses that can then be subjected to quantitative testing.

REFERENCES

Bernstein, B. (1964). Elaborated and restricted codes: Their social origins and consequences. *American Anthropologist, 66,* 55–69.

Blank, M., Rose, S.A., & Berlin, L.J. (1978). *The language of learning.* New York: Grune & Stratton.

Bruce, B. C. (1980). Plans and social action. In R.J. Spiro, B.C. Bruce, & W.F. Brewer (Eds.), *Theoretical issues in reading comprehension* (pp. 367–384). Hillsdale, NJ: Erlbaum.

Camp, B.W., & Bash, M.A. (1981). *Think aloud: Increasing social and cognitive skills.* Champaign, IL: Research Press.

Cummins, J. (1983). Language proficiency and academic achievement. In J.W. Oller, Jr. (Ed.), *Current issues in language testing research* (pp. 108–129). Rowley, MA: Newbury House.

Donaldson, M. (1978). *Children's minds.* New York: Norton.

Dundes, A. (1980). *Interpreting folklore.* Bloomington, IN: Indiana University Press.

Erickson, F., & Mohatt, G. (1982). Cultural organization of participation structures in two classrooms of Indian students. In G. Spindler (Ed.), *Doing the ethnography of schooling.* New York: Holt, Rinehart & Winston.

Hall, E.T. (1959). *The silent language.* New York: Doubleday.

Hall, E.T. (1976). *Beyond culture.* New York: Anchor Press/Doubleday.

Hall, E.T. (1983). *The dance of life.* New York: Anchor Press/Doubleday.

Heath, S.B. (1983). *Ways with words.* Cambridge: Cambridge University Press.

Krashen, S.D., & Terrell, T.D. (1983). *The natural approach: Language acquisition in the classroom.* New York: Pergamon.

Mehan, H. (1979). *Learning lessons.* Cambridge, MA: Harvard University Press.

Mercer, J. (1979). *SOMPA technical manual.* New York: Psychological Corporation.

Michaels, S. (1981). "Sharing time": Children's narrative style and differential access to literacy. *Language and Society, 10,* 423–442.

Ornstein-Galicia, J.L. (1981). Varieties of Southwest Spanish: Some neglected basic considerations. In R.P. Duran (Ed.), *Latino language and communicative behavior* (pp. 19–35). Norwood, NJ: Ablex.

Pea, R. (1982). What is planning development the development of. In D.L. Forbes & M.T. Greenberg (Eds.),

Children's planning strategies (pp. 5–27). San Francisco: Jossey-Bass.

Penalosa, F. (1980). *Chicano sociolinguistics*. Rowley, MA: Newbury House.

Phillips, S.U. (1972). Participant structures and communicative competence: Warm Springs children in community and classroom. In C. Cazden, V. John & D. Hymes (Eds.), *Functions of language in the classroom* (pp. 370–394). New York: Teachers College Press.

Rist, R.C. (1977). On the relations among educational research paradigms: From disdain to detente. *Anthropology and Education Quarterly, 8*, 42–49.

Scollon, R., & Scollon, S.B.K. (1981). *Narrative, literacy and face in interethnic communication*. Norwood, NJ: Ablex.

Sorrell, V., Mike, E.H., Bidtah, L., & Thomas, V. (n.d.). *Cultural conflict: School—community—curriculum.* Central Consolidated Schools District 22, Title VII Bilingual Education Program, New Mexico.

Spradley, J.P. (1979). *The ethnographic interview*. New York: Holt, Rinehart & Winston.

Tough, J. (1977). *The development of meaning*. New York: Wiley.

Tymitz, B.L. (1983). Bilingual special education: A challenge to evaluation practices. In D.R. Omark & J.G. Erickson (Eds.), *The bilingual exceptional child* (pp. 359–377). San Diego: College-Hill Press.

Wilcox, K. (1982). Differential socialization in the classroom: Implications for equal opportunity. In G. Spindler (Ed.), *Doing the ethnography of schooling* (pp. 268–309). New York: Holt, Rinehart & Winston.

Wong, B.L. (Ed.). (1982). Metacognition and learning disabilities. *Topics in Learning and Learning Disabilities, 1*(2), vii.

Nonbiased assessment and treatment of adults who have neurologic speech and language problems

Audrey L. Holland, PhD
Professor
Department of Speech and Theatre Arts
Division of Speech Pathology and
   Audiology
University of Pittsburgh
Pittsburgh, Pennsylvania

SOME TOPICS have not received much attention in the literature because they do not merit much attention. Other topics that are worthy of attention have also been ignored, and the reasons for this lack of effort are obscure and/or bewildering. The subject of this article is an example of the latter. Nonbiased assessment and treatment is a "hot topic" as it relates to the evaluation and management of children with speech and language disorders. It should be obvious that bias itself is no more likely to be outgrown than are the speech–language problems of children on which nonbias issues are focused. Yet it seems that the speech–language pathologist's concern with bias erodes with the client's increasing age to the extent that potential bias is virtually an unmentioned aspect of management of adults with speech and language disorders.

As a result, in deciding to focus on one aspect of this problem, that of nonbiased assessment of adults with neurogenic speech–language problems, one discovers that there are almost too many possible issues to examine thoroughly. This article

Top Lang Disord, 1983, 3(3), 67-75
© 1983 Aspen Publishers, Inc.

deals with some general interpersonal issues that can be discussed without waiting for the substantiating literature to emerge. They represent immediate concerns, and most have practical, if not scholarly, solutions.

To set the stage for the discussion to follow, four brief case histories will be presented. Each will then be used to illustrate a principle of importance in non-biased assessment and treatment for adults.

CASE HISTORY 1

Mr. H is a 37-year-old white male from rural West Virginia who is bedridden and hospitalized in a Veterans' Administration long-term-care facility and has been diagnosed as having rapidly progressing, severe multiple sclerosis (MS). He is no longer capable of intelligible speech and has a concomitent visual problem as a result of the MS. There is no family available to consult. Because Mr. H has enough arm movement to use a fairly standard communication board, the speech–language pathologist constructed a communication board using pictures of functional needs and pictures related to rural West Virginia life style. As an afterthought, the speech–language pathologist also added a large alphabet but did not expect Mr. H to use it, believing that he could not read. Ignoring the pictures altogether, he first communicated via the alphabet of his desire to receive talking books. The speech–language pathologist later learned that he was a high school literature teacher, with a master's degree in theatre arts.

CASE HISTORY 2

Mrs. C is a 75-year-old white female who was referred to speech pathology 5 days after a left hemisphere stroke. According to medical reports, the stroke left her with a "severe comprehension loss and fluent jargon aphasia." After an initial visit that confirmed the medical reports, work was begun to improve comprehension and limit output. At the fourth bedside treatment session, Mrs. C's sister came to visit. She spoke to Mrs. C using a similar "jargon" later identified as the Ukranian language. Mrs. C had grown up in a Ukranian community in Pittsburgh, Pennsylvania, and used that language predominantly in daily life. Subsequent testing in this language revealed only a moderate anomia and comprehension deficit.

CASE HISTORY 3

Mr. W is an 85-year-old widower who had suffered a second stroke that left him with a moderately severe mixed aphasia and dense right hemiplegia. His family placed him in a well-equipped and well-staffed nursing home. A full range of rehabilitation services were available. At the family's request, the speech–language pathologist sees Mr. W three times a week for treatment. Major efforts are directed to motivating him to work on his speech–language deficits. Reports reveal that Mr. W is sometimes uncooperative and seems much more interested in sitting alone and listening to opera on his stereo tape recorder. Both the speech–language pathologist and the family worry that Mr. W is isolating himself from the nursing home community.

CASE HISTORY 4

Mrs. S is a 60-year-old black female with cerebellar disease that has left her with an ataxic dysarthria. After listening to Mrs. S's speech, the speech–language pathologist determined that her speech was different due to her "black dialect" rather than to dysarthria and declined to see her for treatment. During a later interview, the family was observed to speak standard English.

Each of these cases is based on actual experience. Each case underscores the belief that speech–language pathologists working with adults who have neurogenic problems need to be highly sensitive to the broad domain of sociolinguistics. Each case contains an error in sociolinguistic or sociocultural judgment on the part of the speech–language pathologist that had serious implications for the patient.

It is simple enough to point out that for cerebrovascular disease, incidence and prevalence for blacks in this society are considerably higher than they are for whites. Therefore, it behooves the speech–language pathologist, with an interest in aphasia and dysarthria, to prepare for disproportionate numbers of black Americans on his or her caseloads. This point is intensified by the observation that with the exception of Parkinson's disease and possibly multiple sclerosis, incidence and prevalence rates of neurologic diseases that produce speech and language problems do not vary with race in this society (Kurtzke, Kurland, & Goldberg, 1973). Further, one disease that can produce speech or language problems, sickle cell anemia, is limited almost exclusively to blacks.

For other ethnic and cultural minorities in America, incidence and prevalence figures are not so readily available. However, it is probably true that the figures are at or above those for the majority of the society. Even if the figures were lower, the lack of bilingual testing and training materials is such that we are even less prepared to deal with adult Hispanic minorities, for example, than we are with adult black minorities and minority children in general.

What is perhaps even more important and certainly more subtle is that aphasias and dysarthrias mainly result from disorders associated with aging. At this time, there is practically no sociolinguistic literature related to aging, regardless of the racial, cultural, or socioeconomic background of the speaker.

Even for groups in which a healthy sociolinguistic literature exists, it is clear that there is considerably more information on the young than on the elderly. For example, although an elderly black person might have been brought up in the oral tradition of black America, the experiences of the elderly black person are significantly different from more extensively studied younger blacks. These experiences in language are also potentially quite different. In essence, what is known about language differences in young blacks and whites in America does not translate readily into information about elderly blacks and whites. This problem is compounded for America's other ethnic and cultural minorities. The two sources of bias, racism and ageism, coalesce in assessing and treating the bulk of neurogenic speech–language disorders.

The following comments are intended to highlight the need for rudimentary awareness of some sociolinguistic principles among those involved in the practice of neurogenic speech–language pathology, with special emphasis on the problems of the aging. There is little data to rely on. Therefore, these remarks are more common-sense oriented and experiential than they are scholarly. They are offered in the hope that they may serve as an impetus to much needed research and that they may provide a stopgap help to clinicians (and their patients) who frequently face the frightening implications of the deviance–difference distinction in aging persons, be they of the cultural majority or one of its minorities.

Let us return to the four brief case histories introduced previously. What principles do they illustrate? What problems do they exemplify? What mistakes were made?

CASE 1

Principle: In the absence of corroborating evidence, make the fewest possible assumptions. The speech–language pathologist, dealing in this case with a patient about whom little was actually known, handled her specific lack of information by resorting to generalized and stereotyped conceptions of young men from rural West Virginia. As a consequence, she risked insulting the patient and wasted time designing and constructing a device that was inappropriate to his level of language function and cultural interests and that was ultimately abandoned. Are there reasons that explain the errors, and can they be corrected? It must first be recognized that although this patient was young, he was in an institution. This fact illustrates a category of potential problems whose likelihood of occurrence increases with the age of the patient. Specifically, it is often extremely difficult for the speech–language pathologist to obtain the social information (and even the medical information) that is necessary for appropriate treatment planning for patients in chronic care facilities. That the speech–language pathologist in this case resorted to a simple picture board when a more sophisticated language board was more appropriate in part reflects this difficulty as well as the existence of a possible cultural bias. Solving the problem is not simple, and often requires much sleuthing and tenacity, especially in cases such as this one, when the patient's speech is largely unintelligible and visits with the family are not possible. But it is important to emphasize that social service's family contacts should be used almost instinctively if one is tempted to respond to assumptions rather than facts.

A second problem here is less apparent, perhaps, but just as real nonetheless. Assessing reading skills in brain-damaged

---

Assessing reading skills in brain-damaged adults is difficult business, since few standardized measures are available.

---

adults is difficult business, since few standardized measures are available. LaPointe and Horner's (1979) Reading Comprehension Battery for Aphasia is a useful survey, but norms are presently lacking, and when available, they will probably address the aphasic population specifically. I have found it useful, particularly with elderly adults, to simply question reading habits, including how much reading is done (e.g., what sorts of newspapers, books and periodicals are read). A communicative style questionnaire developed for aphasic patients by Swindell, Pashek, and Holland (1982) can be used in this regard as well. The point is not solely to judge reading and communicative *skills*, but to assess the importance of reading (and writing) as a part of communicative style. In the case of Mr. H, his visual deficits compromised his reading skills and his limited-lower extremity movement interfered with his use of an alphabet board. These deficits did not necessarily compromise his interest in the written word, however, and the connection was almost missed due to the assumptions that were made.

Reading is emphasized by this example, but the lack of available material to assess educationally related language behaviors extends beyond reading. Writing and spelling assessment are even more elusive of measurement, and it is often unclear in the case of adults how much of a perceived writing or spelling deficit has been the result of brain damage, of general literacy problems, or of poor schooling. And even if those potential contributory aspects can be disentangled and properly weighted in assessment, the patient's interest in and reliance on school-related language skills still must be worked into the equation.

The power of the yes–no question as a means of seeking such information from motorically involved patients should not be underestimated. In this case, both the requisite background and communicative style information could have been acquired by careful questioning using yes–no questions. Although it would have been time consuming, it would have taken less time than did the constructing of the cumbersome board.

CASE 2

Principle: Cultural minorities exist even in white America. It is especially important to be sensitive to this fact in an aging population. For Mrs. C the tendency toward accepting the ready assumptions that caused the problems in the case of Mr. H was also operating. In Mrs. C's case, however, the assumptions seem to be primarily medical, rather than sociolinguistic. That is, people who speak fluently and who appear to fail to comprehend after a left hemispheric stroke are likely to be aphasic. For Mrs. C, however, the clinician failed to account for her linguistic history. Further, the clinician failed to consider that especially soon after stroke, it is not uncommon to find that bilingual patients are differentially responsive to their most used language, or to their earliest learned language. The obvious solution here is to have a family member (if possible) do the rudimentary testing necessary to demonstrate the language/aphasia barrier, if any question about such language confusion exists. If no family members are available, then another speaker of the language in question must be found and used.

The problem of cultural minority language is perhaps too dramatically illustrated in Mrs. C's case. Often the problem exists in less spectacular ways, and in practice may be even more difficult for the clinician. For example, Holland and Reinmuth (1982) recently identified a still hospitalized postbrainstem stroke patient who was born in and grew up in a Slovak-speaking neighborhood in Pittsburgh. It was unclear whether he (a) was dysarthric, (b) had the rare pseudo-foreign dialect problem that has been reported to occur following a stroke, or (c) had a Slovak accent. We felt the latter to be the most unlikely. However, careful questioning of both the patient and his family convinced us that although he was born and raised in Pittsburgh, he retained throughout his life the features of the Slovak language that he had first learned and, in fact, had no residual speech disorder as a result of stroke.

Particularly as they affect older Americans, some features of cultural differences go well beyond speech and language, but are important for the speech–language clinician to be aware of, for they directly affect treatment. These include cultural differences in responses to the elderly, in regard to disability, and in response to fear and anxiety. For example, the elderly wife who sits all day crying by her husband's bedside might be viewed as disruptive to the healing process by members of some cultures; for those of other cultures the expressed grief might be integral to it.

Although these features might be particularly pertinent to those who live in melting-pot American urban centers, I suspect that they exist in the urban–rural areas as well. In a large city university medical center, many patients are sent there from small towns. The need to be sensitive to the potential of cultural variation for affecting clinical interactions is essential.

CASE 3

Principle: It is more important to preserve the elderly patient's perception of dignity than it is to practice speech intervention. More than any other group of patients, including young children whose parents can advocate for them, the elderly are likely to be "treated" against their wishes. The reasons for this are complex, but some of them fall directly into the sociocultural realm. For example, the general cultural inability to deal with the inevitability of death is one factor that plays a part in any attempts to "do something" about conditions that otherwise might force us to face the terminal nature of life. Family guilt about institutionalization in a society that is struggling to come to grips with its beliefs about it, even when institutionalization is a perceived necessity, also plays a role. In the case of Mr. W, the family pushed for treatment, possibly to assure themselves that they were doing everything they could to help him, and the therapist concurred.

The efforts, however, appeared to be at the expense of Mr. W's own conception of what should be happening to him. Perhaps, for the first time in his life, he finally was able to listen intensively to the music he loved in an uninterrupted fashion. He perhaps felt compromised and embarrassed when he was forced to confront his problems in his clinical interaction with the much younger clinician and to "work" on them in what might easily be perceived as a grade schoollike manner. Perhaps something else underlies his reluctance. Regardless of the reason, however, Mr. W had earned the right, by simple virtue of his age, to choose not to be treated.

Dignity, and one's perception of what constitutes it, must be recognized as an integral part of being old. Part of the process by which the dignity of the elderly can be recognized comes from respecting the wishes of the older person.

A frequent question in relation to direct language intervention with the elderly has to do with how to motivate the elderly patient for treatment. In essence, I do not believe one can "motivate" the elderly client for treatment. At best, one can explain what can be offered and then accept the consequences, which may include rejection of the services offered. Improving what Lubinski (1981) calls "the communication-impaired environment" of long-term care settings (a term that also describes the isolated, home-bound patient's setting) is a meaningful activity for the speech–language pathologist, and often is a much more important activity than direct intervention. (See Lubinski, 1981, for an excellent model.) Listening to an elderly patient, really listening, is often much more important than working on language and speech impairment, if service to the patient is the goal. And, finally, being a predictable and frequent visitor, perhaps holding a hand for even a few moments, has always had clinical value but nowhere are such activities more potent than in working with the elderly.

Regarding cultural differences, it is necessary to remember in general that language styles learned in one's youth persist throughout life. Consider how strange it would be to hear an elderly person say something like, "I was into a real head trip over Prohibition, but I got my act together before the law was repealed," or to hear an elderly black person greet his friend with "Hey Baby, what's happenin'?" Language style across the age span is a little studied phenomenon, but it is one that demands attention

---

It is necessary to remember that language styles learned in one's youth persist throughout life.

---

by speech–language pathologists who work with the elderly, particularly if these pathologists are to respect these persons properly.

CASE 4

Principle: Be extremely aware of dialectal variations (regional, social class, race) and the effects that result from the imposition of speech–language disorders on them. Mrs. S represents one of the most common sociolinguistic dilemmas for the speech–language pathologist working with the dysarthrias and milder forms of aphasia problems. And, unfortunately, the dilemma is one about which little is known in sociolinguistic terms. That is, even though we know something about sociolinguistic variation as it relates to social class, region, gender, race and a great deal about language and speech abnormalities brought about by brain damage, we have virtually no descriptive literature that simultaneously looks at both. The clinician is expected to synthesize information from these two data sources in his or her evaluation of a given patient.

I am not suggesting here that a massive research effort be mounted to look at differential effects on speech production in black and white dysarthric speakers, nor to examine variation among Hispanic and rural white southern speakers with Broca aphasia, and so on, although some such studies would be welcome. Rather, I am suggesting that if a patient has speech and language patterns other than the standard white dialects on which our knowledge of language and speech breakdown is mostly based, it is absolutely necessary to find out about the patient's pretraumatic dialect at the outset of the evaluation. If one is to perform the necessary synthesis of dialect and deficiency, it must be against the background of information about previous speech–language patterns.

There are obvious sources for obtaining such information. The most important is to develop a complete understanding of the dialectal patterns one is likely to encounter in one's *own* geographic area. Although a general study of sociolinguistics is useful in the abstract, it must be supplemented by this more localized study. Second, in the case of a particular potential patient, his or her own description of language change brought about by the neurological condition must be obtained. Third, it is also necessary to compare carefully the differences and similarities between the speech of the potential patient and others of his or her peer group. The patient's family and visitors are the most useful sources of data for this comparison. And finally, the family should also be closely questioned regarding any changes that they perceive in the patient's speech.

In Mrs. S's case, her speech was evaluated, apparently without the requisite corroborating information, by a clinician who was unaware of the phonological characteristics of the regional and racial dialects of her area. As a consequence, the patient's ataxic dysarthria was missed, not by the medical staff particularly, but by the speech–language pathologist.

The difference/deficiency problems highlighted here do not only apply to assessment alone but also to treatment. Disorders of the type discussed here are *always* imposed on *some* sociolinguistic system. The goals for treatment are to restore speech and language skills within the context of the previous dialect, not to change the dialect, or to provide acceptable compensations, again within the confines of the previous dialect system.

It is important to be aware of the potential for dialectal mismatch between clinician and patient, when working with neurogenic speech–language problems. For example, in a fairly systematic procedure I developed in Boston for training auditory memory span, a phrase that patients were required to repeat was "a dozen eggs." The phrase presented no problem to Bostonians, in any of their dialects. Yet in Pittsburgh, where I subsequently used the program, patients consistently repeated that phrase as "a dozen of eggs." This was unimportant to the treatment per se, but it illustrates a subtle dialectal difference. I once misconstrued an aphasic patient's rejection of my production /mɪsəsɪpɪ/ (her home state) as evidence of her auditory comprehension problem. She finally straightened me out by pronouncing it "correctly," that is /mɪzsɪpɪ/. The brain-damaged patient's ability to listen "across dialects" indeed may be lessened by brain damage. This is particularly true in the aphasias with comprehension losses. It behooves the clinician to be aware of this problem. The solution lies not in changing one's speech but in considering dialect-clash as source of perceived miscomprehension.

For each of the four case histories discussed earlier, an opposite decision under different circumstances could have been equally wrong. Mr. H's communication board could have been constructed at too high a level; it could have been too "wordy" and equally useless if his interests and abilities had been overestimated, rather than underestimated. Mrs. C could have been a patient with a true jargon aphasia that the clinician construed to be an exotic foreign language and as a result she could have been denied appropriate treatment. Mr. W's case is less clear, but even the decision not to treat the rejecting elderly person needs to be made primarily on the basis of the no-assumptions principle. Mrs. S could indeed have had no dysarthria; she merely could have been speaking a dialect that differed from the clinician's. If that had been the case, treatment would have been inappropriate. It is this range of possibilities that make the interface between sociolinguistics and language disorders so continually challenging.

•   •   •

I have drawn my examples from my own world of work (Western Pennsylvania) and from the perspective of my own dialect (white, middle-class, distinctive Western Pennsylvania where the /stɪlɚz/, not the /stilɚz/, play /fuʔbɔ/, not

/futbɔl/). Due to both factors, it is important to point out that the intent was to provide examples that have far wider dialectal implications. It is hoped that the implications apply to other areas of regional speech, and as well, for other cultural and language groups, such as Spanish-speaking Americans, that are beyond the range of my personal experiences.

Throughout this discussion, I have grown increasingly aware of the lack of research that has been available to justify my remarks. It is obvious that most of these matters require thorough substantiation, and that research into the sociolinguistics of aging in a pluralistic society is necessary.

What is perhaps less apparent is that training curricula generally have not yet begun to reflect concerns such as these, and that appropriate testing and clinical materials are also notably lacking. As Americans grow older, it is hoped that the plea for more serious consideration of the aging, of all races and cultural backgrounds, will be the result.

REFERENCES

Holland, A., & Reinmuth, O.M. *The natural course of early language recovery in aphasia.* (Progress Rep. NS17495-02; to NINCDS/HHS) Washington, D.C.: Government Printing Office, June 1982.

Kurtzke, J.F., Kurland, L.T., & Goldberg, I.D. *Epidemotology of neurologic and sense organ disorders.* Cambridge, Mass.: Harvard University Press, 1973.

LaPointe, L., & Horner, J. *Reading comprehension battery for aphasia.* Tigard, Ore.: C.C. Publications, 1979.

Lubinski, R. Environmental language intervention. In R. Chapey (Ed.), *Language intervention strategies in adult aphasia.* Baltimore, Md.: Williams & Wilkins, 1981.

Swindell, C., Pashek, G., & Holland, A. A questionnaire for surveying personal and communicative style. In R. Brookshire (Ed.), *Proceedings of the Clinical Aphasiology Conference,* Minneapolis, Minn.: BRK, 1982.

Part IV
Addressing the Needs of Some Specific Populations

Service delivery to Asian/Pacific LEP children: A cross-cultural framework

Li-Rong Lilly Cheng, PhD
Coordinator
Bilingual/Multicultural Program
Department of Communicative
* Disorders*
San Diego State University
San Diego, California

A MAJOR CONCERN in the field of communicative disorders today is service delivery to Asian/Pacific Islanders whose native languages are not English. Issues regarding service provision are emerging and will continue to grow in magnitude in coming years. The purposes of this article are (1) to present general information on the history, cultures, and languages of the major Asian/Pacific immigrant and refugee groups; and (2) to provide information on the types of knowledge required by professionals if they are to work effectively with Asian/Pacific limited-English-proficient (LEP) students.

HISTORY, CULTURES, AND LANGUAGES OF THE ASIAN/PACIFIC POPULATIONS

The influx of Asians/Pacific Islanders to the United States in the last decade has resulted in an increasing number of non-English-proficient (NEP) and LEP stu-

Top Lang Disord, 1989, 9(3), 1–14
© 1989 Aspen Publishers, Inc.

dents in schools. Some are landed immigrants, while others are refugees. Immigrants file for an immigrant visa and wait for a period of time ranging from six months to four or five years before the visa interviews and screening procedures. Immigrants must have a U.S. sponsor, either a close relative or an employer. Many Asian immigrants are citizens from Malaysia, China, India, Hong Kong, Taiwan, Japan, and Korea. Refugees, on the other hand, leave their countries because of fear of persecution; many have risked their lives to escape and have left their families behind. For them the time of transition is filled with unrest, separation, anxiety, and fear. Most refugees are taken to camps until their sponsors arrange passage to the United States. Typically refugees speak no English and have never traveled beyond their homeland.

There are four types of Asian in terms of immigration status and education: (1) first-generation immigrants and refugees are those who came to the United States as young adults; (2) the "one and a half" generation were born in Southeast Asia but are being educated in the United States; (3) the second generation (*ni-sei* in Japanese) were born and educated in the United States; and (4) the third generation (*san-sei*) are those whose parents were born and educated in the United States.

The parents of the LEP populations have different levels of education. Among the refugee populations, some have very little schooling, while others have experienced repeated disruptions in schooling. It is not unusual to find a refugee adolescent with minimal formal education.

The refugee population is younger than the general U.S. population (mean age 32.8). Asian Youth Office of Refugee Resettlement (ORR) data indicate that approximately 40% of the more than 800,000 Southeast Asian refugees admitted to the United States from 1975 to 1986 were between the ages of 6 and 20. Furthermore, more than 200,000 Southeast Asian children were born in the United States over the last decade. Youth is the predominant characteristic of the refugee population: It is estimated that half of all Southeast Asians in the U.S. are under 18 years of age. It should also be noted that in recent years more Indochinese have arrived in the United States from Vietnam, Laos, and Cambodia. A large number of Indochinese refugees are ethnic Chinese. The Hmong and the Mien, who come from the mountains of Laos, are ethnic minorities. More than 100,000 Lao people have come to the United States in recent years. Whereas ethnic Lao people make up 50% of the total Lao population, the rest are composed of Khmu, Tai Dam, Hmong, I-Mien (Yao-Mien), and others.

Clearly there are numerous variables that one needs to consider when working with the Asian/Pacific populations. One important variable is the home language(s) of the LEP individual.

Language patterns of the Asian/Pacific populations

Hundreds of distinct languages and their dialects are spoken in East Asia, Southeast Asia, and the Pacific Islands. They can be classified into five major families, each encompassing several important languages (Ma, 1985):

1. Malayo-Polynesian (Austronesian) family: Chamorro, Ilocano, Tagalog;

2. Sino-Tibetan family: Thai, Yao, Mandarin, Cantonese
3. Austro-Asiatic family: Khmer, Vietnamese, Hmong
4. Papuan family: New Guinean
5. Altaic family: Japanese, Korean

The main languages spoken by Asian/Pacific populations in the United States are Mandarin, Cantonese, Taiwanese, Hakka, Tagalog, Ilocano, Japanese, Korean, Vietnamese, Khmer, Lao, Hmong, Mien, Chamorro, Samoan, and Hindi.

Southeast Asians who emigrate to the U.S. have various bilingual and biliterate backgrounds. Some of them are bilingual or trilingual, whereas others are monolingual. As was noted earlier, some come with prior education and others do not. Some read fluently in many languages; others are illiterate. Moreover, some Southeast Asian groups, like the Hmong, did not have a written language until the 1950s. While the Hmong people have a rich oral history, many are unable to read. These distinctions provide practitioners with a tremendous challenge, as we shall see throughout this issue of *TLD*.

Other important variables include the religious beliefs of the individual and family, which may affect their perceptions of both the world and their handicapping conditions.

Religions

The Asian/Pacific populations have a variety of religious/philosophical beliefs; among the major ones are: Buddhism, Confucianism, Taoism, Shintoism, Animism, Catholicism, and Islamism.

Buddhism, an offshoot of Hinduism, began around the fifth century. Buddha preached kindness and nonviolence. He believed that desire is what causes human misery. Buddhist missionaries first went to Ceylon, which then became the center of Theravada Buddhism. Later, missionaries from Siam, Burma, and Cambodia went to Sri Lanka to seek clarification of the truth (Ma, 1985). Refugees from Laos and Cambodia (now Kampuchea) practice Theravada Buddhism.

Confucianism exerts a strong influence in China and Vietnam. Confucius defined the rules that dictate relationships between father and son, teacher and student, husband and wife, and so forth. His influence spread all the way to Japan and Korea. In another vein, Taoism is derived from the doctrines of Lao Tzu. The basic principle of Taoism, which many Chinese practice, is that one must not interfere with nature but must rather follow its course. Taoism promotes passivity, and those who practice it may display a sense of fatalism about events surrounding them, resulting in resignation and inaction. This basic principle of nonintervention may have a deleterious effect when parents are asked to approve interventions for remediation of language or learning disorders.

Shintoism is the principal religion of Japan, with emphasis upon worship of nature, ancestors, and ancient heroes, and reverence for the spirits of natural forces and emperors. It was the state religion until 1945, before the American occupation.

Animism is another common religion in Southeast Asia. It holds that there are spirits in everything, including one's body, and that demons and spirits exist. Baci, a ritual in animism, is a common practice among the Southeast Asians from Indochina. It is usually performed if one is ill or has to go away on a trip.

The Pacific Islanders have been influenced by Catholicism, and many do practice Catholicism with a mixture of folk beliefs, such as taotaomona/spirits (Chamorro), menehune/spirits (Hawaiian), and the suruhana/healer (Chamorro) (Ashby, 1983). A small portion of Asians are Moslem, scattered from the Malaysian islands to the Philippines. Ancestral worship is a prevailing theme in Asian beliefs, and it is practiced in China, Japan, Korea, and Vietnam. Some Asians may feel that there is nothing that can be done to alter their "karma" (fate) when a family member has a handicapping condition. The Chamorro culture regards the handicapped child as everyone's child and as a gift of God, whereas the Chinese may regard the child as a curse, a result brought about by the wrongdoings of their ancestors.

There are also differences in the child-rearing practices among the various Asian/Pacific cultures. It is not uncommon to find young children taking care of their younger siblings. Discipline may also

---

Children generally are not encouraged to explore and take risks but rather to be cautious and observant.

---

take a different form. A less active, quiet child is often viewed as a good child. Children generally are not encouraged to explore and take risks but rather to be cautious and observant.

Another key variable is the immigration history of the child and his or her family. It is important to understand the major differences among the refugee and immigrant populations in terms of background, such as those demonstrated by the two major groups of refugees, namely the Vietnamese, Chinese, and Hmong (VCH) and the Lao and Khmer (LK).

Immigration background: Home of origin

Refugees: The VCH and LK

Researchers in Indochinese studies have observed tremendous differences within the Indochinese group (Rumbaut & Ima, 1987). For example, there is great diversity in social class among the families of Indochinese students attending U.S. schools. Overall, Vietnamese parents are the most educated, followed by the Chinese-Vietnamese, the Khmer, the Lao, and the Hmong, whose average parental education level is just above Grade One. About 95% of Vietnamese and Chinese-Vietnamese refugees and 75% of the Lao are from urban backgrounds, while more than 50% of the Khmers and 90% of the Hmong come from rural backgrounds. As with any cultural group, heterogeneity within the population must be recognized even though there may be cultural ties and similarities that also link groups together.

The VCHs have similar cultural traits, including sharing of the patrilineal-extended family systems. Patrilineal-extended families were built on a Confucian cultural model that emphasizes family relationships, duties, discipline, filial piety, obedience, parental authority, and respect for the elderly. VCH languages also share some commonalities, in that they are tonal, noninflectional, and essentially monosyllabic.

LK people have common cultural roots, elements of which are borrowed from Indian culture and languages. For example, the Lao and Khmer languages are derived from Sanskrit and Pali. The LKs share similar customs, such as the same form of Theravada Buddhism. The LK group also has a looser neolocal and bilateral system of nuclear family organization than that of VCHs. The Khmer man lives with the wife's family when they are first married, and then sets up his own household. Both parents have authority over family matters.

Professionals in education and allied health services should be sensitive to, and knowledgeable about, the backgrounds of Indochinese students but should be careful to avoid overgeneralization about presumed similarities. Although they have often been referred to as the "boat people," many Indochinese actually traveled long distances on foot to leave their homelands, while others left with the assistance of the United States. The experiences of Indochinese refugees vary greatly. Some left immediately after the fall of Saigon in 1975; others spent many years in resettlement camps at the Thailand border (Walker, 1985). Some families managed to find sponsors to get their families out of their homelands, whereas others lost their families and have suffered great disruptions in their lives (Rumbaut & Ima, 1987). Those who experienced the Khmer Rouge and the Pol Pot era have been severely traumatized.

The VCH and LK cultural groups have different views and expectations. The diversity comes from differences in socioeconomic levels, cultural backgrounds, education, life styles, concepts of illness and healing, self-care practices, child-rearing practices, and family systems (Ebihara, 1968; Libby, 1984; Luangpraseut, 1987; Mitchell, 1987; Scott, 1986; Smalley, 1984; Te, 1987; Wittet, 1983). Misunderstandings caused by cultural differences often result in feelings of vulnerability, mistrust, alienation, stigma, discomfort, and social distance (Goldstein, 1985).

Nonrefugees

Many immigrants from other parts of Asia come to the United States to further their education and then decide to make it their home. Immigrants may elect to petition for permanent residency in the United States. Some immigrants are fluent speakers of English, whereas others have only a limited familiarity with the English language. Even fluent English speakers may prefer to use their first language to communicate at home. Still others, whose English proficiency may be limited, are often employed in jobs where communication in English is not a requirement. Nonrefugee groups include Pacific Islanders, including the people of Guam and the Micronesian Islands, Samoans, and Filipinos.

Pacific Islanders

An increasing number of Pacific Islanders have migrated to the state of Hawaii and the U.S. mainland in the last two decades. The Chamorro people of Guam hold U.S. passports and can travel freely to the U.S. mainland. People from American Samoa are U.S. residents and travel in large numbers to Hawaii, California, and a few other states.

The people of Guam and the Micronesian Islands

A territory of the United States, Guam lies at the southern end of the Mariana Islands in the western Pacific. It is the largest island in the Pacific Ocean between Hawaii and the Philippines—30 miles long and 4 to 9 miles wide. Chamorro is the native language of Guam and also of Saipan, Rota, and Tinian, which make up the Commonwealth of the Northern Mariana Islands. English and Chamorro are the official languages of Saipan, Rota, and Tinian. Residents of the islands speak a variety of languages including Carolinian, Trukese, Yapese, Marshallese, Palauan, Pohnpeian, and Kosraean. There are eleven languages spoken in Saipan and Guam.

The Samoans

Western Samoa is under the rule of the British government, and American Samoa is part of the U.S. territory. During the 1920s some Samoans left to provide the free labor that built the Mormon temples in Hawaii. It was not until the 1950s that large groups of Samoans left for Hawaii and the U.S. mainland. There are approximately 60,000 Samoans living in the United States, and only 30,000 remain on the island of American Samoa.

The indigenous culture of Samoa is a clan culture with an extended family system. The chief (*Matai*), who is elected by the clan members, is responsible for locating resources that include fish, food, land titles, and housing (Shore, 1986). In the Samoan language there is no word for "person," since in the Samoan culture a person is only a part of the whole group. The social system is patrilineal. The chief has authority over titles, although they can also be inherited. Chiefs speak a high form of Samoan, whereas the rest of the people speak "common Samoan." Among the many reasons why Samoans leave their homeland are a search for a better life, access to health care, better education, and an escape from the traditional authoritarian system.

American Samoa is 25 miles by 5 miles and lies 30 miles from Western Samoa. The schools in Samoa are bilingual, using the official languages of Samoan and English. However, many students from American Samoa have encountered academic problems in school and/or are considered to be LEP. Rumbaut and Ima (1987) report that in San Diego county, Samoan students have the lowest grade point average of all groups. Similar reports can be found in Hawaii, where there are also large groups of Samoans.

The Filipinos

There has been a steady flow of immigration from Philippines since the end of World War II. The 1983 Hawaiian census indicated that the Filipino population in Hawaii was over 11% and growing.

The people of the Philippines, an archipelago of more than 7,200 islands, speak a total of 87 mutually unintelligible languages. The major languages are Tagalog, Ilocano, Cebuano, Visayan, and Pampango. Some immigrants from the Philippines do not speak English at home and have little experience with the English language.

KNOWLEDGE REQUIRED TO BECOME A CROSS-CULTURAL COMMUNICATOR

School systems are challenged by the growing numbers of Indochinese students. In neighborhoods where there are large numbers of refugees, professionals such as speech–language pathologists can rely on the natural support system that includes family and community for advice and help. Where resources such as interpreters are scarce, professionals face significant difficulties when trying to provide adequate services in a cross-cultural context.

The question of denying services to culturally diverse populations because professionals are inadequately prepared warrants close scrutiny. Korman (cited in Sue, 1981) describes the dilemma clearly:

The provision of professional services to persons of culturally diverse backgrounds not competent in understanding and providing professional services to such groups shall be considered unethical. It shall be equally unethical to deny such persons professional services because the present staff is inadequately prepared. It shall therefore be the obligation of all service agencies to employ competent persons or to provide continuing education for the present staff to meet the service needs of the culturally diverse population it serves. (p. vii)

Obviously professionals need to become cross-cultural communicators in order to provide adequate services when working with such a culturally and linguistically diverse population.

Obviously professionals need to become cross-cultural communicators in order to provide adequate services when working with such a culturally and linguistically diverse population.

Collecting information: Guidelines for cross-cultural communication

Language learning is affected by many factors. Wong-Fillmore (1985a) indicates that children who are extremely proficient in their home language may not necessarily be the fastest learners of English. In other words, native language proficiency may not be a reliable predictor of success in learning English. Factors leading to successful English acquisition include the number of years devoted to learning English, the amount of English heard, and the kind of English used (Ima & Rumbaut, "Southeast Asian Refugees in American Schools," this issue; Wong-Fillmore, 1985b).

In addition to information regarding the student's language-learning experience, areas such as cultural exposure, educational background, school experience, personal life history, family background, support systems, and health history are essential to a good assessment. A sample questionnaire, presented as an appendix to this article, may be useful for collecting information.

Personal knowledge, skills, and attitudes of professionals

It is of the utmost importance that service providers make a critical examination of their world view, values, beliefs, way of life, communication style, learning style, cognitive style, and personal life history. One should strive for cultural literacy, described by Bjorkland and Bjorkland (1988) as the "broad working knowledge of the traditions, terminology, folklore, and history of our culture." (p. 144) Through these processes, one can gain insight into one's clinical *modus operandi*.

An appreciation and understanding of cultural diversity and affirmation of cultural differences need to be nurtured. Professionals need to develop greater knowledge of the cultural/ethnic composition of this country in order to affirm the existence of these diverse cultures (Cole & Deal, 1986). (For more information on Asian belief systems, see Anderson (1983), Lieban (1979), Moser (1983), and Muecke (1983).)

Knowledge of cultures, languages, and discourse styles

Clinicians need to identify strategies that are culturally and socially relevant. Understanding the differences between oral and literate cultures is relevant in language intervention; for example, as children become acculturated, the language of the curriculum becomes more meaningful. Mastery of academics may be even more difficult for immigrant children because from the beginning there is an absence of shared background in addition to linguistic differences (Gumperz & Hymes, 1972). For example, a child from the mountains of Laos will not know the significance of a Jack-O-Lantern, and a Hmong child may not have had the experience of eating macaroni and cheese for lunch. Chamorro children may be very familiar with typhoons but unacquainted with snow. The Hawaiian student may be quite capable of understanding the details of a volcanic eruption but may fail to appreciate the meaning of a white Christmas.

Speech–language pathologists need to identify "foreground information," or that which is needed to understand the intended meaning of a speaker. Such foregrounding of information may be essential for LEP students in therapy. Highlighting crucial information is the task of the clinician, and Lee ("A Sociocultural Framework for the Assessment of Chinese Children with Special Needs," this issue) provides insight into this process.

Professionals must also question assumptions that are made about what children know (e.g., schema knowledge). Not all students have experienced a birthday party or a family picnic. Furthermore, children may not share assumptions about participant structures (Philips, 1983). Important patterns of verbal and nonverbal behavior learned at home may be quite different from the teacher's expectations. It is rude in the Japanese culture to say "No" in various contexts. One needs to interpret the communicative intent of the answer, since a "Yes" may actually mean "No."

Sociolinguistic rules such as turn-taking, turn-allocation, interruptions, topic shift, topic maintenance, and other conversational rules that underlie the interactions of LEP students must be identified. For example, students from Asia are quiet in the classroom and seldom volunteer information. The classroom is a place where teachers control turn-taking and direct turn-allocations. While these unspoken rules are shared by those who understand them, Asian/Pacific students may need further explanation, exposure, and practice.

Asian/Pacific populations often take meanings literally rather than understanding the implied communicative intent of the speaker. Although LEP students may learn the words and sentences of English, they may operate from a different sociocultural perspective. For example, to Americans the question "Do you have the time?" actually means "What time is it?" Similarly, "Why don't we go to the park?" means "Let's go to the park," and "You like it, don't you?" means "I think you like it." LEP students may have different interpretations and thus may not respond with the expected answers. They may try to give an answer that they believe to be appropriate, such as "Yes, I have the time," rather than "It's two o'clock."

Appropriate usage of the more ritualized sociolinguistic rules—for example, accepting compliments such as "I like your work"; greetings such as "How are you doing?"; leave-taking phrases such as "Goodbye, have a nice day"; or saying "Excuse me"—may have to be taught explicitly.

Clinicians should also increase their knowledge about the home languages of LEP students and try to learn a few words from those languages (Ruhlen, 1975). Learning words in students' languages may set the tone for better communication. However, clinicians must understand that the LEP child's home language (L_1) may be deteriorating while he or she is attempting to become proficient in English.

The discourse systems of Asian/Pacific children include such rules as "Do not speak when you are eating," "Speak only when spoken to," "Do not speak in class," "Be quiet and obedient in class," and "Do not stare at the person you talk to." Whereas these students in an American school may be told by their teacher to ask questions and to challenge assumptions, the same children may be told by their parents at home to be observant and respectful of authority. The significance of such inconsistencies between home and school cultures must not be minimized (Weade & Green, 1985).

Knowledge of family and support systems

Children placed in a new environment must be given time to develop their social circle. Since all encounters are in essence social encounters (Taylor, 1986), children must feel part of a group before they can engage in peer interactions. Fellow students from the same ethnic, linguistic, and cultural backgrounds who tend to be sociable need to be encouraged to work with the newcomers (Erickson, 1979) to show them the rules of the classroom and the school.

Professionals should consult with classroom teachers, who are frequently the best informants about the children's social status. They should also make use of all people who provide support for the child. This may include parents, siblings, friends, neighbors, relatives, and even the community as a whole. For example, to whom does the parent go to seek advice? Who provides assistance when there is a family crisis or emergency? Who makes the decisions about education in the family? Who provides translation for the family if it is needed?

As always, clinicians need to obtain detailed information about the student and his or her family. Once a referral is received, a face-to-face interview with the family should be arranged. If time allows, a home visit by a member of the assessment team should be made. In addition to using the background questionnaire in the appendix, information should be obtained about what the family is like, how the child is functioning, and what child care needs may exist. Questions such as "What is a typical day like?" "What do you do during the weekends?" and "What does your child like or dislike?" would be appropriate.

During any personal contact with an Asian student's family, clinicians should always keep in mind the cultural values associated with the family's background. As is noted elsewhere in this issue, individual family members are expected to submerge behaviors and feelings in a way as to reflect credit on the entire family. Inappropriate behavior on the part of one family member can cause the whole family to be shamed and "lose face." Failure in school may be considered to be shameful behavior; such problems are typically handled within the family as much as possible, without public admission. The same restraint of feelings that is valued in Asian culture may be seen as passive and inhibited behavior in American culture. Professionals need to identify LEP populations, including their language backgrounds, residing in their school district. Especially when only a few students from a particular language group are scattered among different schools in the district, efforts should be made to locate more proficient students who speak the LEP student's language and to enlist their assistance. This may also lead to their families supporting one another. Additionally, service professionals should consider the possibility that peer teaching by more proficient Asian students may be less threatening to the Asian LEP population. Peer instruction may also be more closely matched with the LEP's learning style.

It is imperative that professionals provide assessment and intervention within a cross-cultural framework using all available resources from both cultures.

REFERENCES

Anderson, J.N. (1983). Health and illness in Filipino immigrants. *Western Journal of Medicine, 139*(6), 811–819.

Ashby, G. (1983) *Micronesian customs and beliefs.* Eugene, OR: Rainy Day Press.

Bjorkland, D., & Bjorkland, B. (1988, January). Cultural literacy. *Parents,* p. 144.

Cole, L., & Deal, V. (1986). *Communication disorders in multicultural populations.* Rockville, MD: American Speech–Language–Hearing Association.

Ebihara, M.M. (1968). *Svay, a Khmer village in Cambodia.* Unpublished doctoral dissertation, Columbia University.

Erickson, F. (1979). Talking down: Some cultural sources of miscommunication in interracial interviews. In A. Wolfgang (Ed.), *Nonverbal Behavior* (pp. 99–126). New York: Academic Press.

Goldstein, B.L. (1985). *Schooling for cultural transition: Hmong girls and boys in American high schools.* Madison, WI: University of Wisconsin.

Gumperz, J., & Hymes, D. (1972). *Directions in sociolinguistics: The ethnography of communication.* New York: Holt, Rinehart, Winston.

Libby, M.R. (1984). *The self care practices of the Hmong hilltribes from Laos.* Unpublished master's thesis, University of Missouri.

Lieban, R. (1979). Sex differences and cultural dimensions of medical phenomena in a Philippine setting. In P. Morley & R. Wallis (Eds.), *Culture and curing* (pp. 99–114). Pittsburgh: University of Pittsburgh Press.

Luangpraseut, K. (1987). *Introduction to Lao culture.* Paper presented at the Southeast Asia Education Fair, Stockton, CA.

Ma, L.J. (1985). Cultural diversity. In A.K. Dutt (Ed.), *Southeast Asia: Realm of contrast.* Boulder, CO: Westview Press.

Mitchell, F.S. (1987). *From refugee to rebuilder: Cambodian women in America.* Unpublished doctoral dissertation, Syracuse University.

Moser, R. (1983). Indochinese refugees and American health care: Adaptive comparisons of Cambodians and Hmong. In J.H. Morgan (Ed.), *Third world medicine and social change* (pp. 141–156). Lanham, MD: University Press of America.

Muecke, M.A. (1983). In search of healers—Southeast Asian refugees in the American health care system. *Western Journal of Medicine, 139*(6), 835–840.

Philips, S. (1983). *The invisible culture.* New York: Longman.

Ruhlen, M. (1975). *A guide to the languages of the world (Language Universals Project).* San Diego: Los Amigos Research Associates.

Rumbaut, T., & Ima, K. (1987). *The adaptation of Southeast Asian refugee youth: A comparative study.* San Diego: San Diego State University.

Scott, G.M. (1986). *Migrants without mountains: The sociocultural adjustment among the Lao Hmong refugees in San Diego.* Unpublished doctoral dissertation, University of California, San Diego.

Shore, B. (1986). *Salailua village.* Chicago: University of Chicago Press.

Smalley, W.A. (1984). Adaptive language strategies for the Hmong: From Asian mountains to American ghettos. *Language Science, 7*(2), 241–269.

Sue, D.W. (1981). *Counseling the culturally different: Theory and practice.* New York: John Wiley and Sons.

Taylor, O. (1986). *Treatment of communication disorders in culturally and linguistically diverse populations.* San Diego: College-Hill Press.

Te, H.D. (1987). *Introduction to Vietnamese culture.* San Diego: Multifunctional Resource Center, San Diego State University.

Walker, C.L. (1985). Learning English: The Southeast Asian refugee experience. *Topics in Language Disorders, 5*(4), 53–65.

Weade, R., & Green, J.L. (1985). Talking to learn: Social and academic requirements for classroom participation. *Peabody Journal of Education, 62,* 6–19.

Wittet, S. (1983). *Information needs of Southeast Asian refugees in medical situations.* Unpublished master's thesis, University of Washington.

Wong-Fillmore, L. (1985a). Learning a second language: Chinese children in the American classroom. In J.E. Alatis & J.J. Staczek (Eds.), *Perspectives on bilingualism and bilingual education* (pp. 436–452). Washington, DC: Georgetown University Press.

Wong-Fillmore, L. (1985b). When does teacher talk work as input? In S.M. Gass & C.G. Madden (Eds.), *Input in second language acquisition* (pp. 17–50). Rowley, MA: Newbury House.

Appendix
Background information questionnaire

INSTRUCTIONS: We are going to ask you some questions about your child's medical history, educational history, and related areas. Please be as thorough as you can in your remarks. If I am not clear, please stop me and ask me to say it again. If you don't feel comfortable about answering the question, please let me know. All we want to do here is to obtain as much background information as possible, and, since you are the child's parent, we feel that you have much to contribute.

1. When was your child born?
2. Was this a hospital?
3. How was the pregnancy?
   How was your health during pregnancy?
4. How was the delivery
5. Were any instruments used?
6. Were there any postnatal complications?
7. How was your child's physical development?
   Were there any handicapping conditions?
   If yes, who made the diagnosis?
   When?   How did you feel about it?
8. Was your child ever hospitalized?
   If yes, where?
   When?   Why?
   How long?   Who was the physician?
9. Were there problems in feeding?
10. Were there any prolonged illnesses?
    High fever?   Accidents?
11. Has his/her hearing been checked?
12. Has his/her vision been checked?
13. Has he/she seen a dentist?
    What is the condition of his/her teeth?
14. What is his/her diet history?
15. How is his/her diet now?
16. Does he/she have a pediatrician?
    Who?

Has your child seen any other medical specialist?
If yes, who?
When?   Where?   Why?
17. When did you come to the United States?
    Where did you come from?
    Did you live in a city or in the country?
    Why did you come?
    For refugees: Was he/she ever in a refugee camp?
    How long?   Tell us about it:
18. Was he/she ever on a boat?
    How long?
    Tell us about it:
19. How many brothers and sisters does he/she have?
    Are they all here?
20. Are there any family members who had or have difficulty in speaking or hearing, or problems such as mental retardation, cerebral palsy, cleft palate, or stuttering?
    If yes, please explain:
21. Was your child ever in school?
    Where?   How long?
    What was the language of instruction?
22. How was his/her performance in school?
    Grade?   Attendance?
23. Do you have a report from the school?
    Any comments from the teacher?

24. Was he/she involved in special programs?
   How did he/she do?
25. Was he/she in a day-care or child care program?
   If yes, how did he/she do?
26. Did he/she repeat a grade?
   If yes, why?
27. How was the program similar to his/her program now?
   How was it different?
28. Has your child had sufficient opportunity to learn in school?
29. How many are living in your home?
   Who are they (in relation to child)?
30. Who takes care of your child after school?
   What language(s) does he/she speak?
31. Who makes the decisions at home?
32. Does your child have his/her own room?
   If no, whom does your child share the room with?
   Where does he/she study?
33. Does your child mostly play inside the house?
   Outside?   By himself/herself?   With a sibling?
34. Whom does he/she play with?
   Are they older or younger?
   How does he/she play?
35. What does he/she like to play?
   What toys do you have?
   Does he/she read?   What books and magazines do you have?
36. Do you work?   If yes, what do you do?
   Where did you learn English?
   How long have you been speaking English?
   How do you rate your English?
   When are you home?
37. Does your spouse work?   If yes, what does he/she do?

Does he/she speak English?
When did he/she start to learn English?
When is he/she at home?
38. Do you receive welfare?
   Does your child receive a free lunch?
39. What is your educational background?
   Your spouse's educational background?
40. What languages are used at home?
41. When did your child say his/her first word?
   When did he/she learn English?
   How do you feel about his/her speech now?
   Where did he/she learn English?
   How do you rate his/her English?
42. Do you feel that your child understands everything you say?
   In home language?   In English?
   Explain:
43. What language does your child speak when he/she responds to you?
   What language does he/she understand/speak best?
44. Does your child speak your native language with his siblings?
   Friends?
45. Do your children speak your native language or English among themselves?
46. Does your child mix languages in the same sentence?
47. Does your child frequently use hand and facial expressions to communicate needs rather than words and sentences?
48. Do you help your child with homework?
49. How do you feel about his/her maintenance of your native language?
   Do you send him/her to language school on the weekend?
50. What do you expect the school to do for your child?

51. Do you attend any social functions? Where?
With whom? What are your leisure activities?
52. Do you have difficulty disciplining your child?
His/her siblings?
53. What responsibilities are placed on your child?
On his/her siblings?
54. Does he/she dress himself?
55. Does he/she know your telephone number and address?

56. Do you read to him/her?
What are his/her favorite stories?
Can he/she tell the story back to you?
57. Does he/she watch television?
What is his/her favorite program?
58. Do you think your child is a hard worker?
If so, why?
Do you think your child is lazy?
Why?

COMMENTS:

Considerations in assessing English language performance of Native American children

Gail A. Harris, MS
Co-Director
Native American Research and
Training Center
University of Arizona
Tucson, Arizona

THE PERFORMANCE characteristics of Native American children on measures of intelligence and psycholinguistic ability appear to be culturally determined. Results of studies of Native American children on the Wechsler Intelligence Scale—Revised (WISC-R) suggest that their performance intelligence quotient (IQ) is consistently and significantly higher than their verbal IQ (Lutey, 1977; McShane, 1980; Mishra, 1982). This discrepancy has not yet been clearly explained. Explanations for lower verbal IQ scores have included the possibility of cultural bias inherent in the construction and administration of the instrument, reduced language environments of the children, a cultural emphasis on performance rather than verbal and abstract skills, and possible hearing loss associated with otitis media (Browne, 1984).

This article was supported in part through funding from the Normal Institute of Handicapped Research, grant number 0083C0094.

Top Lang Disord, 1985, 5(4), 45-52

In addition, studies of the performance of Native American children on the Illinois Test of Psycholinguistic Ability (Garber, 1971; Kuske, 1969; Lombardi, 1970) indicate superior scores on visual-motor tasks and reduced performance on verbal tasks. These differences have been attributed to culturally determined child-rearing practices (Kirk, 1972). Inadequate mastery of English continues to be the most serious educational problem facing American Indian children (Rameriz, 1976). The determination of whether this "inadequacy" in English language skills and the discrepancy between performance and verbal tasks is due to bilingualism, biculturalism, or a language pathology has, in part, been the responsibility of speech-language pathologists. These professionals have been faced with the challenge of assessing a child's language skills in a nonbiased manner in order to make an appropriate diagnosis and be able to recommend or provide appropriate intervention.

The professional may make two major types of errors. The first is to assume that a child has a speech or language handicap when, in fact, he or she is using a dialect of English that is appropriate to his or her culture and community. Also, the child probably has greater proficiency in a language that is not tested during assessment. This has been a central theme of discussions concerning nonbiased assessment. An erroneous assumption such as this may create secondary problems for the child, resulting in negative self-concept as a language user, as well as misdiagnosis and inappropriate placement in a special education program.

The other error professionals may make is to conclude that there is no disorder when one indeed exists. This error may result from a lack of confidence in test instruments, the assumption that a non-verbal child is behaving in a culturally appropriate way, or an absence of information regarding aberrant versus dialectal linguistic forms (Terrell & Terrell, 1983). The long-lasting deleterious effect of such a decision may result in drop out or school failure, frustration on the part of the teacher and the child, and, ultimately, language disability in adulthood.

Speech-language pathologists must develop a perspective of the American Indian child as a language learner and user within the linguistic and cultural context of his or her family and community in order to assess the child's language competence adequately. Language clinicians and researchers must consider specific cultural variables when interpreting the performance of Native American children on tests of speech and language. Among these are child-rearing practices and cultural expectations for language use in the home, school, and test environments. The clinician may take specific steps to gain cultural sensitivity and knowledge that will assist in the interpretation of Indian children's performance.

THE RELATIONSHIP BETWEEN CULTURE AND COMMUNICATION

Ethnography of communication refers to the study of speaking, focusing on societal norms and values governing the speech act, as well as the principles and strategies underlying the act (Siler &

Labadie-Wondergem, 1982). Traditionally, the relationship between culture and communication has been the domain of sociolinguists and anthropologists who have conducted ethnographic studies among many of the world's cultures. The increase in the number of minority-language children in the United States, coupled with the dictates of P L 94-142 regarding nonbiased assessment procedures, have forced educators and other professionals, including language specialists, to come face to face with a new skill necessary for clinical competency—that of understanding the effects of culture on communication.

In a study of child-rearing practices in urban Indian families, Miller (1975) reported that the majority of the families, whether their identity tended to be traditional or urban, did not use Anglo child-rearing techniques to any significant extent. Red Horse (1983) contends that, while some gradual changes in cultural values have resulted from intermarriage across racial and tribal lines, these changes do not necessarily bring about middle-class values as a standard for living.

The influence of culture on language use begins with the child-rearing practices of a group. These practices may persist even when external markers (e.g., dress, location, language spoken) of cultural identity are no longer apparent.

Child-rearing practices

Culturally determined child-rearing practices and expectations for child behavior may have a marked effect on the language use of a child. Such practices and attitudes may affect the child's willingness

or unwillingness to speak, the child's average length of utterance, response time, frequency with which the child initiates conversation, and the child's turn-taking behaviors. Significant differences exist between child-rearing practices of Indian tribes and those of the dominant culture. Such differences may yield culturally determined test-taking behaviors that result in lower performance levels on tests such as those used to measure intelligence and language skills.

In many Indian cultures, infants are taught not to cry. Older children are taught to be silent in the presence of an adult, especially if the adult is a stranger (Blanchard, 1983; Weeks, 1975). This background may account for much of the nonverbal behavior and the truncated utterances exhibited by Indian children in classroom and testing situations. Single-word or nonverbal responses are sometimes interpreted as symptoms of a communication or psychological disorder, though they may be culturally appropriate behaviors for certain minority children. Labov (1976) found that children who spoke in truncated utterances in school or during interviews with strangers were highly effective and creative communicators in culturally realistic settings and when interacting verbally with their peers.

The few studies of Indian mother–child interaction and maternal expectations for language behavior have discovered culturally determined differences between Indian and Anglo mothers. Freedman (1979) observed differences between the ways in which Navajo and Anglo mothers got the attention of their infants. While Anglo mothers spoke to their infants con-

While Anglo mothers spoke to their infants continually, evoking arm and leg movement, Navajo mothers were silent, using their eyes to attract their infants' gaze; the Navajo infants responded by gazing back.

tinually, evoking arm and leg movement, Navajo mothers were silent, using their eyes to attract their infants' gaze; the Navajo infants responded by gazing back.

Guilmet (1979) attempted to isolate the cultural factor of maternal attitudes toward verbal and nonverbal activity of preschool-aged children in a study comparing the manner in which Navajo and Anglo mothers described and characterized the speech and nonverbal behavior of their children. Navajo and Anglo mothers viewed videotapes of preschool children involved in play; the children exhibited varied levels of physical and verbal activity. Guilmet concluded that Navajo mothers attribute distinctly different meaning to active speech and physical behavior than Anglo mothers. While the Navajo mothers tended to perceive extremely active speech behavior as discourteous, restless, self-centered, and undisciplined, the Anglo mothers interpreted the same behavior as self-disciplined, exciting to observe, evidence of active learning, and advantageous to the child's development.

Kirk (1972), in a review of ethnic differences in performance on the Illinois Test of Psycholinguistic Ability (ITPA), concurred with earlier studies (Garber, 1971; Kuske, 1969; Lombardi, 1970) attributing the superiority of Papago, Navajo, and Pueblo Indian children in visual-motor sequencing ability to culturally determined child-rearing practices. He postulated that, since Indian cultures rely heavily on visual rather than auditory-vocal channels, this may, in part, account for the children's performance differences on the ITPA.

Indian Headstart children in the Southwest typically score well above average on measures of gross motor, social development, and self-help skills, while scoring below average for fine motor and language skills. These differences may be related to the child-rearing practices of many Southwestern tribes, in which children become independent at a very early age. Indian children are often responsible for caring for younger siblings and spend a great deal of play time outdoors rather than watching television or playing with crayons and books indoors under the supervision of, and in close interaction with, adults.

The social interactions of children with adults and the methods used to instruct children appear to differ markedly between Indian and non-Indian family units. Within many Indian cultures, the responsibility for the care and training of children is often assumed by people other than the parent. These individuals are usually members of the clan or tribal community, such as older siblings, uncles, aunts, or grandparents. Rarely is the Indian child sent to a babysitter or day-care facility for care and supervision by someone who is not a tribal member and who may employ different methods of communication and interaction.

Indian children are typically present as

observers at all tribal events and usually assume a quiet, passive role. Their culture dictates that through such quiet observation the children learn the customs and rituals of the tribe in which they will have an active, vital role as they mature. This practice contrasts with the experience of Anglo children, who are typically excluded from adult events and show impatience when they are expected to sit quietly and listen without being directly involved in a social activity.

Silent listening and watching appear to be the culturally determined methods of learning skills (e.g., weaving, pottery, beadwork) in Indian cultures. Use of speech is minimal in both the instructional model (adult to child) and the performance outcome (child to adult). Typically, demonstration of skill does not involve verbal performance but the display of physical evidence (e.g., a dance) or material evidence (e.g., a completed piece of beadwork). Instead of long periods of observation, non-Indian children receive elaborate verbal instructions describing the full scope of tasks. Verbal interaction and instruction while involved in tasks (e.g., baking a cake or building a model airplane) are characteristic of Anglo parent–child interactions. Western Apache children are chided for "acting like a white man" if they speak in English around the village or if they are too talkative (Basso, 1970, 1979). Therefore, pressuring an Apache child to answer repeated questions, especially to answer in English, may put the child into a cultural conflict. His or her resulting behavior (silence) probably does not indicate a lack of potential or knowledge; instead it may reflect cultural integrity.

In summary, Indian children may not participate verbally in classroom activities and may exhibit minimal verbal competencies during interviews and testing because of social conditions for participation learned in the home or community environment. Indian children's demonstrated preference for, and reliance on, the visual channel rather than the verbal, as well as their widely reported silent behavior seem to reflect the children's early cultural training.

Development and use of tribal language

The development and use of tribal language by young Indian children appears to have different characteristics when compared with the development and use of English in mainstream U.S. culture. Attempts to speak the tribal language before the child is capable of correct articulation are discouraged. Indeed, when the language of a culture is an unwritten or sacred language, with no secular dialect or child-appropriate materials for oral reading, practice in the language may be limited.

When children of the Omaha Indian tribe learn the tribal language, no grammatical slip is allowed to pass uncorrected (Spicer, 1969). As a result, there is no "child talk" or "baby talk" such as observed in English-speaking children. In a recounting of the process for teaching the Menominee language, Montgomery (1982) states that traditional methods discourage early performance of language by the student. Faulty performance is discouraged, often without any explanation of the nature of the student's errors.

In addition to a culturally specific

expectation governing language learning, stringent rules govern adult language use within certain tribes. These include the prohibition of communication between the sexes at certain times and limitations on who may speak to tribal elders and medicine people. Basso (1970) relates that "the critical factor in the Apache's decision to speak or keep silent seems always to be the nature of his relationship to other people" (p. 216). In specific situations within Apache tribal culture, silence is expected. These include meeting strangers, interacting during initial stages of courtship, parental greeting of children when they come home after a long absence, and being with people who are sad. While these situations differ, they are similar in that the participants perceive their relationship with the other person in each situation as "unpredictable or ambiguous" (Basso, 1970, p. 225).

Professionals who are unaware of these restrictions on verbal interaction should be cautious of interpreting behaviors that are culturally appropriate as pathological or deviant. A child's reluctance to speak, use of restricted codes, or refusal to engage in verbal communication with an examiner must not be interpreted as an indication of a lack of communicative ability. In some instances, these behaviors reflect appropriate cultural patterns. Thus culturally determined child-rearing practices and expectations for child behavior (including language behavior) may yield culturally determined test-taking behaviors and lower performance levels on certain instruments used to test intelligence and language skills.

Different scores on a measure may conceal the underlying fact that an attribute or skill is phenomenologically normal within each culture's terms or constraints. Goldschmidt (1971) discusses cultural differences in the context of the Greek word *arete*, which describes the composite qualities a person should ideally possess according to the consensus of a community. If the goal is to understand the character of an individual's behavior, whether normal or pathological, the context of the value system within which the individual was raised must be known. Behavior is meaningful only when set against the arete of an individual's childhood culture.

THE ASSESSMENT PROCESS

Ethnographic analysis of the assessment process reveals several factors that might affect the performance of minority-language children, especially Native American children. Wolfram (1983) discusses the three sociolinguistic levels related to testing: (a) linguistic form, (b) task characteristics, and (c) social context. All are important factors to consider in interpreting a child's performance on language measures.

Language assessment, even for monolingual and monocultural English-speaking children, is more an art than a science. Standardized measures of language performance in English abound, but most do not stand up to psychometric scrutiny (McCauley & Swisher, 1982). Professionals serving bilingual and bicultural children may select from among available tests to measure English skills; however, many of the embedded test items reflect cultural or linguistic biases that may negatively affect the child's performance. Furthermore, none of these tests provide normative data that are appropriate for the Native American population. The need for normative data appropriate for each Native American population presents an awesome and perhaps impossible task given that approximately 300 distinct tribal languages exist, with wide variations of use within tribal units.

Even if the Native American child is a monolingual English speaker, the assessment process may contain bias related to (a) the social situation and interaction of the testing environment; (b) the linguistic task characteristics of the instruments; (c) the administration procedures (which may limit or govern practice and feedback); (d) the "acceptable" responses; and (e) the normative data provided for interpretation.

Because of the paucity of research regarding Native Americans, language specialists serving this population must (a) review the available standardized tests and determine which are the least biased; (b) adapt existing tests to meet specified needs; (c) devise appropriate methods of informal language assessment; and (d) calculate norms of performance on the measures they use that are appropriate to their specific population.

Test administration

Typically, formal assessment procedures are carried out in a clinical or school setting with an adult stranger who does not share social class or minority membership with the child. Furthermore, the assessment process is directed by the adult, so that the adult determines what will be discussed and how long the process will continue.

Typically, formal assessment procedures are carried out in a clinical or school setting with an adult stranger who does not share social class or minority membership with the child.

Studies have indicated that Indian children tend to be nonverbal in totally teacher-directed activities, especially activities in which verbal responses are demanded of the participants (Dumont, 1972; Philips, 1972; Philipsen, 1972). Numerous interpretations of a testing situation are possible. The individual being tested may be fearful and apprehensive, or see it as a competitive challenge and an opportunity for social interaction.

Given the cultural orientation of Indian children previously discussed, the formal testing procedure is more likely to be one in which the Indian child will not exhibit his or her true level of linguistic competence.

The Indian child may be unwilling to ask questions or to admit confusion. The child may desire to please the tester or to finish the task quickly, falsely stating that he or she understands the task. The response time allowed for a child may have to be increased. The pragmatic rules of some cultures require contemplation of questions prior to response to indicate that the question is considered valuable and worthy of thoughtful consideration. Such latency of response should not be interpreted as a processing problem.

The first stage to all assessment practices, that of "establishing rapport," takes on new meaning and presents unique challenges when the client is a member of a minority group, especially if the examiner is not a member of that group. The professional must take ample time to interact with the child before the formal testing process to assure that the child understands the task to be performed and what type of responses are expected from him or her.

The linguistic task characteristics of formal assessment, which include methods of giving directions and the language structure of the test itself (e.g., "Tell me all about this"; "Here is a dress" then "Here are two _____"), may be biased against minority children. The typical response of Southwest Indian children on the Verbal Expression subtest of the ITPA when instructed to "Tell me all about this" was, for example, "It's a nail." When encouraged to elaborate, they would generally repeat the label or say nothing at all.

More expansive utterances were generally elicited from these children when they were instructed to retell a story to the examiner (e.g., the Story Retelling Task of the Goldman-Fristoe Test of Articulation) from pictoral representations, or when allowed to describe a recent event of relevance to the child and his or her community. Wolfram (1983) states succinctly that "the more distant an individual's everyday speaking style is from the style of testing tasks, the greater potential for task interference" (p. 29).

Test interpretation

To circumvent the bias intrinsic in standardized testing, the professional should identify regional, tribal, or community dialectal features, as well as cultural factors relative to language use. Only then may appropriate judgments be made regarding the language performance of children in the school district or community. As these differences are documented, the examiner may adapt the list of responses deemed appropriate for specific items, facilitating appropriate diagnoses of disorders and identifying curricular recommendations to classroom teachers and curriculum committees regarding the children's instructional needs. Such adaptations should, of course, be noted on the protocol and in the test report.

It must be stated that while the testing methods that are used and the linguistic responses that are expected in formal assessments may not be familiar to the child, they are the sort of methods and expectations that the child must face repeatedly during his or her academic career. Ways of helping the child respond to such demands should be considered by the educational team, which includes the speech-language pathologist, the psychologist, and the classroom teacher.

Local norms

There has been some controversy regarding the efficacy of establishing local norms for standardized instruments. Some professionals believe this practice is prejudicial because it lowers performance expectations for some children. Others believe that the only appropriate diagnosis is achieved by comparing an individual's performance against that of his or her community peer group.

Evard and Sabers (1979) review procedures for improving the validity of speech and language tests for use with ethnic or racial groups. These procedures include (a) developing a new test; (b) modifying test items or required responses on existing tests; and (c) developing new norms for existing tests.

The development of local norms for existing tests seems an efficient and fair method for speech-language pathologists to use. Evard and McGrady (1974) found that as specific norms were developed for ethnic and racial groups (e.g., Papago Indian, Mexican American, Black, Anglo), the number of children identified as speech or language impaired decreased.

Bayles and Harris (1982) and Tomoeda and Lennertz (1984) used a similar procedure in studies involving Native American children. The resulting local norms were found to be a useful standard, even though they were lower than published test norms. These local norms appear appropriate within their communities for distinguishing disorder from difference.

SUGGESTIONS FOR GAINING CULTURAL SENSITIVITY

Finally, an increased awareness and sensitivity to the cultural patterns that exist within a community will help the professional make clinical judgments about language use by community members. It is important to note that the information offered here may not apply to all Native American tribes; thus the suggestions offered may not be appropriate for every community setting. However, the following suggestions may be helpful:

- Be aware that tribes are distinct and sovereign nations, and that levels of acculturation vary markedly both inter- and intratribally.
- Be willing to attend tribal social events. This may result in: (a) an increase in your status within the community; (b) an increase in the willingness of parents and children to interact with you freely; (c) an increase in your understanding of the community; and (d) an opportunity to observe parent–child interactions.
- Discuss your desire to make appropriate judgments and bring about effective intervention with individuals who can provide information about the tribe's culture, language structure and use, tribal attitudes toward disabilities, and mistakes your predecessors may have made. Researchers have been unwelcome in many Indian communities because of past studies that were conducted without the tribe's permission and without sharing the results of the studies with tribal members. Many traditional Indian beliefs about handicaps and disabilities are different from the beliefs and explanations of modern medicine. These beliefs must be identified and respected, especially in case history interviews with parents. Sensitivity to these issues will have a great effect on the development of a complete and acceptable intervention strategy.

•   •   •

The concept of biased assessment suggests images of prejudice, discrimination, and stereotyping. In addition, it refers to error in decisions, predictions, and placement of members of particular ethnic and racial groups (Cleary, Humphreys, Kendrick, & Wesman, 1975). The result of assessment errors is that children do not receive appropriate services. Despite the paucity of linguistically appropriate tests, however, it is important to assess language skills. Any child's performance on a test is a reflection of past learning in both formal and informal environments. As noted by Salvia and Ysseldyke (1978), the level of acculturation is the most important characteristic in evaluating a child's performance on a test, although sometimes it is the most ignored.

To appropriately measure and evaluate the English performance of minority-language children on measures of speech and language, the examiner must be familiar with the behavioral characteristics of the cultural group as they relate to language learning and language use. The level to which the particular children employ the traditional linguistic-cultural practices of their ethnic minority group must be determined in order to assess performance appropriately.

The elimination of bias in decision making will not be achieved through the development of new test instruments alone. Children's performance must be compared to that of their cultural age-mates. In addition, their level of mainstream acculturation must be assessed. The ecological/ethnographic perspective allows for evaluation within the contexts of home and school, peer group and community, including the interrelationships between these contexts (Bailey & Harbin, 1980). Although assessment in the first language of the bilingual and bicultural child is not addressed here, this aspect of assessment is not unimportant; indeed, it is critical. However, present emphasis has been on certain cultural factors as they may affect performance of bicultural children whose primary language is not English.

REFERENCES

Bailey, D.B., & Harbin, G.L. (1980). Nondiscriminatory evaluation. *Exceptional Children, 46*(8), 590–595.

Basso, K. (1970). To give up on words . . . silence in western Apache culture. *S.W. Journal of Anthropology, 26*(3), 213–230.

Basso, K. (1979). *Portraits of "The Whiteman" linguistic play and cultural symbols among the Western Apache.* London, UK: Cambridge University Press.

Bayles, K., & Harris, G. (1982). Evaluating speech-language skills in Papago Indian children. *Journal of American Indian Education. 21*(2), 11–20.

Blanchard, E.L. (1983). The growth and development of American Indian children and Alaskan native children. In G.J. Powell (Ed.), *The psychological development of minority group children* (pp. 115–130). New York: Brunner/Mazel.

Browne, D.B. (1984). WISC-R scoring patterns among native Americans of the Northern Plains. *White Cloud Journal, 3*(2), 3–16.

Cleary, T., Humphreys, L., Kendrick, S., & Wesman, A. (1975). Educational uses of tests with disadvantaged students. *American Psychologist, 30*, 15–41.

Dumont, R. (1972). Learning English and how to be silent: studies in Sioux and Cherokee classrooms. In C. Cazden, V. John, and D. Hymes (Eds.), *Functions of Language in the Classroom* (pp. 344–369). New York: Teachers College Press.

Evard, B.L., & McGrady, H.J. (1974). *Development of local language norms for Papago Indians, Mexican Americans, Blacks, and Anglos.* Paper presented at the annual meeting of the American Speech-Language-Hearing Association. Las Vegas, Nevada.

Evard, B.L., & Sabers, D.L. (1979). Speech and language testing with distinct ethnic-racial groups: a survey of procedures for improving validity. *Journal of Speech and Hearing Disorders, 44*(3), 271–281.

Freedman, D.G. (1979, January). Ethnic differences in babies. *Human Nature Magazine*, pp. 36–43.

Garber, M. (1971). *Ethnicity and measures of educability: Differences among Navajo, Pueblo, and rural Spanish-American first graders on measures of learning style, hearing, vocabulary, entry skills, motivation, and home environment processes.* Unpublished doctoral dissertation, University of Southern California.

Goldschmidt, W. (1971). Arete-motivation and models for behavior. In I. Galdstone (Ed.), *The Interface Between Psychiatry and Anthropology* (pp. 55–87). New York: Brunner/Mazel.

Guilmet, G.M. (1979). Maternal perceptions of urban Navajo and Caucasian children's classroom behavior. *Human Organization, 38*(1), 87–91.

Kirk, S.A. (1972, October). Ethnic differences in psycholinguistic abilities. *Exceptional Children,* pp. 112–118.

Kuske, I.I. (1969). *Psycholinguistic abilities of Sioux Indian children.* Unpublished doctoral dissertation, University of South Dakota.

Labov, W. (1976, Fall). Systematically misleading data from test questions. *Urban Review, 9,* 146–169.

Lombardi, T.P. (1970). Psycholinguistic abilities of Papago Indian school children. *Exceptional Children, 36,* 485–493.

Lutey, D. (1977). *Individual intelligence testing: A manual and sourcebook* (2nd ed.). Greeley, CO: Carol L. Lutey Publishing.

McCauley, R., & Swisher, L. (1982, November). *Psychometric review of language and articulation tests for preschool children.* Paper presented at the annual meeting of the American Speech-Language-Hearing Association, Toronto.

McShane, D. (1980). A review of scores of American Indian children on the Wechsler Intelligence Scales. *White Cloud Journal, 1*(4), 3–10.

Miller, D. (1975). *Native American families in the city.* San Francisco: Institute for Scientific Analysis.

Mishra, S.P. (1982). The WISC-R and evidence of item bias for native American Navajos. *Psychology in the Schools, 19,* 458–464.

Montgomery, J.A. (1982). Natural text and delayed oral production: an indigenous method for teaching American Indian languages. In F. Barkin, E.A. Brandt, & J. Ornstein-Galicia (Eds.), *Bilingualism and language contact: Spanish, English and Native American lan-*

guages. New York and London: Teacher's College, Columbia University.

Philips, S. (1972). Acquisition of roles for appropriate speech usage. In R.D. Abrahams & R.C. Troike (Eds.), *Language and cultural diversity in American education* (pp. 167–183). Englewood Cliffs, NJ: Prentice-Hall.

Philipsen, G. (1972). Navajo world view and cultural patterns of speech: a case study in ethnorhetoric. *Speech Monographs, 39,* 132–139.

Rameriz, B. (1976). Background paper on American Indian exceptional children. Reston, VA: National Advisory Council on Education, Council for Exceptional Children.

Red Horse, J. (1983). Indian family values and experiences. In G.J. Powell (Ed.), *The psychosocial development of minority group children* (pp. 258–272). New York: Brunner/Mazel.

Salvia, J., & Ysseldyke, J.E. (1978). *Assessment in special and remedial education.* Boston: Houghton-Mifflin.

Siler, I.C., & Labadie-Wondergem, D. (1982). In F. Barkin, E.A. Brandt, & J. Ornstein-Galicia (Eds.), *Bilingualism and language contact: Spanish, English and Native American languages* (pp. 93–99). New York and London: Teacher's College, Columbia University Press.

Spicer, E.H. (1969). *A short history of the Indians of the United States.* New York: Van Norstrand Reinholt.

Terrell, S.L., & Terrell, F. (1983). Distinguishing linguistic differences from disorders: The past, present, and future of nonbiased assessment. *Topics in Language Disorders, 3*(3), 1–8.

Tomoeda, C., & Lennertz, M. (1984, November). *Performance of Apache children on the Test of Language Development.* Paper presented at the annual meeting of the American Speech-Language-Hearing Association, San Francisco.

Weeks, T. (1975, November). *The speech of Indian children: Paralinguistic and registral aspects of the Yakima dialect.* Paper presented at the annual meeting of the National Council of Teachers of English, San Diego, CA. (ERIC Document Reproduction Service No. ED 128 838)

Wolfram, W.A. (1983). Test interpretation and sociolinguistic differences. *Topics in Language Disorders, 3*(3), 21–35.

Learning English: the Southeast Asian refugee experience

Constance L. Walker, PhD
Assistant Professor
Department of Curriculum &
  Instruction
University of Minnesota
Minneapolis, Minnesota

OF THE MANY immigrant groups that have sought new lives in the United States over the past two centuries, surely Southeast Asian refugees are among those whose arrival has provided the most widespread challenge to established societal institutions. Fugitives from a modern war, they find themselves attempting like so many before them to start a new life in a new land. Yet the stark contrasts between their past rural, agrarian lives and the computer age to which they come have resulted in unique difficulties with adaptation and resettlement.

The way in which a society assists in resettlement and absorbs new people depends both on the adaptive characteristics of the newcomers themselves as well as the nature of the society to which they come. The past decade has witnessed the immigration of Southeast Asian refugees, with settlement in all 50 states and the territories of Guam and Puerto Rico. Who are these immigrants, and how difficult has their adjustment been? Southeast

Top Lang Disord, 1985, 5(4), 53-65
© 1985 Aspen Publishers, Inc.

Asian refugees' social and historical background, as well as their linguistic and cultural characteristics, have influenced their learning of English. All of these factors have implications for instruction and intervention.

While the total number of refugees from Southeast Asia has been smaller than that of other immigrant ethnic groups, the refugees join a rapidly increasing Asian American population. Americans of Asian and Pacific Island origin have increased 120 percent since 1972, numbering 1.5 percent of the total population ("Asian Americans," 1984). Approximately 700,000 Southeast Asian immigrants have joined the national population. These refugees have come from Vietnam, Laos, and Cambodia, most since the 1975 fall of South Vietnam. Of the total Southeast Asian population in the United States, 85 percent are Vietnamese, 10 percent are Laotian (including Hmong), and 5 percent are Cambodian. Among Laotian nationals, 65,000 members of a Lao ethnic group called Hmong (Yang, 1984) have resettled in the United States. Hmong, along with many Laotians, were recruited by the Central Intelligence Agency during the Vietnam War to conduct clandestine maneuvers in the region against the Communist Pathet Lao. These rural agrarian peoples were the target of elimination at the close of the war—like other Southeast Asians who had assisted the American effort, they were marked for death. Many were processed for resettlement at once, while others were left to die or find their way to camps in Thailand.

Refugee movement of Southeast Asians to the United States is considered to have occurred in two "waves." The first, from 1975 to 1976, followed the fall of Saigon. Largely Vietnamese, this group was ethnically homogeneous, consisting primarily of urbanized, educated professionals who had been exposed to Western culture through both French colonization and American involvement in the region. The second wave, since 1976, has involved immigrants of varying ethnic and educational backgrounds: Vietnamese, ethnic Chinese from Vietnam, Cambodians, Laotians, and Hmong. This group has tended to be less educated and with less economic means than earlier arrivals (Thuy, 1983). Primarily from a rural background, these people had had little or no exposure to Western culture or urban living. Few had ever had any contact with formal education, literacy, or training. They possessed few job skills and faced considerably more difficulty in adjusting to their new lives.

Cultural groups from Southeast Asia possess a common bond of geography and ancient history. Old traditions and cultural heritage have been altered throughout the years by domestic and foreign conquest, with the history of the region reflecting the colonization of the land by Western European entities. Fundamental cultural characteristics have changed little, however, through the centuries—cultures of the region are characterized by strong family ties and community and clan interdependence. Since the individual is secondary to the family and community, individualism is subordinate to the needs and desires of the immediate and extended family. A strong respect for authority characterizes Asian cultures. Elders, parents, and teachers maintain a place of esteem in the social hierarchy of cultures that revere authority, experience, and knowledge (Nguyen, 1984). The tendency in Southeast Asian cultures is to marry young, with large families believed to be the reward of a good life.

ADJUSTMENT TO THE NEW WORLD

As a result of displacement, Southeast Asian refugees found themselves part of a complex plan of resettlement throughout the United States. The shortsighted policy that arranged for settlement in all 50 states on an equal basis failed to take into account one very important point: the need for human comfort with loved ones often precludes the success of any policy or plan for distribution. "Secondary migration," as it is called, occurred dramatically among Southeast Asian populations and still occurs today for a variety of reasons. Families move to join other families, or to join with friends made during the long years in resettlement camps in Thailand, Singapore, Indonesia, or the Philippines. Plans for gradual integration of refugees in communities throughout the country failed as refugees congregated in large numbers in Washington, D.C., and in major cities in California, Texas, and Minnesota. Yet even the insulation of ethnic enclaves failed to stem widespread culture shock. Frustration, anger, alienation, depression, guilt, and anxiety were to follow on the heels of resettlement, and were documented by social service agencies serving refugee communities. One study of Hmong communities in four states (Meredith & Cramer, 1982) found that 92 percent of those interviewed reported stress-related illness.

The shock of adjustment cannot be underestimated. Southeast Asians who have settled in the United States are still referred to as refugees because of their nonvoluntary immigration history. In other words, a great majority of Southeast Asian refugees left their homes because of war and persecution, and would not have emigrated had not circumstances forced their departure. Adjustment and resettlement will be significantly more difficult for this group for a number of reasons. Urban living is a new world for many of rural background, who have lost the skills, status, and roles that were theirs in the old culture. Much of the refugee population is unemployed or underemployed, and a large number are on public assistance. Many have insufficient job skills, and often those who do get training still cannot find work (Problems of jobs, 1984). The cycle of welfare dependence is part of the new culture of resettlement. Minimum-wage jobs that might be available provide no benefits and cannot support a family. Stress, anxiety, and emotional health problems arise; anxiety among refugees is high (Smither & Rodriguez-Giegling, 1979), with adaptation to a new culture becoming more difficult as individuals become older. Clashes between traditional values and the requirements of a technological society are numerous. Researchers studying the problems of resettlement among this population are examining cultural characteristics to determine areas of conflict with the new culture. Psychoreligious forces form ways of thinking that are so basic to a culture that they have a profound impact on cross-cultural adaptation (Liem, 1980).

The dilemma of adjustment involves

determining which part of the old culture can be retained, which can be modified, and which must be abandoned. Given such vivid cultural differences as those between East and West, the adjustment of Southeast Asian refugees to American technological society in the 20th century must be considered the most dramatic in U.S. history.

ORIENTATION TO LEARNING

Learning to learn is a dimension of the cultural information that is passed from adult to child in a family network. The ways in which people learn are a reflection of their culture's framework for teaching and learning, which is in turn embodied in the values that society wishes

---

The ways in which people learn are a reflection of their culture's framework for teaching and learning, which is in turn embodied in the values that society wishes transmitted to its young.

---

transmitted to its young. While much has been written about approaches to teaching and learning across cultures, very little is known about the predispositions to learning in one culture that differ fundamentally from those of another. Still less is known about the effect of a cultural discrepancy between the nature of early learning and the requirements of formal learning.

Asian cultures generally have been depicted as encouraging rote, passive learning. Education in Southeast Asia has more recently experienced a hybridization of ancient Asian traditional values and the imposition of colonial influences (primarily French) that have affected both the overall structure of schooling as well as individual classroom practices. Some who have studied Asian culture (Wang, 1977) believe oral language to be discouraged in Asian learning, and cross-cultural infant studies by Caudill and Weinstein (1969) present evidence that vocal response in Japanese infants is not encouraged to the levels evident in American infants. Clearly, social and cultural environments influence the verbal interaction of children; cultures that stress receptive learning and passive behaviors instill in children a manner of behavior that reflects those values.

The achievement characteristics and acculturative behaviors in other American ethnic groups show changes with subsequent generations. Younger children exhibit schooling behaviors that indicate the strong influence of the American school culture, while older children with prior life and/or schooling experiences have a more difficult time with adjustment and acculturation. Definite changes have been noted in refugee students over time (California State Department of Education, 1982), as well as evidence of more acculturated behavior among Southeast Asian students born in the United States (Weimer, 1980). Yet the influence of culture on learning cannot be underestimated and is crucial to understanding the particular adjustment difficulties of refugee students.

Students who received any education in Southeast Asia had difficulties adjusting to American schools for a number of reasons.

Their familiarity with rote learning made it difficult to adapt to the active nature of American classrooms. This conflict between passive acquisition of knowledge (an Eastern approach) and Western dynamic approaches that stress questioning and searching has meant difficulties for both teachers and students (Nguyen, 1984; Ree, 1980). Volunteering and assertiveness often present difficulties for Southeast Asian students. Hmong children are raised to be respectful and passive in their interaction with adults. They seldom challenge the teacher or exhibit independent behaviors. Most Southeast Asian students arrived with limited study skills and were ill prepared for American classrooms. Most Vietnamese children, particularly early arrivals, had had strong academic preparation in their first languages (L1) and showed a strong desire for achievement. Those who had attended school were accustomed to a formal, highly structured classroom setting (Wei, 1980) where modesty and humility meant never wishing to be singled out for individual recognition or attention (Nguyen, 1984). The strongest clash of cultures and resulting difficulty in adjustment at school occurred for those refugees who arrived with no literacy skills or experience in formal school settings. Adults often saw their children become the first family members to ever attend school, then began their own experience with English as a Second Language (ESL) and vocational classrooms.

Teaching English has been the primary focus of educational programs serving Southeast Asian refugees for the practical reason that, before individuals can get work, they must have the language.

Before students can learn subject matter in English, they must have enough proficiency in English to be able to learn *through* English. Few bilingual programs exist that provide for subject matter instruction in the L1 while refugee students learn English. Thus for most refugee students, children and adults alike, their experience with American schools is a "sink-or-swim" situation. A successful outcome depends on personal, social, and economic variables, but predisposition to learning in Western cultural settings seems to have a strong influence over final outcome. Cultural distance between home and school can only add to the difficulty of becoming proficient in English and succeeding at learning (Walker, 1980).

LEARNING ENGLISH

Language acquisition is a natural, unconscious process that cannot be taught. The learner can be helped to acquire proficiency in the language, to "acquire" language in a natural way, by using language for real communication (Krashen & Terrell, 1983). Language learning involves acquiring the phonetic system (the sounds of the language), the morphologic system (how words are formed in the language), the syntactic system (the structure and grammatical system of the language), and the semantic characteristics of the language (the actual meaning of the utterances spoken and heard). The term "linguistic proficiency" refers to an individual's level of mastery over each of these aspects—his or her internal knowledge of how the language works. (Young children acquire linguistic knowledge *without* formal instruction in the language system).

The development of full language proficiency is a creative process in which the learner tests hypotheses about the target language and builds a mental structure of how it functions. Yet knowing how the language works, linguistic proficiency does not guarantee fluent communication. Knowing when, and in what ways, and with whom, and in what manner to use the language requires the more complex "sociolinguistic proficiency." Learning appropriate patterns of discourse means learning a verbal repertoire for each social context in which speech is used. Since this ability develops slowly through interactional experiences in childhood, native speakers have proficiency in both the forms and functions of a language—"communicative competence" (Savignon, 1972). This level of proficiency—the ability to use the language correctly in both form and function—is most difficult to achieve in second language learning.

Southeast Asian refugees bring to the language-learning experience certain cultural, linguistic, and personality variables that directly influence their ability to develop proficiency in English, which is required for school, for work, and for interaction with society at large. What are these variables, and how are they different for men, women, and children? Clearly, the most difficult challenge in the resettlement process is learning English. Southeast Asians interviewed for a large study on resettlement (Reder, Cohn, Arter, & Nelson, 1984) cite learning English as their primary and most difficult task. The need to know English for employment is crucial, and the relationship between English fluency and successful resettlement and employment is a strong one.

Without English, getting employment is next to impossible.

Individual background characteristics have been found to exert strong influences on English language learning: sex, age, education in the homeland, literacy, and bilingualism all have an effect on success. In all age groups, men seek more English language training and develop more proficiency in English than women (Reder et al., 1984). Women are often isolated at home, and the absence of child-care facilities denies them access to English language classes or job training programs. Elderly refugees have difficulty with language classes, citing their age and fear as keeping them from learning English ("From One Culture," 1984). Many refugees find it difficult to learn English in formal educational settings, yet often have little access to English-speaking neighbors or friends who might help them use the language informally. Thus contact with English is limited to classroom settings. Prior education in the homeland and literacy in another language have a positive influence on L2 learning. Indeed, both formal studies and anecdotal information support this contention.

Children, though demonstrably better L2 learners than adults, have exhibited sociocultural conflicts in school settings. Differences within and between cultures in the areas of cognition, perception, and learning styles may have some influence on the development of English language proficiency. More important, however, is the danger of evaluating the early English proficiency common in younger children as sufficient for success in academic learning. L2 learning by children has been shown to be advantageous in many of those communities that have offered bilingual and ESL programs during a transition period prior to mainstreaming. But the complexities of learning through a second language and achieving success in school in that language require a level of language proficiency that is far beyond superficial (Cummins, 1979).

Certainly the resettlement factor itself has an impact on the learning of English. Evidence of trauma, depression, and social adjustment problems (all indicative of culture shock) substantiate the tremendous difficulties involved in learning a new language and adapting to an alien culture. Attitude and motivation are strong determinants of successful language and culture acquisition. The trauma of resettlement has had, for many Southeast Asians, a negative effect on self-esteem and motivation, often resulting in feelings of isolation and inadequacy. Successful English language development is less likely to occur when there are personal, economic, or health problems. While many refugees have had successful adaptation experiences with language and culture, far more remain marginal in their English capabilities. The strong desire to learn English is often overshadowed by other needs, and refugees remain divided in their opinions of ESL instruction and bilingual schooling (Downing, 1984). Some feel that language instruction does not meet their needs; others fear first language (bilingual) instruction for their children. Achievement, motivation, and career aspirations are high among young people, yet some delay plans for study in favor of marriage and children; for them, supporting a family may well preclude full-time study.

LINGUISTIC DIFFICULTIES

Linguistic differences between the first languages of Southeast Asian refugees and English, combined with cultural characteristics of the learners, are significant predictors of success in English. The nature of Southeast Asian languages and their effect on English language acquisition have only recently begun to be examined. Phonological, morphological, and syntactical differences exist between English and Vietnamese, Hmong, Lao, and Cambodian. Beyond these surface dimensions of language, there are differences in cultural values, communicative style, and world view as well. Laotian words are polysyllabic, and Khmer (Cambodian) consists of one- or two-syllable words. Hmong and Vietnamese are monosyllabic, tonal languages, members of the Sino-Tibetan and Austro-Asiatic language families respectively. Hmong words contain an initial consonant, a vowel sound, and a final tone. Tonal languages are characterized by pitch changes within a word that affect lexical meaning. Each lexical item has a particular tone associated with it; thus words pronounced with differing tones have differing meanings. Using an incorrect tone amounts to mispronunciation or saying a completely different word from the one intended. Speakers of non-tonal languages have great difficulties mastering the varying tones of Hmong, Lao, or Vietnamese; the lack of tonal significance in English (except for intonation) may present problems to an individual who has a developed ear for different tones.

Considering the unique characteristics of Southeast Asian languages, several linguistic difficulties may be expected to arise when speakers of those languages seek to acquire English. Learners acquire new strategies in the L2, and often confront linguistic elements not present in their L1. Since Southeast Asian languages have no final consonants, adding and distinguishing them in English is a major part of developing English proficiency, espe-

---

Since Southeast Asian languages have no final consonants, adding and distinguishing them in English is a major part of developing English proficiency, especially for Hmong speakers.

---

cially for Hmong speakers. Unlike English, these languages do not have a system of verb tenses, and the verb ending does not change to agree with the subject. Tense is evident in the context of a sentence or with a system of markers that function somewhat like English auxiliaries, denoting questions, negatives, and time relationships. Thus the use and recognition of tenses in English is part of the difficulty in developing proficiency, and the need to match subject and verb proves formidable.

Yet regardless of the contrasts between the L1 and English that present linguistic difficulties, it is learning the cultural dimensions of the language and developing sociolinguistic proficiency that are often the greater tasks. The cultural referents of linguistic terms in an L2 are particularly difficult to master. For example, for the single English word *you*, other languages may require the speaker to use several different terms, depending on the status, age, or relationship of the referent. Kinship terms that are elaborate in Hmong and are used extensively in that language (National Indochinese Clearinghouse, n.d.) are not nearly as prevalent in English. Terms related to technology have proven particularly problematic for Southeast Asian refugees. Incorporation of new vocabulary in their own languages has been the result. Recognizing terms and concepts in English that were heretofore not part of their culture requires both cognitive and linguistic adjustment.

Particular pronunciation difficulties have arisen with consonant clusters in English (*cl, dr, cr,* and *br,* to cite just a few), and, like many other ESL students, Southeast Asians have difficulty with the irregularities of spelling and grammar in the new language. Older learners often cannot rely on developing L1 literacy in English classes, and teachers and students alike have found a need for different strategies and a longer time commitment than might be expected for learners who are literate in their L1. Cohn (1984) found in her analysis of Hmong resettlement in Orange County, California, that Hmong adults felt the need for more time to develop English proficiency. Even L1 literacy cannot ensure successful development of literacy skills in English—speakers of Lao and Cambodian who are literate may experience difficulty in reading and writing English because the orthographies are different. Lao and Cambodian have modified alphabets related to ancient Sanskrit, while Vietnamese and Hmong use Roman alphabets; thus their literate speakers have a visual head start in the process of learning to decode English.

WHAT HELPS IN THE ACQUISITION OF ENGLISH?

Success in English is affected more by economic, social, and circumstantial factors than by ESL programs, teachers, materials, and curricula. While educators may prefer to think that their efforts at language teaching make the largest contribution to proficiency, learner characteristics and outside experiences and circumstances have a far greater impact on the ultimate development of L2 proficiency.

Bilingualism (prior to entry to the United Stated and most common among Vietnamese who speak French and Hmong who speak Lao) exerts a positive influence on English development. Certainly, any level of English language proficiency prior to entry also helps. Refugee camps that are departure points for U.S.-bound refugees offer initial instruction in ESL for exiting refugees. In combination with education in the homeland, early exposure to English offers the learner greater opportunity for later success.

Youth is an important predictor of L2 learning success for Southeast Asian refugees (Sweeney, 1984; Reder et al., 1984). Young children learn English quickly in the school setting, and in many cases become the "culture brokers" of their families. Generally better risk-takers (an important factor in L2 learning success), they serve as the linguistic and cultural link between their parents and the outside world. While their parents participate marginally in the English-speaking world, English-proficient children become the connection. The full implications of this power enjoyed by children for family relationships remain to be seen, but the proficiency of the second generation will certainly have a profound impact on the family. Studies of Hmong communities cite differences between younger children and high school students in their adaptation to English. Southeast Asian students overall experience greater difficulty in secondary settings where they are attempting to succeed at both English and academic learning. These students are influenced much more strongly by economic and social pressures, feelings of inadequacy, and difficulty with the literacy requirements of a secondary curriculum.

Affective factors play a major role in L2 acquisition. Research has shown that positive attitudes toward the L2 enhances proficiency, while motivation to learn the language and willingness to make mistakes aids greatly in becoming proficient (Gardner & Lambert, 1972). Self-confidence and feelings of security, as well as an absence of shyness, contribute as well. The trauma of adjustment for many Southeast Asian immigrants has meant that these important affective factors have been suppressed. Among those who exhibit strong English proficiency, these positive influences have played an important role.

Time spent in the United States, although significant, does not seem to be a major factor influencing proficiency in English. Many older refugees have been able to acquire only minimal English since their arrival, and they are often isolated from English speakers. Experiences are the more important gauge; integration with native speakers and contact with the language environment are strong factors that aid in developing English skills. Those Southeast Asian language speakers who demonstrate good English skills tend to have English-speaking friends or co-workers, have taken or are taking English language training, and receive some exposure to the media. Employment itself seems to facilitate proficiency in English, but only for those who have already attained a high level of proficiency (Reder et al., 1984). Refugees with low-level English skills are often employed in situations in which language skills are not required for performance on the job.

For adults who are beyond secondary school, success in English depends on enrollment in formal ESL instruction. Attendance at these ESL classes is crucial to the acquisition of language skills. Studies report low attendance at formal classes (Downing, 1984), with Southeast Asians often feeling that courses are not geared to their needs. Unwillingness to attend is often coupled with inability to attend because of transportation, time, work, or family problems. Attributing lack of attendance to low motivation fails to consider that goals for the acquisition of English must range further than simple mastery. With few opportunities or requirements to use the new language with native speakers, the L2 learner may feel no need to master English for its own sake. A parallel to this situation exists in the case of native English speakers living abroad in "American" communities at corporate sites, academic settings, or military installations. Often these Americans do not seek opportunities to develop proficiency in the language of the host country. Their lives may be carried on principally within their own linguistic environment,

and many perceive no need to learn the target language.

Acquiring an L2 demands the coalescence of a number of personality, social, and circumstantial variables related to the language learner. Educators, social service workers, community agencies, and resource personnel must take these myriad factors into account when examining the success of English language learning and cultural adaptation. Serving the instructional needs of Southeast Asian communities requires considering all of these factors and adapting to learning needs through careful curriculum development and instructional strategies.

IMPLICATIONS FOR TEACHING AND INTERVENTION

The unique characteristics of Southeast Asian learners of ESL require that those who serve them in teaching, guidance, and counseling pay particular attention to linguistic, cultural, and sociohistorical factors that may influence their adaptation and success with English and American culture. This group has brought new challenges to American public schooling, particularly to those who must help in the struggle for English language proficiency. Professionals have learned much about these brave people and their needs, and continue to seek better ways to help them. Research on L2 teaching and learning as well as studies of teaching practices in bilingual settings serving ethnic minority populations have yielded several important lessons that are crucial to understanding the Southeast Asian refugee language learner.

First, individuals learning a second lan-

While certain individuals in the population may have language disorders, assessment in the L1 would be necessary to determine the nature of the disorder and to recommend appropriate treatment.

guage are not disordered. People with limited proficiency in English are simply linguistically *different*. While certain individuals in the population may have language disorders, assessment in the L1 would be necessary to determine the nature of the disorder and to recommend appropriate treatment.

Second, the need for survival is the foundation for L2 instruction. The luxury of memorizing dialogues and conjugating verbs must be left to proponents of traditional language teaching pedagogy; for these learners, the development of communicative skills in English is a matter of necessity. The goal of communicative competence requires learning key vocabulary and building fluency in basic communication patterns. Language skill areas can then be acquired in a natural order: listening, speaking, reading, and writing. New L2 learners must not be expected to read material that they cannot command in oral English, nor must they be expected to write material that does not reinforce other skill areas. Communicative competence-based language development comes first—formal, grammar-based ESL can come later.

Third, the development of oral language skills precedes the ability to handle decontextualized material (written pages,

workbooks, tests, text materials) that offers no face-to-face paralinguistic cues to aid in understanding. Thus learners may demonstrate oral language skills (listening and speaking) that far exceed their ability to handle complex academic tasks requiring writing and reading. An observer may conclude from oral skills that a speaker's overall personal communication skills are sufficient for handling more complex academic work through English. This assessment of language proficiency will prove erroneous when actual literacy tasks are undertaken. The ability to use English in academic, decontextualized situations requires a high level of language skill. This skill takes time to develop, and requires practice and continual feedback from instructors. The most difficult skill area to master in a second language is writing—which is the last area in which refugee students nonliterate in L1 will demonstrate strong proficiency. Those refugees with prior literacy in their L1 may be more successful in communicating through reading and writing, given limited opportunities to express themselves in oral English.

Fourth, although a nonnative English speaker's proficiency is generally judged on the basis of an accent, the quality of pronunciation should be addressed only when it interferes with intelligibility. Many refugee students (particularly adults) will never speak English without some degree of phonological interference. If the goal is to develop strong communication skills in English, pronunciation exercises should be at the bottom of the priority list. Once the learner has a good vocabulary and an excellent mastery of English grammar, practice drills may be introduced to aid in the improvement of pronunciation.

Fifth, certain characteristics of English instructional settings have been shown to encourage the use of English in the classroom. A trained, experienced staff with positive attitudes toward the learners and sensitivity to their cultural background provides an environment in which students feel comfortable in their use of the L2. The use of bilingual personnel in ESL settings has been found to be beneficial to refugee students. Several studies have found that when the first language is used for assistance in the classroom, no corresponding decrease in students' English was found (Reder et al., 1984; Troike, 1978).

Finally, research in L2 teaching, both for foreign language education and ESL, has found that an eclectic approach to instruction seems to work best in the development of L2 proficiency (Saville-Troike, 1976). In the past, the structuralist view broke language down into component parts for learners to master individually. More modern views, such as the notional-functional approach to language teaching, regard language as communicative in nature, consisting of a variety of strategies used to achieve certain functional goals. Successful L2 teaching methodology requires combining these two approaches in an eclectic instructional framework. While younger learners would not be expected to benefit from discrete-point grammar instruction, older learners often want a structural framework on which to organize the target language. With the goal of developing functional language competence, an eclectic approach uses a variety of strategies to integrate the four language skill areas—listening, speaking, reading, and writing—which are best developed when they support and reinforce each other.

•   •   •

The long-term impact of Southeast Asian refugees on American society will not be known for years. The immediate impact has been significant. Schools and social service agencies, initially ill prepared to serve these newcomers, have adapted to their needs in several ways. Still, the development of bilingualism and biculturalism will most certainly continue to be a long and painful process. Second language and culture learning are at best difficult and at worst debilitating. Southeast Asians have encountered unique difficulties in the task of acquiring another language and culture. Their very survival as a people depends on their ability to preserve what they can of old traditions and to adapt to new American ways. With some Southeast Asians the gap is wide; for others, the transition has been easier. For all, immigration has meant a new life, new language, new culture. How well they adapt may well depend on Americans' understanding of their unique linguistic and cultural characteristics, together with a willingness to assist in the process.

REFERENCES

Asian Americans: A "model minority." (1984, December). *Newsweek*, p. 40.

California State Department of Education. (1982). *A handbook for teaching Vietnamese-speaking students.*

Los Angeles: Evaluation, Dissemination and Assessment Center, California State University.

Caudill, W., & Weinstein, H. (1969). Maternal care and infant behavior in Japan and America. *Psychiatry, 32(1)*, 12–43.

Cohn, M. (1984). *The Hmong resettlement study. Site report: Orange County, California* (Contract No. HHS 600–82–0251). Washington, DC: Office of Refugee Resettlement, U.S. Department of Health and Human Services.

Cummins, J. (1979). Linguistic interdependence and the educational development of bilingual children. *Review of Educational Research, 49(2)*, 222–251.

Downing, B. (1984). *The Hmong resettlement study. Site report: Dallas-Ft. Worth, Texas.* (Contract No. HHS 600–82–0251). Washington, DC: Office of Refugee Resettlement, U.S. Department of Health and Human Services.

From one culture to another: Hmong briefing classmates. (1984, March). *St. Paul Dispatch*, p. 1C.

Gardner, R.C., & Lambert, W.E. (1972). *Attitudes and motivation in second language learning.* Rowley, MA: Newbury House.

Krashen, S.D., & Terrell, T.D. (1983). *The natural approach. Language acquisition in the classroom.* San Francisco: Alemany.

Liem, N. (1980, May). *Vietnamese-American cross-cultural communication.* Paper presented at the 30th Annual International Conference on Communication: Human Evolution and Development, Acapulco, Mexico.

Meredith, W., & Cramer, S. (1982). Hmong refugees in Nebraska. In B. Downing & D. Olney (Eds.), *The Hmong in the West: Observations and reports* (pp. 353–362). Minneapolis, MN: Southeast Asian Refugee Studies Project, Center for Urban and Regional Affairs, University of Minnesota.

National Indochinese Clearinghouse (n.d.). *Indochinese refugee education guides. General information series: The Hmong language—Sentences, phrases and words.* Arlington, VA: National Indochinese Clearinghouse.

Nguyen, T. (1984, Spring). Positive self-concept in the Vietnamese bilingual child. *Bilingual Journal*, 9–17.

Problems of jobs, language persist for Asian refugees. (1984, March). *Minneapolis Tribune*, p. 1A.

Reder, S., Cohn, M., Arter, J., & Nelson, S. (1984). *A study of English language training for refugees* (Public Report, U. S. Department of Health and Human Services, Office of Refugee Resettlement). Portland, OR: Northwest Regional Educational Laboratory.

Ree, J.J. (1980). English for Asians as a second language: Problems and strategies. In J.H. Koo & R.N. St. Clair (Eds.), *Bilingual education for Asian Americans: Problems and strategies* (pp. 15–22). Japan: Bunka Hyoron.

Savignon, S. (1972). *Communicative competence: An experiment in foreign language teaching.* Philadelphia, PA: Center for Curriculum Development.

Saville-Troike, M. (1976). *Foundations for teaching English as a second language: Theory and method for multicultural education.* Englewood Cliffs, NJ: Prentice-Hall.

Smither, R., & Rodriguez-Giegling, M. (1979). Marginality, modernity, and anxiety in Indochinese refugees. *Journal of Cross-Cultural Psychology, 10*, 469–478.

Sweeney, M. (1984). *The Hmong resettlement study. Site report: Portland, Oregon.* (Contract No. HHS 600–82–0251). Washington, DC: Office of Refugee Resettlement, U. S. Department of Health and Human Services.

Thuy, V.G. (1983). The Indochinese in America: Who are they and how are they doing? In D. T. Nakanishi & M. Hirano-Nakanishi (Eds.), *The education of Asian and Pacific Americans: Historical perspectives and prescriptions for the future* (pp. 103–21). Phoenix, AZ: Oryx Press.

Troike, R. (1978). Research evidence for the effectiveness of bilingual education. *NABE Journal, 31(1)* 13–24.

Walker, C.L. (1980). *Locus of control and attribution responses of bilingual Spanish-English children.* Unpublished doctoral dissertation, University of Illinois, Urbana-Champaign.

Wang, P.C. (1977, November). *The effect of east/west cultural differences on oral language development.* Paper presented at the annual meeting of the American Council on the Teaching of Foreign Languages, San Francisco.

Wei, T.T.D. (1980). *Vietnamese refugee students: A handbook for school personnel.* Cambridge, MA: National Assessment and Dissemination Center for Bilingual Education.

Weimer, W. (1980). Factors affecting native language maintenance. In R.V. Padilla (Ed.), *Theory in bilingual education. Ethnoperspectives in bilingual education research* (Vol. 2). Ypsilanti, MI: Department of Foreign Languages and Bilingual Studies, Eastern Michigan University.

Yang, D. (1984, February). *The acculturation and resettlement of Hmong in the United States.* Paper presented at a conference on Southeast Asian Refugees: A People in Transition, Merced, CA.

Working with Asian parents: Some communication strategies

Maryon Matsuda, PhD
Associate Professor
Department of Communication
  Disorders
California State University
Los Angeles, California

PROVIDING quality speech and language services for Asian minority children is a challenge for language specialists. Part of this challenge involves holding meaningful conferences with Asian parents concerning their children's communication disorders. By law, and in accordance with principles of effective intervention, speech–language pathologists are required to contact and meet with parents of children receiving therapy.

This article will focus on conferences that are held to make initial recommendations for professional services and/or placement in special programs. This type of conference is often the first face-to-face meeting between the speech–language pathologist and parents. It is critical that during such conferences professionals establish personal credibility and rapport with parents. The communication interaction that takes place in these conferences will affect the parents' decisions regarding the recommendations made, and they will

Top Lang Disord, 1989, 9(3), 45–53
© 1989 Aspen Publishers, Inc.

influence the tone and direction of future contacts.

From a communication perspective, these conferences are likely to be among the most challenging for clinicians. It is when recommending special services and/or special program placement that clinicians are most likely to encounter resistance from the parents to the information being shared with them. Since parental consent to recommendations is necessary before the recommendations can be implemented, clinicians must be prepared to persuade the Asian parents that the recommendations they have made are in the best interest of their children.

Communicating effectively with Asian parents requires understanding of Asian cultures, sensitivity to individual differences among Asian parents, and awareness of one's own cultural biases. According to Barnlund (1975), "people tend to avoid those who challenge their assumptions, who dismiss their beliefs, and who communicate in strange and unintelligible ways" (p. 16). Unintentionally and out of ignorance, professionals do on occasion challenge the assumptions of Asian parents, dismiss their beliefs, and communicate to them in ways that appear to the parents to be strange and unintelligible.

Improving the communication between language specialists and Asian parents requires that aspects of Asian culture that contribute to communication breakdown be identified.

WHO ARE THE ASIANS?

"Asian" is a term used to identify individuals from diverse ethnic groups who live in various countries and speak many different languages and dialects, but who share a similar cultural heritage rooted in Buddhist, Confucianist, and Taoist philosophies and doctrines. This shared cultural heritage has led to a similar world view (i.e., perceptions, values, beliefs).

Unlike American society, which might be described as horizontally stratified, Asian societies are vertically stratified. That is, the social structure of Asian societies demand verbal and nonverbal recognition of status. One must know whether the person to be addressed is of higher, equal, or lower status than oneself before speaking. Status will determine the interactants' roles as well as their verbal and nonverbal behavior. An individual's status is situational; that is, one's status is always relative to the status of the other participants in the situation. Knowing the status of the other participants in a communication situation is so important that Asians are often reluctant to address strangers whose status is unknown to them (Barnlund, 1975; Ishisaka, Nguyen, & Okimoto, 1985; Phommasouvanh, 1981). Asian cultures are patriarchal and male dominated; within the family, the father has the most status.

In Asian cultures the communication interaction is very structured and predictable. As was just noted, the individual's status in the situation will define the role that he or she is expected to play in communication. These roles are usually defined by tradition and are often highly formalized. For communication to proceed smoothly, each participant must behave in the expected manner by using verbal and nonverbal behaviors appropriate to one's role. When participants do not behave as expected, confusion and communication breakdown can result. For instance, a situationally identified authority figure who does not assume this role will lose credibility.

Whereas American culture emphasizes individualism, Asian cultures are group oriented. Not having a group identification is tantamount to having no identity (Doi, 1971). An individual will belong to a number of groups in a lifetime, generally including family, peer, community, and employer. Membership in these groups means lifelong obligations to the groups; for example, one's obligation to the family is to save face, or to avoid bringing shame upon the family. Failure to live up to this obligation could mean rejection by the family.

Saving face has more to do with appearance than with substance. Therefore, although all children are different, they are raised to give the appearance of being as much like the other members of their peer group as possible. This is true regardless of whether individual differences are positive or negative. Positive differences are deemphasized, and negative differences are concealed if possible. A conspicuous difference will almost always bring shame upon the family.

Because being a member of a group is so important, the ability to work harmoniously within a group is highly valued. This means being sensitive to the needs of others, showing emotional restraint, and working for the good of the group rather than for personal gain or recognition. In this context it is desirable to be indirect in what one says and passive when confronted with negative situations. The goal of group problem solving is to reach consensus, not to compete for acceptance and approval of one's own idea or position at the expense of others in the group. Directness and forthrightness are not valued, and people who display these traits are considered to be rude and impolite.

Although the characteristics just described can be found among all of the Asian cultures, these cultural similarities should not be overgeneralized. The historical and socioeconomic development of various countries from which Asians have emigrated has tempered these similarities. Moreover, differences in life experience, social and economic status, and educational background, in addition to individual personalities, intellectual capacities, and physical health, further blur the Asian "identity." Although Filipino, Chinese, Taiwanese, Japanese, and Koreans are all Asians sharing similar cultural roots, their historical development has been very different, producing divergent experiences and perceptions. These differences are, in turn, reflected in the ways in which cultural values are manifested behaviorally. In addition, length of residence in the United States influences the degree of immigrants' acculturation. Therefore, Asian parents, in spite of their many cultural similarities, reveal considerable variability in their responses.

VIEWING LANGUAGE-DISORDERED CHILDREN FROM AN ASIAN PARENT'S PERSPECTIVE

All parents, Anglo as well as Asian, react to the disability label. In each case, parents' reactions will be influenced by how their culture views disabilities, their causes, and their treatment.

In each case, parents' reactions will be influenced by how their culture views disabilities, their causes, and their treatment.

At present very little is known about the identification and treatment of speech and language disorders in specific Asian cultures, or about cultural attitudes and behaviors toward individuals with such disabilities. However, from research in the areas of social work, mental health, exceptional children, and education, it is possible to draw some inferences.

In most Asian cultures, if the child has a disability that does not manifest itself physically in some way, the child is not perceived to have a disability (Carlin & Sokoloff, 1985; Cheng, 1987). For this reason, psychosocial problems may go unrecognized and untreated until they manifest themselves physiologically or the child's behavior becomes sufficiently disruptive or bizarre that it cannot be ignored (Lock, 1986; Weisz, Rothbaum, & Blackburn, 1984). Thus Asian parents may find it difficult to accept the clinician's recommendation that their child, who has been diagnosed as language-delayed but who has no overt physical disability, should receive therapy or be placed in a special class. In such cases the mother is likely to experience a deep sense of inadequacy because she has failed to train her child properly. The parents are likely to attribute the child's atypical behaviors to willfulness or to a physical disorder (Carlin & Sokoloff), or they may simply deny that there is a problem. Because of these attitudes, the Japanese do not have special classes for children with learning difficulties. McGrath (1983) observes that "the Japanese make no effort to single out slow or gifted pupils for special classes. Nor are inadequate students held back; the shame is thought to be too great" (p. 66). If the child does not do well in school, it is because he or she is not trying hard enough (McGrath).

Even if the parents agree with the clinician that their child has a problem, they may still refuse to accept the clinician's recommendations for special services. The parents may feel that therapy is not the most appropriate way to handle the child's problem.

Major handicapping conditions that the family cannot deny, such as serious emotional disturbance, mental retardation, and physical/sensory disabilities, are recognized and cause considerable stigma (Chan, 1986). Cases of severe language delays, language deviations, or language disorders with associated physical handicap may fall into this same category.

Even when the handicapping condition is obvious, Asian parents may still refuse to accept the clinician's recommendation of professional help, since in many Asian cultures a child's handicap is likely to be attributed to moral, spiritual, or superstitious causes; thus it cannot be cured or corrected through secular means. Moreover, speech and language therapy is unknown in some Asian countries, and the methods used may be unfamiliar to such parents. If a physiological function were thought to be the cause of the language problem, a culturally appropriate medical person would be contacted (Chan, 1986), not a language specialist.

INTERPERSONAL STYLES OF ASIANS

In describing the interpersonal styles of Asians, Kim (1985) observes:

Intuition rather than logical reasoning plays a central role in the Eastern interpersonal understanding of how one talks, how one addresses the other and why, under what circumstances, on what topics in what varied styles, with what intent, and with what effect. Verbal articulation is less important than nonverbal, contextual sensitivity and appropriateness. Eastern cultures favor verbal hesitance and ambiguity to avoid disturbing or offending others. (p. 405)

Because this view of communication is so different from the Western view, it has frequently resulted in negative impressions between Asian and Western communicators. For instance, many Japanese are frustrated by Americans' " 'flippant' attitude toward formalities, their 'insensitivity' to differences in status, their 'embarrassing' critical remarks, their 'prying' questions, their 'unnatural' physical intimacy, their predilection for 'premature' decisions" (Barnlund, 1975, p. 41). Americans, on the other hand, are "baffled by the rituals that seem 'endless', conversations that seem 'pointless', by long silences that 'waste time', by humor that seems 'childish', by delays that are 'inexcusable', by 'evasive' statements, by the 'distant and cold' demeanor" of the Japanese (Barnlund, p. 41).

These impressions are more than likely further exacerbated when the communication is between unequal status participants. Asians generally tend to use repeated head-nodding, avoidance of direct eye contact, and minimal spontaneous verbalization, and to refrain from making critical comments, as a way of showing deference toward an authority figure.

Another aspect of the Asian interpersonal style that can result in a communication breakdown between clinicians and Asian parents is the difficulty that Asians have with saying "no." Direct disagreement is considered to be confrontational and thus a threat to the harmony of the group. Among the Vietnamese, a "yes" response might be a polite acknowledgment of a question. It may also be used because a person believes that this is the desired response or because he or she does not wish to appear rude (Brower, 1982). In Japan, a "no" response is considered to be "offensive and insulting" and is avoided whenever possible (Barnlund, 1975, p. 136).

Miyamoto (1986–87) describes the differences in interaction styles between Japanese and Americans in terms of "subjective self-awareness" and "objective self-awareness," or the degree of sensitivity to others. He remarks that "Americans give more attention to the *subjective self* (one's own feeling, motives, etc.) and less to the *other person* than do Japanese, whereas among the Japanese there occurs an almost perceptible sequencing of attention: first to the other, second to objective self, and finally to subjective self" (p. 37).

However, not all communication breakdowns are attributable to cultural differences; some are the result of very basic experiential differences. Therefore, these differences must also be taken into consideration in conferences with Asian parents: (1) For many Asian parents a parent conference is an unfamiliar experience. They are entering a communication situation for which they have no frame-of-reference. (2) The clinician may have identified a disability that the parents do not recognize as a disability, and may have recommended a kind of treatment with which they are unfamiliar or that they find unacceptable. (3) Recent immigrants in particular are unfamiliar with the services that are available to them in this country and with the cost of those services.

Communicating effectively with Asian parents requires establishing credibility and rapport with them. This, in turn, involves understanding and accepting cultural differences, adapting to individual needs, and communicating in familiar and intelligible ways.

COMMUNICATION GUIDELINES

- Be status-conscious. Establish your role and the roles of the parents through formal introductions when possible; then adopt the role of the authority figure.
- Try to reach consensus on your recommendation. A compromise should be viewed as a first step toward acceptance of a recommendation rather than as a refusal.
- Be pragmatic. Address immediate needs and give concrete advice.
- Respect cultural beliefs and incorporate them into your therapy, if possible.
- Try using indirect approaches, such as history taking and modeling, rather than direct questions to gather information.
- Be patient and quiet. Silent gaps in

the interaction should be thought of as opportunities to reflect on what has been said.
- Be informative. Give parents all of the information that they will need, including costs and ways of meeting these costs, if appropriate.
- Pay attention to nonverbal cues.

For example, begin by acknowledging the parents' need to identify the status and position of the professional through use of a formal introduction by a respected third party, when possible. The introduction should include the clinician's title, education, and experience. Not knowing the clinician's status is tantamount to not knowing how to talk or how to interpret information in this communication situation. Clinicians should try to avoid doing this introduction themselves, if possible, because they should not appear to be boastful. This is a personality trait that is frowned upon by Indochinese people (Ishisaka et al., 1985) as well as other Asian cultures. Thus a third party introduction will both enhance the clinician's initial credibility and facilitate communication.

Having established one's status as an authority figure, the clinician should assume that role. In recent years it has been stressed that parents should be active participants in their child's educational process, and clinicians have been encouraged to elicit suggestions and ideas from parents during the decision-making process (Warren & Roger-Warren, 1985).

Having established one's status as an authority figure, the clinician should assume that role.

This style of interaction is unfamiliar to most Asians and could easily be misinterpreted. Brower (1982) found that Vietnamese parents expected school authorities to be "authoritative and directive." This means that once the clinician knows what the parents are willing to accept (i.e., when consensus appears to have been reached), the clinician should be prepared to tell the parents exactly what they should do to change or improve their child's behavior. These suggestions should be tangible, specific, and short-term; that is, suggestions should be feasible and calculated to bring about immediate and noticeable change in the child's behavior.

Asian parents often find it difficult to accept speech and language disorders that are not the result of physical abnormalities, particularly if the child's behavior is neither disruptive nor bizarre. Using indirect means, assess the parents' attitudes and feelings toward their child and ascertain how they normally cope with the child's behavior. This information will assist clinicians eventually to present their recommendations in the manner most acceptable to the parents. For instance, if the clinician wants to know about the amounts and types of interaction that the child has with the family, the "American way" would be simply to ask the questions, "How much time does J spend interacting with family members?" and "What kinds of things do you do with him?" An indirect approach might entail talking about children's television shows if the clinician suspects that the child spends a lot of time watching television. The clinician might encourage a discussion of which shows the child enjoys watching, why he or she likes those particular shows,

and other activities that the child enjoys (or at least devotes time to), whether alone or with others. An indirect approach is time-consuming, but the quality of the information obtained is well worth it, and the clinician's original questions do get answered.

History taking is another indirect interaction style that has been used successfully to gather information (Ishisaka et al., 1985). This technique encourages parents to talk about their lives, including their immigration to the United States. During the course of the conversational narrative parents will disclose naturally the information that the clinician is seeking. If, for example, the clinician is interested in gathering information related to possible physiological and/or psychological trauma that might be contributing to the child's language delay, inquiring about the family's immigration and resettlement in America would be appropriate. As the parents are giving an account of what happened, the clinician can empathize with their hardships or good fortune while also asking about the child. Such an approach enhances the clinician's credibility and rapport because it demonstrates personal interest and concern for the family. It also yields the desired information.

Modeling is another useful technique. In this approach, the clinician engages in social conversation by sharing personal feelings and problems during the conference. The purpose of this technique is to demonstrate for the parents how to talk about their feelings and problems, and to indicate to them that it is acceptable for them to do so (Ryan, 1985).

An indirect communication style is effective because it does not require the parents to disclose information, especially about those matters that they find embarrassing. Furthermore, it is useful to the clinician in that it provides an opportunity to identify potential areas of disagreement so that direct confrontation can be avoided, harmony can be maintained, no loss of face occurs, and consensus can be reached. For clinicians who serve Asian populations, a more indirect style of communication will generally be appropriate. Miyamoto (1986–87) found that even with second-generation Japanese Americans who had successfully acculturated in other ways, an indirect style of communication was more desirable. If a more direct approach becomes appropriate, the clinician can easily switch styles without having initially offended the parents with the direct approach.

It is important not to rush Asian parents into making a decision. If they are not fully committed to the decision, their responses become meaningless because they are no longer being candid. An example of this is positive head-nodding and the use of "yes." If clinicians interpret these behaviors as signifying agreement, they may be right, but it is also possible that they may be wrong, which might not become evident until the parents refuse to sign the consent form. The parents may have been nodding their heads and saying "yes" in order to avoid or delay the confrontation that they foresee.

Nonverbal misinterpretation is thus another source of communication breakdown. The use and interpretation of nonverbal cues are particularly hazardous because familiar overt gestures may convey different underlying meanings across cultures.

Among the familiar nonverbal behaviors that are a source of misinterpretation are eye contact and the smile. Asians generally consider direct eye contact to be rude and an invasion of privacy. The eyes are like windows to a person's emotional state, and that is considered personal. The smile can also be a source of miscommunication. On the smiling behavior of Americans, a Vietnamese student observes: "The reason why certain foreigners may think that Americans are superficial . . . is that they talk and smile too much" (Barna, 1985, p. 332).

Clinicians should avoid conveying disapproval nonverbally. Saving face is so important that any indication of disapproval of what the parents are saying or doing will tend to inhibit discussion, or they may revert to telling clinicians what they think they want to hear. In this situation, disapproval is construed by the parents as loss of face. When a conflict arises in which Asians must choose between honesty and saving face, they will most likely choose to save face. It is not that dishonesty is valued, but rather that saving face is valued so highly (Carlin & Sokoloff, 1985).

• • •

The sources of communication breakdown between speech–language pathologists or other language specialists and Asian parents have been presented to heighten professionals' awareness of why seemingly useful and appropriate recommendations are sometimes rejected by Asian parents. Following the guidelines provided may not ensure parental acceptance, but they should assist professionals to achieve better communication outcomes.

REFERENCES

Barnlund, D.C. (1975). *Public and private self in Japan and the United States.* Tokyo: Simul Press.

Barna, L.M. (1985). Stumbling blocks in intercultural communication. In L.A. Samovar & R.E. Porter (Eds.), *Intercultural communication: A reader* (4th ed.). Belmont, CA: Wadsworth Publishing.

Brower, I.C. (1982). Counseling Vietnamese. In D.R. Atkinson, G. Morten, & D.W. Sue (Eds.), *Counseling American minorities: A cross cultural perspective* (2nd ed.). Dubuque, IA: William C. Brown Co.

Carlin, J.E., & Sokoloff, B.Z. (1985). Mental health treatment issues for Southeast Asian refugee children. In T.C. Owens (Ed.), *Southeast Asian mental health: Treatment, prevention, services, training, and research.* Washington, DC: National Institute of Mental Health.

Chan, S. (1986). Parents of exceptional Asian children. In M.K. Kitano & P.C. Chinn (Eds.), *Exceptional Asian children and youth.* Reston, VA: The Council for Exceptional Children.

Cheng, L.L. (1987). *Assessing Asian language performance: Guidelines for evaluating limited-English-proficient students.* Rockville, MD: Aspen Publishers.

Doi, T. (1971). *The anatomy of dependence.* San Francisco: Kodansha International.

Ishisaka, H.A., Nguyen, Q.T., & Okimoto, J.T. (1985). The role of culture in the mental health treatment of Indochinese refugees. In T.C. Owens (Ed.), *Southeast Asian mental health: Treatment, prevention, services, training, and research.* Washington, DC: National Institute of Mental Health.

Kim, Y.Y. (1985). Intercultural personhood: An integration of Eastern and Western perspectives. In L.A. Samovar & R.E. Porter (Eds.), *Intercultural communication: A reader* (4th ed.). Belmont, CA: Wadsworth Publishing.

Lock, M. (1986). Plea for acceptance: School refusal syndrome in Japan. *Social Science and Medicine, 23*(2), 99–112.

McGrath, E. (1983, August 1). Schooling for the common good. *Time,* pp. 66–67.

Miyamoto, S.F. (1986–87). Problems of interpersonal style among the Nisei. *Amerasia, 13*(2), 29–45.

Phommasouvanh, B. (1981). Aspects of Lao family and social life. In Asian American Community Mental Health Training Center, *Bridging cultures: Southeast Asian refugees in America.* Los Angeles: M & N Lithographers.

Ryan, A.S. (1985). Cultural factors in casework with Chinese-Americans. *The Journal of Contemporary Social Work, 66*(6), 333–340.

Warren, S.F., & Roger-Warren, A.K. (1985). Teaching functional language: An introduction. In S.F. Warren & A.K. Roger-Warren (Eds.), *Teaching functional language: Generalization and maintenance of language skills.* Austin, TX: Pro-Ed.

Weisz, J.R., Rothbaum, F.M., & Blackburn, T.C. (1984). Standing out and standing in: The psychology of control in America and Japan. *American Psychologist, 39*(9), 955–969.

A socio-cultural framework for the assessment of Chinese children with special needs

Alice Lee, MS
Bilingual Evaluator
ESOL/Bilingual Programs
Montgomery County Public Schools
Rockville, Maryland

THERE IS an old Confucian curse: "May you live in interesting times." Apparently this ominous warning has come to haunt us once again. Due to geopolitical upheavals and rapid socioeconomic changes, immigrants are pouring into the United States from every corner of the globe. Educating children with culturally and linguistically diverse backgrounds presents both a challenge and a problem.

The Asian population consists of a diverse group representing many nationalities (see Cheng, "Service Delivery to Asian/Pacific LEP Children," in this issue). This article focuses on only one ethnic group, the Chinese. To illustrate the complexity of subcultural diversities, the differences existing among many Chinese immigrant groups will be described. Examination of such cultural characteristics as languages, religions, philosophy, and family life is required in order to assess a child from the Chinese population.

Top Lang Disord, 1989, 9(3), 38–44
© 1989 Aspen Publishers, Inc.

CHINESE IN AMERICA

Early Chinese immigrants came to the United States, mostly from the southern province of Guangdong, as miners, builders, and farmers. Economic hardship at home and prospects of quick wealth in *Gum Shan* (Golden Mountain) were powerful motives for many to join the gold rush in California in the late 1840s. With increased social and political turmoil in China in the early decades of the twentieth century, Chinese from other provinces also emigrated. The number of Chinese immigrants rose steadily after the repeal of the Chinese Exclusion Act in 1943 and the abolition of the national origin quotas in 1965 (Lee & Yip, 1986). By 1980 the U.S. census showed that there were 806,040 ethnic Chinese living in the United States.

More recently Chinese have come from the People's Republic of China, Taiwan, Hong Kong, and Southeast Asia. Because many have fled their countries as refugees, the composition of these recent waves of immigrants differs from that of past generations. There are fewer laborers; professionals and technicians emerge as the most numerous groups of new Chinese immigrants.

Many Hong Kong Chinese who are apprehensive about 1997, when the British government will return the colony to Chinese control, are also emigrating to the United States in search of economic opportunity. Additionally, there is a considerable number of Taiwanese parents who send their children, sometimes as young as 10–12 years of age, to live with relatives in the United States in order to escape the rigorous school system in Taiwan and take advantage of the United States educational system.

Among Vietnamese refugees are a large number of "boat people" who are of ethnic Chinese origin. These families fled Vietnam on small crafts and were traumatized by both their escape and their subsequent stay in refugee camps for periods ranging from several months to years. Many of these refugees remain immersed in Chinese culture and traditions (see Ima & Rumbaut, "Southeast Asian Refugees in American Schools," in this issue).

The fact that these different groups of Chinese have all come to the United States seeking better socioeconomic conditions and educational opportunities provides a serious challenge to educational policy makers and to special education professionals. To work effectively with this group, some appreciation of their cultural characteristics as well as their languages is essential.

CULTURAL CHARACTERISTICS

Chinese languages

Chinese is a major branch of the Sinitic family of languages. While there are many forms of spoken Chinese, Mandarin is the majority dialect that has been adopted as the "official" language of the People's Republic of China (where it is know as *putonghua,* or common speech) and of the Republic of China (where it is known as *guo-yu,* or the national language). Other than Mandarin, Chinese dialects include the Wu dialect of the Shanghai area, the Min dialect of Fujian province, Toishanese (Taisanhua), and Cantonese of Guangdong. Since most of the early immigrants in this country were from the Toishan and Canton provinces, Toishanese and Cantonese are still the most commonly spoken dialects in the Chinese sections of this country's cities. (For more information about Chinese languages and dialects, see Cheng, 1987.)

Chinese words are essentially monosyllabic, and tonal differences help to distinguish between homophones. Polysyllabic words are compounds of basic monosyllabic words, many of which convey a meaning of their own but cannot be used independently. Chinese words are uninflected and thus do not change to indicate number, tense, gender, or subject/object. Word order and auxiliary words are used to show grammatical relationships.

Despite the diversity in the spoken language, there are two versions of written script that serve as important unifying factors in Chinese civilization. The earliest archeological finds containing Chinese script date from the Shang period (ca. 1766 B.C. to ca. 1122 B.C.). By that time, the Chinese writing system had already moved beyond simple pictographs, and many of its words and characters differ very little from modern Chinese.

Religious and philosophical influences

The influence of religion and philosophical thought on the Chinese way of life have been profound. Ancient, classical Chinese religion has four major components: "ancestor worship, the worship of Heaven with its subordinate system of naturalistic deities, divination, and sacrifice." (Yang, 1973, p. 645.) These essential elements have intermingled with Buddhism and Taoism in the religious life of

the people. Ancestor worship, still practiced by many overseas Chinese, has played an important role in maintaining the cohesion and continuity of the family organization (Yang, 1973).

The most important philosophy to influence Chinese culture is Confucianism, named after its formulator in the sixth century B.C. It is not a religion but is essentially a system of ethics for human relationships and government. Emphasizing moral regeneration, Confucius urged courage, moderation, filial piety, and loyalty to the state and its leaders. Education and the cultivation of personal virtues are thought to transform one into a person of moral worth. Oriented toward this world, Confucius did not speculate about the supernatural or afterlife. *The Analects*, a collection of his sayings, is probably the most important book in the development of Chinese thought.

Christianity, although introduced into China as early as the sixth century A.D., did not significantly affect Chinese religious and social life until the mid-nineteenth century, when Western missionaries, backed by the political and military power of the West, began to establish churches, schools, and hospitals in China. In spite of their efforts, the missionaries never succeeded in christianizing China. Christian churches, financed and run largely by foreigners, failed to take root as indigenous institutions. After the Communist takeover in 1949, the Chinese government sanctioned atheism. Recently, however, the Communist government has once again allowed some churches to open for religious services. In the United States, some Chinese have embraced the Christian faith and are active in church and other religious activities. There are many Chinese Christian churches all over the United States, and they serve as important centers for social interaction in Chinese-American communities (Lee & Yip, 1986).

Family relationships

The Chinese family unit provides cohesion, strength, and meaning to its members. The Chinese word for family depicts "a pig under a roof," thus signifying the agrarian roots of the past. Today the typical family still values responsibility, cooperation, and mutual support. Close-knit and hierarchical, the family remains the social unit that transmits moral precepts and cultural values. Each family member fulfills a role based on age, gender, and generation. Reverence for the aged and their experienced and traditional authority has important ramifications in family relationships.

The Confucian ideal of the value of education is accepted by most Chinese. When given the opportunity, everyone is expected to excel, which can be done if only one tries hard enough. To many Chinese, academic achievement is the ultimate goal that will bring glory and respect to the family. Considerable sacrifice and pressure are exerted on both parents and their children to achieve success in school.

Close-knit and hierarchical, the family remains the social unit that transmits moral precepts and cultural values.

WORKING WITH PARENTS OF SPECIAL NEEDS CHILDREN

Working with Chinese parents and their special needs children is a highly complex task that requires cultural knowledge, sensitivity, and a high degree of professionalism. (See also Matsuda, "Working with Asian Parents," in this issue.)

The most critical element is the sense of traumatic interruption of an old, familiar life that is experienced by recent emigrees to the United States. In addition to making a continuous adjustment to new surroundings, jobs, and neighbors, now they must learn to cope with their children's exceptionalities.

EDUCATIONAL EVALUATIONS

Assessing Chinese children is both difficult and challenging. In the evaluation of Asian and other language-minority children who are suspected of having learning handicaps, understanding their cultural adaptation is perhaps the most important element. Successful assessment of Asian children for whom no standardized instruments in their language group exist often depends on informal instruments and on the professional judgment of the evaluator.

Usually the educational diagnostician or perhaps a language specialist is the first to see the child. There has been an increase recently in the number of preschoolers being referred because of suspected educational handicaps. The following discussions of two case histories reveal the difficulties inherent in assessing culturally and linguistically diverse children.

Case #1: Mary

Mary, a 3½-year-old Chinese girl, attended a Child-Find clinic designed to assist in early identification of children with special needs. She was born in the U.S. and is the middle child of Mandarin Chinese parents. Both Chinese and English were spoken in the home. Her initial screening was administered by an English-speaking early childhood specialist. Mary passed the vision and hearing screening, scored at the cut-off point for her age in language, and was at the lower end of the average range for motor and conceptual development. However, she could not catch a ball, exhibited a tremor when cutting with scissors, and demonstrated very little expressive language. When she attempted to speak English, most of what she said was unintelligible. Following a team decision, Mary was referred for a bilingual educational and speech–language evaluation.

Since there were no standardized Chinese tests available, assessing Mary's strengths and needs required a significant effort. The evaluation relied on informal measurements, interviews, observations, and consultations with the child-care coordinator and her student interns to provide information about Mary's social interactions with peers and adults.

While Mandarin was the language spoken by the adults at home, English was often used among siblings. An informal Chinese language assessment showed that Mary verbalized very little in either Chinese or English. The few words she uttered in English and Chinese were not clearly articulated. Mary's mother believed that her reluctance to speak was

due to motivational or behavioral factors rather than to an inability to do so.

In addition, a joint bilingual speech–language evaluation was completed by an English-speaking speech–language pathologist working with the author, a Chinese-speaking evaluator. Special consideration was given to Mary's culturally and linguistically divergent background. Using both formal and informal measurements, Mary was assessed over several sessions. The presence of the Chinese evaluator proved to be important, as she translated oral directions into Chinese and made conversational comments that made Mary feel more at ease during the testing sessions.

Formal assessment included the Expressive One-Word Picture Vocabulary Test and the Fluharty Preschool Speech and Language Screening Test. Interpretations of the test results were made with linguistic and cultural considerations in mind. For example, it is common for Chinese speakers to omit the final /s/ and to distort or delete the /l/ phoneme. The speech–language pathologist, in consultation with the Chinese-speaking evaluator, concluded that Mary showed delays in English phonological development and attentional problems. Her English lan-

---

The speech–language pathologist, in consultation with the Chinese-speaking evaluator, concluded that Mary showed delays in English phonological development and attentional problems.

---

guage structure appeared to be age-appropriate, with some minor syntactical errors that are typical of a second-language learner. Her Chinese language proficiency was limited in terms of listening comprehension, use of some simple words, and short phrases. It was recommended that Mary receive speech and language services (Blumberg, 1987).

Case #2: Eric

Eric, a three-year and one-month-old Chinese child, was screened at a Child-Find clinic for a possible language delay. His mother, a single parent, was born in Vietnam of ethnic Chinese origin. She came to the United States alone after spending one year in a refugee camp in Malaysia. She spoke three languages: Vietnamese, Chinese, and English. Eric had been exposed to at least two languages at home, since members of his extended family also spoke Vietnamese and Chinese. Eric had a limited Chinese vocabulary and knew even fewer English words. He was evaluated by a monolingual English-speaking speech–language pathologist and was recommended for diagnostic therapy while attending a daily program for language-delayed children.

In a diagnostic teaching situation, the speech–language pathologist could not complete the speech–language evaluation. The inappropriateness of the English normed tests, the unavailability of an interpreter, and the child's lack of social and academic experiences in addition to developmental delays may be some of the reasons for the incomplete formal speech-language assessment. Under these circumstances, R. Clausen (personal communica-

tion, October 10, 1988) suggests that the following diagnostic questions should be asked:

- Is the child developing receptive skills faster than expressive skills?
- Is the child demonstrating soft signs of learning disabilities, such as problems in retention, sequencing, oral/motor functioning, or topic maintenance?
- Is the child progressing at the same pace as others in the group?
- Is the child struggling to communicate in his or her native language? How does the child communicate with peers speaking the same native language? With family members? With siblings?
- What do other professionals working with the child think about his or her speed or proficiency in learning English—for example, the English for Speakers of Other Languages teacher?
- How does the child communicate with his or her English-speaking peers?
- What does the child do to communicate?
- Is the child acquiring English sounds appropriately?
- Does the child use any language to get the attention of others?

Eric's language difficulties appear to be the result of his lack of familiarity with English and confusion resulting from exposure to several languages. Currently it would seem that Eric's language difficulty is associated with cultural and linguistic differences rather than with a clinical language disorder. However, his overall progress and language development will be monitored over time by his school's educational management team.

• • •

Assessing culturally and linguistically diverse children is a difficult but not impossible task. Employing a multidisciplinary educational model, classroom teachers, speech–language pathologists, special educators, administrators, and parents who work with bilingual/bicultural staff and/or experienced interpreters can serve culturally and linguistically diverse children. However, educators and other specialists must broaden their knowledge of second-language acquisition and the acculturation process. While gathering all relevant data, education specialists must take time out to think through cultural issues and their implications. As certain patterns and relationships emerge, previously puzzling questions may be answered. Meaningful assessment should be followed by intervention, whether in the form of specific learning strategies, speech–language services, and/or other programming options. Educational institutions must develop plans to accommodate the diverse cultural needs and issues related to exceptional students, their parents, and the professional school staff that serves them.

REFERENCES

Blumberg, I. (1987). Bilingual speech–language evaluation. Unpublished confidential speech report.

Cheng, L. (1987). *Assessing Asian language performance*. Rockville, MD: Aspen Publishers.

Lee, A., & Yip, K.C. (1986). *Ethnic reminder: The Chinese-Americans*. Rockville, MD: Department of Human Relations, Montgomery County Public Schools.

Yang, C.K. (1973). The role of religion in Chinese society. In H. Meskill (Ed.), *An introduction to Chinese civilization*. Boston: D.C. Heath.

Index